Unspoken Interactions

Exploring the unspoken dimension of learning and teaching in creative subjects

edited by Noam Austerlitz

Published by
The Centre for Learning and Teaching in Art and Design (*cltad*)
2-6 Catton Street
London
WC1R 4AA

Unspoken Interactions:
Exploring the unspoken dimension of learning and teaching in creative subject
edited by Noam Austerlitz

ISBN 978-0-9541439-9-2
British Library Cataloguing-in-Publication Data.
A catalogue record for this book is available from the British Library

Designed by Meg Richardson, Pelinore Press

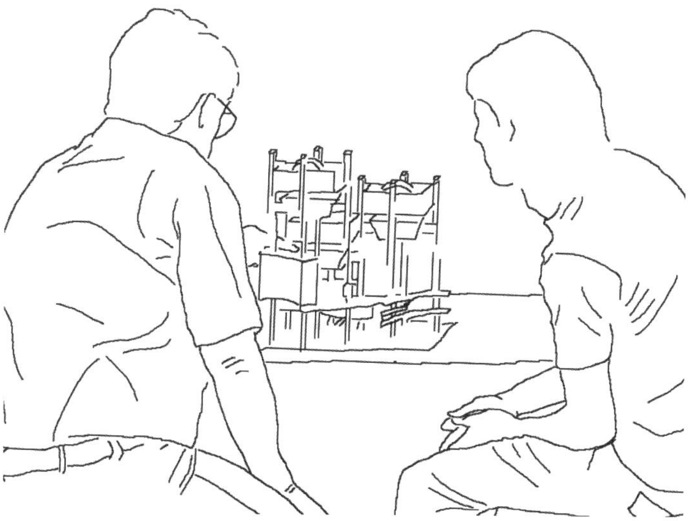

Studio interactions
Reproduced by permission of the artist

Asnat Austerlitz

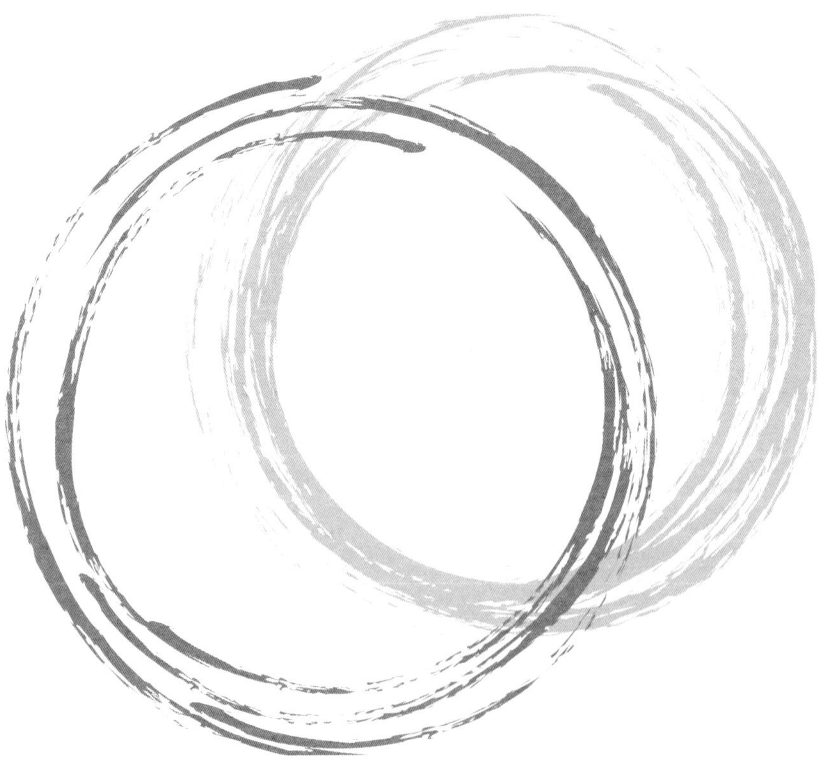

Acknowledgments

This anthology and the processes leading to it could not have been produced without the fundamental support of these organisations and people. I would first and foremost wish to express my appreciation to of the people who took part in the 'Unspoken Interactions' project and most particularly to the authors who enthusiastically devoted so much of their time and creative energy. The lively exchanges of ideas with thoughtful educators were vital for generating this collaborative project and gave the anthology its final shape.

The production of this book is also the result of the hard work of many other people in the University of the Arts London, particularly the Creative Learning In Practice CETL team (Alison Shreeve, Becky Parker, Cara lee Roth, Ellen Sims), and Felix Lam from CLTAD. Many thanks also to Diana Aronstam for her assistance with creating the mind map.

I would like to thank Professor Linda Drew for encouraging the initial connection with the CETL and for supporting my research fellowship in the University of the Arts.

I wish to express my deep gratitude for the financial support which enabled the project through my visits to the UK. This support was kindly given by the following organizations:

The British Technion Society and the Joan & Reginald Coleman Cohen Exchange Program
The America-Israel Cultural Foundation
The Creative Learning in Practice Centre for Excellence in Teaching and Learning (CLIP CETL) at the University of the Arts-London.

Noam Austerlitz

Contents

Section 2
The emotional landscape in practice

Section 3

Supporting the individual journeys in the emotional landscape

Foreword

As the Director of Creative Learning in Practice Centre for Excellence in Teaching and Learning (CLIP CETL) I have been privileged to work with Noam Austerlitz for the last two years while he has been a Visiting Research Fellow at Chelsea College of Art at the University of the Arts London. This collaboration focused on 'unspoken interactions in art and design', an exploration of issues around learning in art and design which are not part of the general approach to teaching one might find addressed in text books on teaching for example.

Creative Learning in Practice is a Centre for Excellence in Teaching and Learning (CLIP CETL). It is one of 74 centres awarded to institutions by the Higher Education Funding Council for England for a period of five years from 2005-2010. Our remit is to invest in excellent practice and to disseminate that to others. We include a range of activities that reward tutors in creative arts to innovate, take risks, research and share their approaches to teaching and learning with others.

Through the CETL we were able to support Noam's research fellowship in the University of the Arts London and the 'Unspoken Interactions' project which involved colleagues with the research he had undertaken for his PhD and to build on that research.

The collaboration between us has been an interesting and profitable one. Noam has enthused and enlivened the debate about learning and teaching in creative, practice-based disciplines by raising awareness of the importance of emotions and social interactions in learning. The interest has grown from a few people involved in research into learning in art and design, to include over 100 staff members who have expressed a specific interest in the topic. About thirty people took up the challenge to actively reflect on emotions and interactions in their work with students and have, or are in the process of, formalising these into projects or research topics.

We now have a selection of viewpoints from colleagues who have written up their work exploring specific issues in creative learning in practice which are based on emotions or social interactions and we are delighted to be able to present them here in this anthology.

We hope you enjoy reading them and we hope it will inspire you to undertake your own research and to contribute to the future debates about learning to practice.

Alison Shreeve

Director, CLIP CETL

Introduction

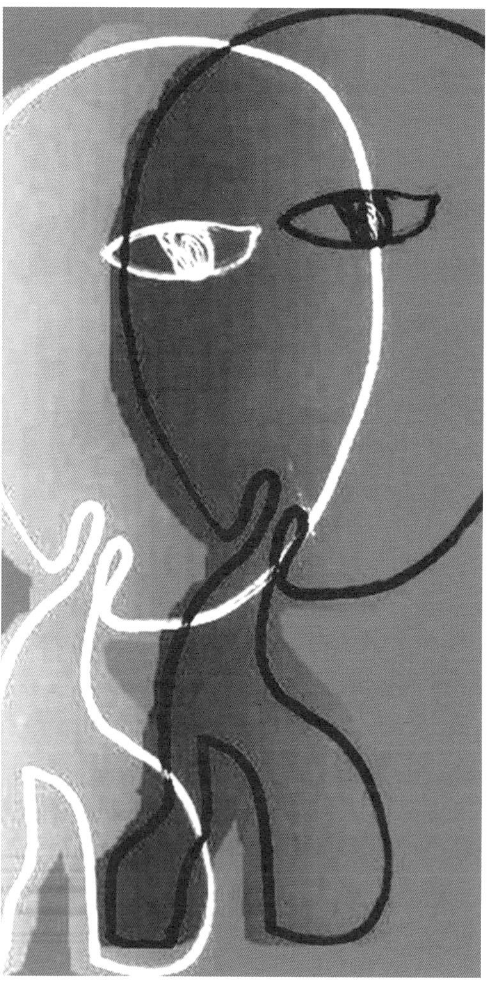

Alchemy Yewande Okuleye

Reproduced by permission of the artist

Introduction: Exploring the unspoken dimension of learning and teaching in creative subjects

Author: Noam Austerlitz

Noam Austerlitz

Right now you are holding a book. You have already felt its texture, smelled its pages and looked at the cover. These impressions and bodily sensations have probably evoked some reflections, memories and maybe elicited an emotional response. Though you haven't read it yet, you already know a lot about this book. Nevertheless, when we think of reading an academic book, our minds are prepared to acquire knowledge through our intellectual faculties, thus we are seldom consciously aware of other ways in which we interact with it. Even at this very moment, as you are, I hope, sitting in a relaxed position ready to read and learn, even in this undisturbed situation, your emotions and bodily sensations are spontaneously involved.

These affective aspects of everyday life have a major effect on the way we recognise the world around us; yet at the same time they are taken for granted. We seldom take a moment to reflect on the way we feel – for example why we feel particular emotions, how they are generated and how we express or acknowledge them. We also do not regard these ways of interaction with the world around us as a meaningful, valuable source of knowledge. We become aware of these experiences only in extreme situations but as a rule we just go with the flow and cope with our social interactions. Such coping often means applying various learned strategies to ignore, hide, obscure or deny emotional responses from others and even from our conscious self.

Recent years have witnessed a growing interest in emotions as an integral part of the phenomena of everyday life. Emotions are no longer the exclusive realm of psychotherapists but have become an established area of inquiry and scholarly writing that have a significant effect on contemporary Western culture. Emotions research is currently at the centre of multidisciplinary discussion. Innovative studies from the fields of neuroscience, cognitive psychology, sociology, anthropology and philosophy are shedding new light on the importance of emotions (Ben-Ze'ev, 2000; Damasio, 1994, 1999; Ekman & Davidson, 1994; Frijda et al., 2000; Lazarus, 1991; Ortony et al., 1988; Rorty, 1980).

Following such studies, we can outline three dimensions that encompass the affective domain's effect on our everyday experience:

- Emotions impact on the way we interpret our interactions with the world around us, and most significantly our social interactions.
- They influence the way we are motivated, act and react.
- They structure the way we give meaning to and reconstruct our perceptions of ourselves and others in a particular 'lifeworld'.

These dimensions of human existence are often denied and left out of everyday discussion and even more so when it comes to academic discourse. While, for example, discussing with colleagues an academic paper we will probably refer to its contents and share a few intellectual observations; however we will most likely not describe feelings and personal reflections that are elicited while reading. This is probably because:

- we were almost unaware of them when they happened;
- we rarely think of these ways of knowing as relevant information in this context;
- we tend to see such kinds of interpretations as inferior to intellectual ones;
- we tend to see these private matters as unworthy of disclosure or inappropriate for discussion.

This anthology deals with exactly these unspoken yet influential aspects of daily life, and particularly with their implication for the education of artists and designers.

Higher education aims to change peoples' lives by providing them with opportunities to reconstruct or reconsider the ways they interact with the world around them. This transformative process is emotionally laden and is highly dependent on the quality of students' social interactions. Hence it will be stressed through this entire book that as educators we cannot afford to ignore such influential factors in learning situations. Students are whole, thinking, feeling human beings and to learn is to undergo change. Such interactions, engaging with and constructing new knowledge in socially organised environments, require the engagement of the whole person, not simply the marshalling of some kind of disembodied intellect.

Such an approach that recognises higher education as a holistic process of personal development, reconstruction of identity and becoming part of a professional community of practice through legitimate peripheral participation (Wenger, 2006), is currently gaining increasing support. Recent works point to the importance of emotions in educational encounters in higher education (Boler, 1999) and seeing students as 'affective and embodied selves' (Beard et al., 2007), in spite of the discourse of skills currently being promoted by government in the UK. Consequently, tutors' emotional intelligence is seen as a crucial factor for success in classrooms (Mortiboys, 2005). Recent works in that area explored issues such as first-year emotional journeys (Bird et al., 2007), accounts of relationships and emotions in students' perceptions of assessment (Crossman, 2007) and the effects of students' emotions on their self-esteem (Clegg et al., 2006). Dall'Alba and Barnacle (2007) advocated an 'ontological turn for higher education' that emphasises a more holistic approach, 'promoting the integration of knowing acting and being'. According to this approach:

> Knowledge remains important, but the focus is no longer knowledge transfer or acquisition. Instead, knowing is understood as created, embodied and enacted. In other words, the question for students would be not only what they know, but what they are becoming.
> (ibid., p. 683)

Implementing such an approach seems relevant to any educational practice that seeks to promote a deep approach to learning (Ramsden, 1992). However, I believe that when it comes to higher education in creative subject areas, this ontological turn becomes more vital and underpins the approach wishes to facilitate transformative processes which will enable students not only to learn new skills but also to become proficient, innovative practitioners.

Students come to art and design schools with hopes, ambitions and fears. They are frequently striving to become the next star artist or famous designer. They wish to express their originality and, for many of them, it is the first time they have been encouraged to develop their own personal agenda. For students, the university is the means of fulfilling their dreams, but they first have to learn to cope with a very unfamiliar kind of pedagogy.

This pedagogy, which is unique to higher education, has proved itself to be effective in many ways also because it requires personal involvement and intrinsic motivation. This and other characteristics of this pedagogy have a potential to increase the role of the affective domain in both learning and teaching. Among these characteristics we can outline areas with particular potential for becoming emotionally laden, for example the nature of the creative act, which requires a never-ending (at times frustrating) process of improving, and the open discussion, which exposes not only the creative process outcomes but also the ideas and private thoughts around it. In addition, as students wish to progress but have limited knowledge and experience, they need to constantly deal with tutors' feedback and face critical assessments.

Moreover, since engaging with creative acts requires students to reflect in and on action (Schön, 1983) they potentially are in a relatively high state of awareness with regards to their performance and to the impression they make on others. This reflective awareness can by itself increase emotionality and affective impact on both creative and educational processes.

The effect of emotions on teaching and learning in creative subject areas

Such unspoken and often unacknowledged emotional interactions have been the focus of my inquiries since 1999 when I started looking into the nature of such interactions and examined their effects on architecture students' experiences. I was particularly interested during these years in experiences in studio courses where the pedagogy is based on a long tradition of apprenticeship but also has to conform to academic requirements such as marking procedures and design tasks with a time-span limited to one semester.

My interest in architectural education originated from my background as an architect and also from being an architectural design tutor. Consequently, I investigated mostly architecture students' experiences. In the last two years, which Ihave spent working with educators from various fields of art and design, my impression has been that the most fundamental characteristics of learning and emotions I found in architecture are common to the pedagogy of all creative disciplines.

Observing students in their studio classrooms reveals only the tip of the iceberg – the most interesting and significant information about these phenomena is in most cases out of sight. According to my experience of researching emotions in such situations, revealing the nature of emotional experiences depends much on conversations with students (Austerlitz, 2007). Therefore, a researcher should establish an empathic trustworthy interaction with students to promote a discussion of emotions and their meanings. This research approach follows the assumption that, although emotions obey schematic patterns of reactions (Oatley, 1992), they are also socially constructed (Harre, 1986). Therefore, an affective experience is a sequence of subjective spontaneous interpretations of information, schematic reactions and meanings attributed to the whole experience. It is thus essential to explore the way students construct their emotional experiences and to give voice to the meanings that are consequently created. During the time spent in studio courses, I have been observing students' reactions while interacting in their studios and discussing these with them afterwards. When I analysed this data I looked for common emotional patterns. These inquiries led me to identify some major loci for emotional responses.

The first locus in which emotions are elicited is the kind of educational tasks students are expected to undertake. These, by their very nature, are ill-defined and open-ended problems and therefore have often been characterised as 'wicked problems' (Rittel & Webber, 1973). The activity in such disciplines as architecture, filmmaking, fashion marketing, graphic design etc. has neither one correct end-result nor one way to get there. Hence it cannot be addressed by any linear pre-structured method (Cross, 2001). Engaging with these open-ended tasks is accompanied by an intensified emotional component associated with the uncertain nature of the tasks. Calling for students' creative individual interpretation to a given task often raises their hopes and personal involvement; nevertheless it also forces students to deal with ambiguity and uncertainty regarding the path towards personal accomplishment.

The second locus of students' emotions may arise around interactions with tutors. As this is part of any pedagogy, I believe that in the particular pedagogical tradition of the art and design school, there is an increased significance in student-tutor interaction as the dominant educational factor. In such a pedagogy, which deals with the ambiguous nature of learning tasks, both parties need to cooperate and negotiate meanings. This interaction has an even greater potential to become emotionally saturated when it comes to subjective assessments of products and creative processes.

The third locus of emotional responses is interactions with peers and the particular kind of group dynamic characteristic of the pedagogy of creative subject areas. Students are often learning in relatively small groups, spending long hours together, sometimes collaborating to perform a joint task. In such a social environment, a high level of disclosure and exposure to one's peers is also a common phenomenon. Also, students' work and the progression of their work are more public than for their counterparts in other academic subjects.

Students' experiences are often a conglomerate built from prior expectations, interpretations of occurrences, previous coping strategies (as well as new strategies developing while they are on the course), actual behaviours and psychological impacts. Nevertheless, it is asserted here that such phenomena can and should be analysed and that once this conglomerate is unpacked it becomes more comprehensible. Such unpacking obliges discerning between three levels of information regarding the emotions elicited during the analysed educational episode:

- The episode's origins and how it has arisen – for example, the participant's background and prior expectations, specific causes of the elicited emotions, what kinds of coping strategies have being applied.
- The kind of interactions that developed or evolved during the episode.
- The impact of the emotions discerned, on learning and teaching.

It is apparent that emotions, as a fundamental aspect of human life, have an effect on almost all examined dimensions of learning and teaching in observed cases of design studio courses (Austerlitz and Aravot, 2007). Yet following an analysis of the data gathered through my inquiries, as well as other studies observing art and design students' learning, it is possible to suggest areas where both educators and researchers might pay particular attention:

- The generation of emotions in relation to the creative act.
- The generation of emotions in relation to challenges of the teaching method and its unique characteristics.
- The role of expectations and standards (formed by prior experiences).
- The effect of emotions on students' motivation (both the kind and level).
- The effect of emotions on the quality of interaction with tutors.
- The emotional construction of group dynamics.
- The overall impact of particular emotions on students' learning approaches.
- The overall impact of the emotional experience on the transformative level: the reconstruction of self-identity and professional identity.

Locating such loci of the emotions' potential impact and recognising their significance is a crucial step towards engaging with these aspects of art and design education. Yet awareness is only a first step towards progressing and realising this knowledge in actual learning situations.

As this is relatively unknown territory, we need to be careful before jumping to conclusions regarding the ways we should or should not change educational practice. Indeed, although identifying a 'problem' is half way towards a 'solution', the other half requires in-depth knowledge of the implications of this perspective in specific cases of art and design courses.

At this moment, we can see the outlines of the 'promised land' but have only vague ideas about its nature. Gathering particular details of this territory is an important step. We need to learn much more about the mountain peaks of pride and joy, the deep valleys of frustration and the cliffs of fear. We also need to find trails that will allow us to tour this territory and benefit from what it has to offer.

The expedition

Following my experience of researching emotional interactions in design courses I came to the following conclusions:

- It is a researchable area open to analysis and intellectual interpretation.
- Careful, well-designed research can clear some of the mist covering this area and inform academic debate around these largely unspoken issues.
- Uncovering this huge area is obviously too big an assignment for one researcher.

These conclusions motivated me to look for allies who might join this research quest and engage in academic discussion. Including more people was not just driven by the mission's size but also for more ontological and epistemological reasons i.e. the nature of emotional interactions as a researched phenomena and the diverse options to investigate it. This project is led by the belief that such a research area obliges one to adopt a multi-perspective examination and that only by combining several viewpoints can a valid picture be obtained. This led to a visiting research fellowship and cooperation with the Creative Learning in Practice Centre for Excellence in Teaching and Learning (CLIP CETL) at the University of the Arts London (UAL).

Together we set out to recruit a group of explorers who would become part of this expedition. We hoped that among staff members of a university that is dedicated primarily to teaching and researching subjects around art, design and communication, we would find people willing to join this research group. The other reason for recruiting collaborators among UAL staff was that this research project, in addition to its objective of generating new knowledge about emotions and social interactions, has also a clear agenda to increase university staff awareness of the new perspective portrayed earlier and thus to become a driver for change within the university.

This approach follows the 'action research' philosophy (Elliott, 1991; Levin & Greenwood, 2001; Park, 2002), which allows more fluid boundaries between researchers' roles of collecting and interpreting data and the active roles researchers play in their research field. The 'unspoken interactions' project's first step was therefore to establish such a 'participatory action research' group that included people holding various positions in the university.

By presenting workshops and seminars to the university staff we have been able to achieve two goals: raising awareness of the area under discussion and providing opportunities for staff members to become part of the research group.

As in any expedition, we needed a group of people from diverse backgrounds and with varied skills. In this case, it was realised that in order to obtain a multilevel examination of theoretical, empirical and practical aspects of the research question we would need professional researchers, tutors and support staff.

Fortunately the response to our calls for participation were outstanding. More than 100 staff members from the university expressed their interest in the project and from this group more than 20 people were interested in taking an active part in the research. These participants were presented with a wide-ranging research question:

How should theoretical concepts of emotions and social interactions be incorporated in practices to enhance education in creative disciplines?

It was assumed that once researchers, tutors and support staff who have active roles with students in the university colleges reflected on that question, and contrasted it with their own experiences of higher education, they would be able to suggest some original ways forward with the research.

The goal set for the participants of this project was to eventually compose an academic paper relating to this question. However, for many, this was, at that stage, a distant and questionable target. Thus, the second phase of the research process was focused on moving from a general interest in the subject towards locating more specific areas of interest and lines of questioning, and identifying a relevant approach to examining it. Participants were invited to identify one issue/concept/theme as their focal point of investigation. It was recommended that this should be an aspect of their own educational practice or research field, one that they regarded as most related to or affected by emotions and specific social interactions. It was a requirement of the project that the investigation was associated with a particular aspect of art and design pedagogy and, in addition, that it would be focused around a specific area, such as a particular course, a teaching method or a distinct group of students. Linking the investigation to the participants' own experiences and biographies was again highly encouraged.

This requirement – to focus a research interest – was not an easy task, since for most participants this was their first experience of research in this area. Many people, even experienced educators and researchers of higher education, are not used to dealing with emotional interactions in an analytical way. Therefore, the faults, while commencing a research project of this kind, are many, and most participants were confused at the outset. One of the risks in researching everyday-life phenomena from a subjective viewpoint – and more so in the area that lies between emotions and education – is becoming sentimental about it. When it comes to reflecting, analysing and theorising emotions, an over-romantic approach can often become a fault, as it obscures the researcher's sight.

This resulted in some participants becoming unclear about the phenomena in focus: confusing the questions with their own personal agendas, making subjective observations and referring to them as facts, and jumbling together a few theoretical perspectives, were only some of the risks which the participants faced.

Hence, participants have been challenged to find an individual path through the vast territory of unspoken interactions in art and design higher education.

In order to assist them with this task, they were asked to define three parameters for the research:

- The theme of inquiry – define a theme that is related to your interactions with students (while tutoring, counselling or researching).
- The researcher's role – define your position in relation to the research question and the perspective you wish to bring to the discussion.

- Theoretical framework in use – define your writing position and the theoretical background you wish to apply while enquiring (for example cognitive/psychoanalytical/sociological/educational theories).

As this was an action research process, it was essential that the first two parameters of the research were associated with the participant's role in the university. This was for two reasons: first, it was a year-long project with a very limited budget and we could not expect participants to commence large-scale research, and second, we required the investigation to be developed around issues that were related to the participant's everyday interactions with students, so that the practice and the research would inform each other. Participants were required to find a thought-provoking subject of inquiry that they regarded as relevant and viable for themselves and for others who deal with similar situations.

As a starting point for defining the third parameter, a theoretical perspective, the participants were introduced to the research approach I adopted and developed for my PhD thesis. This was done through workshops, personal meetings, correspondence with authors and providing recommended papers for reading (Austerlitz, Aravot & Ben Ze'ev, 2002; Austerlitz & Aravot, 2006; Austerlitz & Aravot, 2007; Austerlitz, 2007). This perspective was offered as an example for a research approach that deals with both emotions and design pedagogy. Nonetheless, participants were not obliged to base their inquiries on this approach and they were absolutely encouraged to bring in and apply any other theoretical perspectives they regarded as relevant.

Identifying and defining the parameters for the individual inquiry was actually an ongoing process that constantly reconstructed the inquiry matrix. Such a process of finding an appropriate research path and clarifying its boundaries enabled participants to be more focused, yet to remain flexible and to move between the personal and the general. Thus they could link their observations, memories, students' reports and subjective interpretations to a more theoretical level of interpretation.

Voyage journals: presenting the anthology papers

Each one of the papers assembled in this anthology is a result of an exceptional voyage within such a three-dimensional matrix. Though these are specific case studies, we presume the readers will recognise similarities to their own experiences. Readers will be able to trace each paper's structure through identifying the parameters that build the research matrix as described above. Thus, for example, Andrea Lioy's paper will be read as a tutor's report of his interactions with students in an extra-curricular activity. That report includes self-report, observations of students' experiences, analysis of affective and intensive interactions, and links of these occurrences to a number of educational theories. A totally different kind of matrix would be that of Olivia Sagan's paper, which investigates the concept of 'space' in students' experiences. As she explores this fascinating aspect, she moves between personal memories of being an art student and a theoretical analysis that brings in Winnicott's psychoanalytical perspective.

As one might expect, the varied backgrounds participants brought to the project proved to be as fruitful as the inquiry itself. The process yielded papers not only covering diverse fields of interest, but also based on different forms of investigation. The authors applied one or more of the following forms of investigation:

- theoretical inquiries applying theories from relevant academic areas (psychology, sociology, educational theory etc.);
- empirical research applying qualitative research methods to gather information on students' experiences from their point of view;
- reflective investigations by tutors and counsellors who are actually engaged with students.

Consequently, the anthology's papers portray the knowledge generated in the research process and shed new light on distinct cases of interactions in art or design courses. For example, Su-Lynn Tan's paper explores the way students interact with and around sketchbooks. To interrogate this, she chose to bring in her own memories as a student, her observations as a tutor of her students' reactions and an analysis of data from interviews with students. A different kind of investigative method is the one described by Silvia Sovic, who used a qualitative research approach utilising interviews with a large cohort of more than 140 students.

The anthology's papers could be categorised according to a number of various classificatory systems. It was eventually decided to sort them into three sections.

The first section – **Mapping the terrain** – includes papers that are more theoretical and relate to general issues. In a way, these papers portray the nature and some boundaries of the 'unspoken interactions' territory. Sagan's paper discusses the concept of space, both as a physical and conceptual aspect in learning. She examines the nature of the creative space and analyses interactions with that space and, from there, the way it effects transformative processes. Ben Jonson looks at the role of emotion in tutor-student interactions in the context of the studio experience from both a practical and a theoretical perspective. He brings into that discussion the issue of the tutor-student power relationship, theories of learning approaches, and emotional intelligence. The third paper provides evidence from a large-scale study into the international student experience (a distinct and growing group of students in the UK). In this paper, Silvia Sovic deals with stress – a conglomerate of negative emotions – while she applies mostly cognitive psychology theories. The paper discuses students' reports of what stresses them and what their strategies are for coping with that stress. In the last paper in this section, Julia Gaimster portrays a unique emerging kind of educational space, as she discuss the advantages and risks of interacting in virtual realities as part of an art and design educational environment.

The second section – **The emotional landscape in practice** – is central to this action research project as it includes papers by tutors. These papers contribute to our understanding of tutors' perspectives on their teaching. These papers are built around fundamental questions any tutor should ask, such as: what are the emotions that motivate my students? What causes my students' emotions? How could my emotional interactions with students be of benefit to the educational and creative processes? What is the role of the tutor in such interactions and what is the role of interactions among the peer group?

Tan examines students' interactions with and around sketchbooks, a well-accepted tradition among practitioners and students in creative disciplines. She investigates how this aspect of teaching and learning in graphic design courses is affected by emotions. Tan highlights issues of exposure and disclosure of private spaces that in turn arouse fears, envy and embarrassment as dominant emotions. The paper also raises questions around the issue of student-tutor and peer relationships, which facilitate or inhibit the revealing or sharing of sketchbook work. Katrine Hjelde also discusses student-tutor interactions, while she investigates her own actions in art studios. She focuses on the role of passion as a vital emotion for any creative act and she explores her role as tutor in facilitating passionate work by students as well as demonstrating passionate tutoring. Lioy's paper also describes a model of enthusiastic tutoring that encourages students to explore their situation, as students, by means of creative writing. He analyses the effects of creating an enabling, yet demanding, educational environment, which leads to both intense student-tutor interactions and to supportive group dynamics. Cathy Greenhalgh describes the distinctive case of filmmaking courses.

This is an excellent example where an educational environment is dealing with emotional interactions, not as a by-product, but as one of the primary educational outcomes of the course. Learning to deal with group dynamics, and emotional and embodied interactions, on film sets is crucial for future practitioners of this discipline. Thus the paper demonstrates the ways in which the course staff try to deal with these aspects and support such learning. The last paper in this section, by Yewande Okuleye, is a sensitive self-study in which the author takes two voices, one as a former art student and the other as the accomplished artist she is today, and includes her observations on the tutor as a role model, even a sage, with a significant impact on the student's creative soul. Her paper focuses particularly on happiness as a central emotion for healthy art making. She distinguishes between a profound (at times painful) search for being happy with the results versus a tendency to look for enjoyment coming from pleasing others and superficial contentment coming from a laid-back yet dull creative process.

The third section – **Supporting the individual journeys in the emotional landscape** – also deals with students' emotional experiences, but from the perspective of supporting students outside everyday student-tutor interactions. All the papers in this section recognise that students in creative subject areas are facing unique challenges that require special attention and support. Both Ken Ewings' and Daphne Hampton's papers discuses these challenges and student support from the perspective of university support staff. Ewings describes students' difficulties, which he faces as a counsellor, and the differences between the kinds of support that should be offered by tutors and the kinds that could be provided by counsellors. Hampton discusses newcomers' experiences and the way newcomers could be best supported. In addition, she brings forward evidence regarding how they approach using student support services. Alison James and Noam Austerlitz recognise that emotions, both negative and positive, have a role in any constructive process. Thus, they suggest using personal and professional development (PPD) reports and learning logs – a self-evaluation process performed by students in many courses – as tools for reflecting on the emotional aspects of learning and creating. It is suggested that both tutors and students can benefit from analysing the emotional journey the students have been through and looking at the way it contributes to a student's personal growth.

Opportunities for exchanging ideas

Though all the authors are associated in one way or another with UAL, they had few opportunities for interacting with each other and exchanging ideas. Most of the time authors were exploring on their own within the matrix they created around the phenomena they identified. Though they did have opportunities for corresponding from time to time with 'base camp' (me) to receive further directions and advice, developing ideas around such complex phenomena in isolation could be a serious handicap. Hence, once papers started to shape up, we created a peer reviewing process within the group of authors in order to provide a testing ground for ideas and to develop clarity around the structure of the writing. In addition to this, another route for exchanging ideas was introduced by calling on scholars, who also have roles in UAL, to write a commentary on one of the papers. Through that, we achieved two additional goals. The first was doubling up the scholarly responses to the questions under discussion, and the second was involving more staff members in the process and, through that, increasing the project's impact.

The commentaries that accompany each of the papers in the anthology add insights on the papers, links to more theoretical background reading and bring further reflections to light on unspoken interactions.

Conclusions

This anthology aims to increase readers' awareness of unspoken interactions in the learning process. However, awareness itself is only a starting point for generating knowledge about particular aspects of this massive terrain and discussing the implications for educating creative practitioners. The authors of this anthology have responded to the challenge of deepening our understanding of such aspects, allowing the readers a glimpse into what is happening under the surface in art and design schools. Though each of the papers brings forth a different perspective and explores a different situation, preliminary meta-analysis of the anthology content reveals some common arguments.

Authors of this anthology agree that art and design schools are emotional spaces and thus many of them see tutoring as emotional labour (Hochschild, 1983), although they do not use this term. This is to say that their ability as educators to facilitate a deep approach to learning to an increasing number of students from diverse backgrounds depends on their aptitude to fully interact with them. This includes, among other things, interacting with students' emotional reactions. Many of the authors acknowledge that the creative process is an inevitable source of emotions, but they also recognise the duty of tutors to recognise these emotions as a valuable part of creating and learning. While reading the anthology, one will find evidence of almost every kind of emotion. Fear of failure and of others' critical judgments, envy, embarrassment, frustration and anger, but also creative passion and a search for happiness, the joy of interacting with peers and pride in achievements are all part of this intensive academic environment. Many of the authors come to the conclusion that providing a safe space for learning includes embracing all these emotions as part of the educational process. Many of the papers can thus be seen as particular suggestions for applying that approach. Following a central idea arising from several papers is the call for applying the concept of containment (Bion, 1970) and creating a holding environment (Winnicott, 1971) for students' developmental process. In the context of this anthology, this concept may be understood as a call for an educational practice that enhances emotional student-tutor relationships rather than suppressing these aspects.

When emotions are discussed in the context of higher education, they are often regarded as a problematic issue that students and tutors need to overcome in order to get to a higher, calmer, more intellectual mode of learning. During their investigations, the authors have come to see that this approach diminishes the value and the place of emotions. They realise that emotions and social interactions around them are forms of vital tacit knowledge. Thus a more effective teaching should recognise all emotions and all kinds of interactions as generating skills and knowledge.

Artists, designers and other practitioners define their professional identity while they negotiate meanings and act in socially constructed realities . It is asserted throughout this anthology that in order to do so they apply tacit knowledge regarding their embodied self, emotions and social interactions at least as much as any other kind of knowledge they hold. Awareness of embodied aspects of experience, dealing affectively with stressful criticism, moving between personal agendas and interacting with stakeholders, and facing the emotional roller coaster that all of these create, are only some examples of the skills that every creative practitioner should master. The authors of this anthology all agree that higher education institutions must see themselves as responsible for these aspects of teaching and learning, as well as those based on more visible skills and explicit knowledge.

As I said previously, it was not our intention to bring forward hard facts or to find a universal truth through undertaking this collaborative inquiry. On the contrary, this anthology intends to bring together 12 views of experiencing emotions and interactions in learning and teaching art and design, each representing the examination of a singular aspect or particular area where emotional interactions take a dominant role in students' and tutors' lives.

It is hoped that as these pieces come together the jigsaw puzzle image starts to develop. It is also our hope that some of the papers here will bring the readers to rethink their own educational practice and, with the suggested perspective in mind, to question themselves and their own small pieces of higher education territory – and even to undertake a journey of adventure and inquiry into mapping the role of emotions in learning and teaching.

Discussing the role of unspoken interactions is not the privilege of a few scholars isolated in an academic ivory tower. The discussion itself is a way forward; it is the driving force of ideas that should dive under the surface into the aquifer of educators' minds and from there be applied in numerous ways.

This anthology invites you, the reader, to discover the new terrain of unspoken interactions as it is portrayed by a group of courageous explorers. The order of reading and the ways of interacting with the ideas in the papers is entirely up to you. Therefore, in order to help you find your way around this anthology, a mind-map of the leading themes and concepts under discussion is provided at the end of the book.

We wish you a thought-provoking and affect-stimulating reading and hope that it will find ways to enter your own educational practice.

References

Austerlitz, N. (2007), 'The internal point of view: Studying design students' experience in the studio via phenomenography and ethnography', *Art, Design & Communication in Higher Education*, **5** (3), pp. 3–12

Austerlitz N. & Aravot, I. (2006), 'The emotional structure of student-tutor relationship in the design studio', in *Enhancing Curricula: Contributing to the Future, Meeting the Challenges of the 21st Century in the Disciplines of Art, Design and Communication*, proceedings of the 3rd cltad International Conference, pp. 79–94 (London: cltad)

Austerlitz N. & Aravot, I. (2007), 'Emotions of design students: a new perspective for the design studio', in Salama, A. & Wilkinson, N. (eds.), *Design Studio Pedagogy: Horizons for the Future*, pp. 233–246 (UK: Urban International Press)

Austerlitz, N., Aravot, I. & Ben-Ze'ev, A. (2002), 'Emotional phenomena and the student-instructor relationships', *Landscape and Urban Planning*, 60, pp. 105–115

Beard, C., Clegg, S. & Smith, K. (2007), Acknowledging the affective in higher education *British Educational Research Journal*, **33** (2), pp. 235–252

Ben-Ze'ev, A. (2000), *The Subtlety of Emotions* (Cambridge, Mass.: MIT Press)

Bion, W.R. (1970), *Attention and Interpretation* (London: Tavistock)

Boler, M. (1999), *Feeling Power: Emotions and Education* (New York: Routledge)

Clegg, S., Bradley, S & Smith, K (2006), 'I've had to swallow my pride': help seeking and self-esteem', *Higher Education Research & Development*, **25** (2), pp. 101–113

Cross, N. (2001), 'Designerly ways of knowing: design discipline versus design science', *Design Issues*, **17** (3), pp. 49–5.

Crossman, J. (2007), 'The role of relationships and emotions in student perceptions of learning and assessment', *Higher Education Research & Development*, **26** (3), pp. 313–327

Dall'Alba, G. & Barnacle, R. (2007), 'An ontological turn for higher education', *Studies in Higher Education*, **32** (6), pp. 679–691

Damasio, A.R. (1994), *Descartes' Error: Emotion, Reason, and the Human Brain* (New York: G.P. Putnam)

Damasio, A.R. (1999), *The Feeling of What Happens: Body and Emotion in the Making of Consciousness* (New York: Harcourt Brace)

Elliott, J. (1991), *Action Research for Educational Change* (Milton Keynes: Open University Press)

Ekman, P. & Davidson, R.J. (1994), 'Affective science: a research agenda', in Ekman, P. & Davidson, R.J. (eds.) *The Nature of Emotion: Fundamental Questions*, pp. 411–433 (New York: Oxford University Press)

Frijda, N.H., Manstead, A.S.R., & Bem, S. (2000), *Emotions and Beliefs: How Feelings Influence Thoughts* (Cambridge: Cambridge University Press)

Harre, R. (ed.) (1986), *The Social Construction of Emotions* (Oxford: Blackwell)

Hochschild, A.R. (1983), *The Managed Heart: Commercialization of Human Feeling* (Berkeley, CA: University of California Press)

Lazarus, R.S. (1991), *Emotion and Adaptation* (New York: Oxford University Press)

Levin, M., & Greenwood, D. (2001), 'Pragmatic action research and the struggle to transform universities into learning communities', in Reason, P. & Bradbury, H. (eds.) *Handbook of Action Research: Participative Inquiry and Practice*, pp. 103–113 (London: Sage Publications)

Mortiboys, A. (2005), *Teaching with Emotional Intelligence, a Step by Step Guide for Higher Education and Further Education Professionals* (London: Routledge)

Oatley, K. (1992), *Best Laid Schemes: The Psychology of Emotions* (Cambridge: Cambridge University Press)

Ortony, A., Clore, G.L., & Collins, A. (1988), *The Cognitive Structure of Emotions* (Cambridge, UK, and New York: Cambridge University Press)

Park, P. (2002), 'Knowledge and participatory research', in Reason, P. & Bradbury, H. (eds.) *Handbook of Action Research: Participative Inquiry and Practice*, pp. 81–90 (London: Sage)

Ramsden, P. (1992), *Learning to Teach in Higher Education* (London: Routledge)

Rittel, H.W.J. & Webber, M. (1973), 'Dilemmas in a general theory of planning', *Policy Sciences*, **4**, pp. 155–169

Rorty, A. (1980), 'Explaining emotions', in Rorty, A. *Explaining Emotions*, pp.103–126 (Berkeley: University of California Press)

Schön, D. (1983), *The Reflective Practitioner: How Professionals Think in Action* (New York: Basic Books)

Wenger, E. (2006), *Communities of Practice – Learning, Meaning and Identity* (Cambridge, New York: Cambridge University Press)

Winnicott, D.W. (1971), *Playing and Reality* (London: Tavistock/Routledge)

Section 1

Mapping the terrain

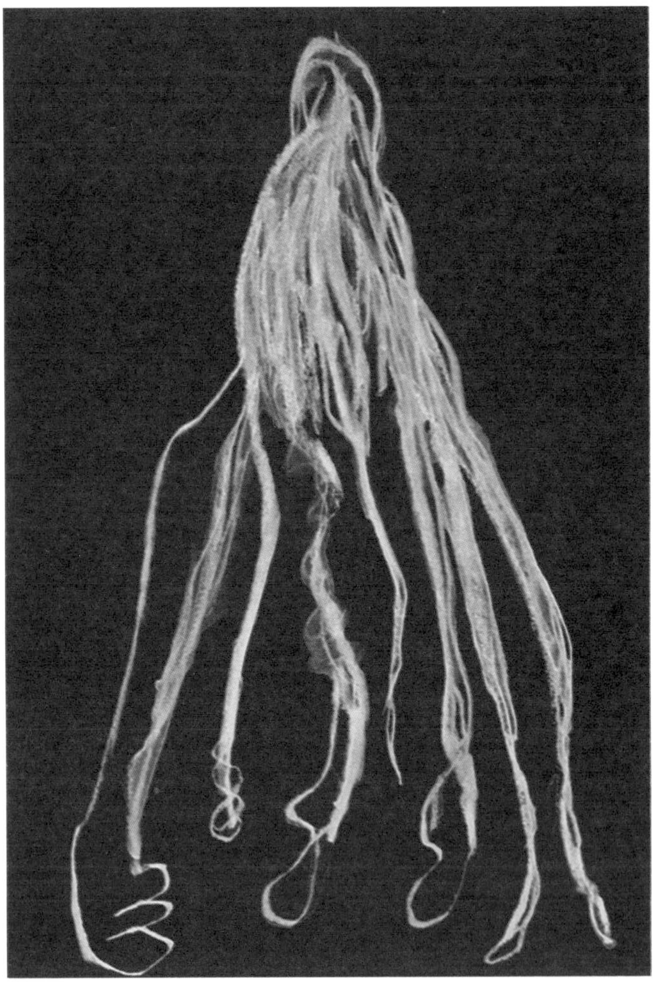

Amy Yewande Okuleye

Reproduced by permission of the artist

1

Playgrounds, studios and hiding places: emotional exchange in creative learning spaces

Author: Olivia Sagan

Commentary: Geoffrey Makstutis

Keywords

creativity,
emotion,
identity,
space,
transitional

Olivia Sagan

> The present epoch will perhaps be above all the epoch of space
> (Foucault, 1986)

I wonder where you're reading this now. Did you choose to read it in a particular place? How do you feel about that space, and how is that space impacting on your reading of this paper, your enjoyment or not, empathising or not, boredom or not? Is space really that important, that it can affect the way we read, understand, learn, express ourselves? Maybe not. But this paper discusses the possibility that for some, spaces are that important, that alive, that dynamic – because they are filled with emotion, or residual emotion.

Introduction

This paper aims to do three things, in a short space, which immediately tells you something about me and space. I fill it, cram it, then find that crammed space oppressive and set about stripping it into a minimalist expression. Something there, one might interpret, about needing the fullness before being able to be calm in a void. When I painted, I did pretty much the same thing. I thickly and lusciously over-painted, then, exhausted, I'd white-emulsion over the whole thing and go for a one liner, as though, that one line somehow contained and condensed all my previous superfluity. In my research now, there is a similar pattern of behaviour with the research space. I collect, magpie-like, all and every scrap of data (some call it ethnography) – I develop multi-perspective interpretations. Multi-dimensional speculations. Multi-layered readings. Then, boom: a one-line finding about a tiny something in something tiny.

But I digress… back to the three things: firstly, I want to give an overview of some selected ideas about space which I find pertinent to our thinking about emotions and the educational creative space. Secondly, I want to briefly illustrate how some of these ideas came into play in a research project I undertook with a group of mentally ill learners. Thirdly, I want to extract from both these sections and apply the ideas and findings to our understanding of pedagogical encounters in art and design spaces.

I will now leave a space for you to reflect on this, and decide whether you want to continue reading.

OK.

Spaces in learning and learning spaces

One of the first learning spaces I ever taught in was a designated space under a particular tree, highly sought after for the shade it offered from the blistering sun that would hit us within an hour of school starting. Clearly, we were not in Harringay, where my own primary school classroom, some 15 years before that, was a quaint blend of tall arched windows and parquet flooring lightly carpeted with chalk dust near the blackboard. Both spaces I recall acutely – and in both spaces, *happy* learning took place for me, whether as pupil or teacher; but this may of course be down to the recasting of thoughts through rose-tinted memory. What such memories enable, however, is a perception of 'emotional and affective dimensions of learning as (also) contributing to a positive educational experience.' (Dirkx, 2001, p. 67). In both instances, emotions positively infiltrated the learning and the learning space – and the latter would forever become a *happy* space, which, in turn, 'magically' *enabled* learning. However, the opposite is also possible, as testaments to failed, thwarted, 'difficult learning' (Britzman, 1998) teach us.

Since both of these instances of learning, I have taught and learned in spaces less sanguine though no less memorable. The white, bare-walled high security unit of a psychiatric hospital comes to mind, with its ingrained stench of piss and despair. There, learning was arduous and sometimes desperate, though spotted with short breaths of relief in the form of hope, humour or rest, the three elements Immanuel

Kant so aptly claimed were given us to counterbalance the miseries of life. There, the best of intentions became quickly eroded and the lightest of lessons swiftly turned turgid in a space tragically difficult to imbue with positive emotion.

Literature on education, from government policy to pedagogical research, is replete with references to the learning environment and its potential to 'motivate learners and promote learning as an activity' (HEFCE, 2006, p. 3). Yet while we all have some idea of the constituent factors of a *good* learning space, there is in fact a dearth of studies exploring what this might actually be, and what, if any, is its impact. But there is more that I find puzzling. The three examples I give above (tree, Harringay, hospital) are, in my mind, saturated with *emotion*. And while there has been a surge in the levels of interest in the complexity of emotional factors of learning (Salzberger-Wittenberg et al., 1983; Todd, 1997) and teaching (Carlyle & Woods, 2002; Troman & Woods, 2001; Woods & Carlyle, 2002), emotions are still regarded somewhat as 'baggage' and split off from the rationalist, cognitive task of learning. There is also an absence of the study of space and emotion as being inextricably linked in learning;[1] a tired, Cartesian insistence on splitting off the 'out there' of space with the 'in here' of affect. Craib (1997) goes so far as to suggest that this proliferation of binaries (with which we are intensely preoccupied in the field of education) is not only Cartesian but *psychotic*, while for Michael Rustin (2001, p. 213) the fracturing and atomising of current educational policy and practice constitutes 'an attack on thinking'.

What *is* so threatening about an *embodied, emotional subject* – one who impacts emotionally on the space in which she/he learns, and is, in turn, impacted on by the space and emotions in it?

But there also remains something intrinsically 'malestream' (Tanesini, 1999) about this preoccupation with binaries – with a discourse of 'emotional space' being associated with a clichéd notion of women, femininity and the emotional. Furthermore, our reluctance to consider, holistically, the emotionality of space, or the spatial in emotionality is redolent of a classicism and ethnocentricity in which one (the privileged, the male, the white) posits space as *neutral*, 'open' for all. Spaces, in fact, and the emotions they provoke, contain or deny are not neutral at all, but branded with particular race, class and gender 'affiliations'. Spatial organisation is also a mechanism through which 'othering' (De Beauvoir, 1949/1972; Said, 1978) takes place. As certain spaces come to be implicitly recognised as more powerful, less powerful subjects/activities/courses can be relegated elsewhere. We all, in addition, have a sense of space and territory which is a potent part of our identity; think of the wonderful saying 'you can take the girl out of the hood, but you can't take the hood out of the girl …'. That identity is built in direct relation to what is sometimes 'devalued territory' (Taylor, 2004) and a liminal space (Turner, 1997), one which is either physically or psychologically experienced as a midway, borderline space which shares none of the recognition or security of orthodox, delineated spaces. Liminal space, however, may ironically also offer freedom and possibility. In playing truant from school (way after my halcyon days in Harringay), and having no set space to occupy as I was always 'elsewhere', I was given the freedom to roam the then sleazy streets of Soho and Chinatown. It was a space in which a troubled teenage identity could be bizarrely moulded through dank basement record shops and poetry readings in the dim backrooms of crammed bookshops. Liminal space can be isolating, but it can also offer the possibility of resistance and even rebellion with one's 'fellow liminars' (Sibbett, 2003).

> Learning can provide a space for contesting and critiquing the dominant hegemony in society; it has the potential to be a liberating and empowering experience. Yet education is also contradictory, as it reproduces the dominant social order.
> (Merrill, 2004, p. 75)

So despite the spatial rhetoric of 'student-centred' learning, and the fantasy of democratisation through 'open-access' and e-learning with virtual tutors in cyberspace, educational discourse is riddled with embedded ideas of top, bottom, and … elsewhere, out there, perhaps in the 'community' spaces to where participation has to be 'widened'.

Metaphors, one might argue, are merely linguistic and do not accurately represent how we organise or use 'real' space in educational institutions. However, post-structuralists from Derrida and Foucault on have argued forcefully that the subject is constructed through language; subject positions being constituted through the larger discourses of society (Davies & Harre, 1990). In being so constructed, we embody and reproduce the very discourses that have constructed us. Certain 'knowledge' is enscripted onto our bodies, and this is the mechanism for the self-regulation (Foucault, 1977) that we undertake. This helps to explain the comfort or discomfort we feel in particular public spaces. Such public and social spaces are also the means by which different forms of capital (Bourdieu, 1989) to which one has access, come to have currency:

> So when one enters a physical space such as a bar, school or home, one brings with one, embodied, certain quantities of different

> capitals. It is the physical embodiment of the different positions that the body has previously been able to inhabit. So one is always moving in and out of spaces carrying and sometimes increasing the value of different capitals. Although for some groups this may not be possible.
> (Skeggs, 1999, p. 214)

So if language structures how we think and feel about the social, and if embodied experience of space helps constitute our identity, then the spatial metaphors through which we teach and learn may powerfully reproduce inequalities in society. The waters are further muddied when emotions are thrown into the fray, as being inextricably linked to language and space. Being top of the class *feels* very different to being bottom of it. Within art education, we have a sublime muddying of the waters, for we form part of, and think through, an educational discourse stiff with highly *emotive* metaphorical notions of top and bottom achievement. In addition, we are working with an artefact, a product, which is created (and criticised) within a certain *physical* (studio) space which has a high potential of 'being emotionally saturated' (Austerlitz & Aravot, 2002, p. 87). And finally, the creation of that artefact (to be 'exhibited' in yet another stratified space) is historically regarded as a product of self-expression, which is, if nothing else, an emotional process.

Later on, I'll give an example from my research of how an individual may (or may not) negotiate the emotional terrain laid down by this blend of discourse, space and self-expression in order that learning can progress.

Learning: finding a space small enough to contain anxiety

OK, back to me. When I was three or four, my favourite place to run and hide from the turbulence that was my home was behind a small cupboard door. When the door was open, the alcove created between door, cupboard and wall was tight and snug and private. Within a year it would be too small for me and my picture book, but for an important space of time, it was perfect. I felt safe. To this day, I like a quiet, small corner to study in. Not wanting at this juncture to enter into dense interpretations of this, let's just posit, for argument's sake, that one's feelings towards space are not only *socially* constructed through a given social order and its discourse, but *psychologically* constructed too, through our own individual histories. In this psycho-social approach (Frosh, 2003), the social and the psychic are mutually constitutive.

This is what a recently graduated student from a foundation degree had to say about her learning, shared space and how it related to her background:

> I found it difficult ... all this sharing of space ... I couldn't get things done ... cause, when I was growing up, you know, it was just me and my mum ... she'd be over there, and I'd be over here and I'd have my paints and things, she always really encouraged my creativity ... and it was quiet, you know, nice ... a nice space ... (Stephanie)

What seems to be being alluded to, in both my experience and Stephanie's (neither of which is unique), is the idea of transitional space (Winnicott, 1971)

> … in which aspects of the self are created and transformed in relationships with others and with the matrices of culture.
> (Day-Sclater, 2003, p. 326)

Transitional space is the 'facilitating environment' par excellence. Stephanie in the quote above had a strong internal model of this. It arguably sustained her through later years of disruption, interrupted learning and phases of failure. When she returned to study as a mature student, she needed to recreate something of that early experience of interaction, trust and creativity, and found the studio space and the crit less than conducive, spending her most productive time at home.

Transitional space is one of the more useful, as well as poignant and textured, concepts of space nestled within psychoanalytic theory. It is to a small selection of these to which I now turn. In order to get a grip on any psychoanalytic theory or application of it, it helps to hold in mind the concept of the 'defended subject' as best articulated by Hollway and Jefferson (2000). This draws mainly on Kleinian models of the individual as driven by very rational, though unconscious, urges to keep levels of anxiety down. The defended subject can be interpreted as engaging in behaviours and thought processes that have, as their aim, the warding off of the unpleasant sensation of increased anxiety. Hollway and Jefferson have been able to offer stimulating analyses (Hollway & Jefferson, 2001) of how and why individuals sometimes follow apparently illogical deductive reasoning, or engage in acts and behaviours which are not, at first glance, apparently in their favour. They offer a most persuasive argument for looking seriously at the impact and meanderings of the unconscious in the social, including, of course, learning and teaching. What's important to us at this point is that the notion of *anxiety* and defence, as being at the core of human experience, provides a context to look at notions of space within psychoanalysis. Popping back to me in my cupboard, for example, I could offer an interpretation of that particular space and its constituent elements as being intrinsic in my surviving high levels of anxiety at that point in time. So instrumental was that space in offsetting the anxiety, that I would carry this memory (and others, unconsciously) of certain elements being prerequisites in any space that would be considered as safe, and, by extension, potentially creative.

But psychoanalysis has done more than offer us images of the porousness of the human condition. It has given us an unimaginably (because now taken for granted) important way of thinking about both our *internal* and our *external* space. It has helped examine how we negotiate movement from the internal, with its thoughts, imaginings, phantasies etc. to the external, with its enacting, projections, and so on. It is easy to see the importance of this internal, external and intermediate (transitional) space for both learning (in which we take from the outside, combine with internal subjectivity, and reproduce, in a given form back into the external) and artistic endeavour (in which we draw deep on the internal in order to express, externally, something which is a fusion of psycho/social elements). Winnicott's transitional or *potential* space has been used and explored richly in contemporary work on learning (Richards, 2002) and creativity (Gosso, 2004). It is a space (which can be both physical and/or abstract) which is the

> … space between symbol and symbolized, mediated by an interpreting self, (the) space in which creativity becomes possible.
> (Ogden, 1992, p. 213)

Transitional space offers potential, and is the prototype of a successful infant/primary caregiver dyad, in which the infant is 'held' physically and/or emotionally. Importantly, it is a space where one is allowed enough risk to learn, develop and create, a space where the natural anxiety provoked by learning and development is contained. It is a space in between inner and outer world, where interrelationships and creativity occur (Winnicott, 1971). Whether we are in a learner/tutor one-to-one, a peer interactive space, a desk crit or an exhibition space, a meeting of inner and outer world and intersubjectivity is occurring.

The idea of containment (Bion, 1984) is also useful in any discussion of learning, for it is the capacity, again based on pre-verbal interaction, for a caregiver to accept, hold and detoxify the infant's projections of fear, anger and anxiety. In showing/modelling a capacity for mentalisation, for a tolerance of the difficult, the ambivalent, the ugly, the caregiver 'contains' and detoxifies the raw, sensory experience. This containment is essential in the management of anxiety necessary for learning:

> If well enough contained, anxiety can (therefore) act as a source of creative, task-related energy, as reflected in the phrase 'anxious to learn'. Unconscious anxiety, however, is an all too powerful inhibitor of learning.
> (French, 1997, p. 484)

The model followed in much of today's educational practice, for the containment of anxiety and any 'emotional disturbance', is to relegate the emotion elsewhere, literally, to another space, often student support systems and/or counselling. While these are both important aspects of an effective learning framework (Coren, 1997) a reliance on these enables us to 'clean' the immediate teacher/student space and maintain an illusion that it is emotion free, intellectual, cognitive. It also continues the fallacy that students are the main drivers of emotional exchange, while we teachers are often equally anxious or defensive, and similarly prone to casting past experiences and their emotional residue into the teaching space (Britzman & Pitt, 1996), creating an emotionally fraught learner/teacher terrain. Arguably, our role is both more responsible and more creative:

> In clinical settings, it is the capacity of the therapist to contain anxiety and process ambivalent feelings as well as projections … and feed these back in intelligible and digestible forms. Similar dynamics can apply in adult learning too (teachers and activists may contain and process a whole range of feelings, often unconsciously) yet relatively little attention is paid to these dimensions of learning.
> (West, 2007, p. 13)

But there is more to the job of containment, and of co-constructing a transitional space along with the student, in which one feels safe, stimulated, inspired and valued. It is not only part of good pedagogical practice; it is also the role of the institution to contain anxiety (Obholzer & Zagier-Roberts, 1994):

> In secure organizations social influence is exercised in a framework dominated by an awareness of mental states, concerns, thoughts, and feelings of individuals within the system – that is, a capacity for mentalization.
> (Fonagy, 2003, p. 223)

For any initiative towards widening participation or greater democratisation of public/learning spaces to be fundamentally successful, the possible fragmented mind-states, anxieties and emotional memories of thwarted creativity need to be faced as part of the package of working with students from disadvantaged, non-traditional or 'high-risk' backgrounds. We in art institutions need to consider the spaces we are (re)creating – and question to whom they 'belong' and which/whose purposes they serve. Reception areas, for example, seldom 'receive'; studios are rarely studious, and classrooms invariably have more room for some classes than others.

Many of the students that widening participation initiatives are hoping to attract have not just walked out of domestic and social situations in which their emotional development, learning and creativity have been carefully nurtured. Their relationship with learning spaces may be dense with past confusion, anxiety, hostility or even humiliation. In research I carried out with very disadvantaged learners with mental health difficulties (Sagan, 2002; Sagan, 2007b) social disadvantage was the norm, and high levels of anxiety were repeatedly experienced as part and parcel of learning.

Learners referred to several characteristics of the provision that they felt enabled them to continue and persist, rather than drop out of one more learning situation. Among these there were few surprises; learners wanted a local, safe space in which they felt ownership over the course and its contents. They wanted to be treated like adults and accepted and understood for any shortcomings. They wanted to make friends and socialise with others who shared their worries about learning, about not 'measuring up'. They wanted less prescription and more time to talk about the business of learning. And they wanted consistency – of teacher, time, place and pedagogical approach. However, interestingly, one of the elements of the teaching provision which was to emerge as being instrumental in containing anxiety and developing a transitional space in which individuals felt more able to engage in symbolisation and reflexivity, was the biographic narrative interviews being carried out as part of the *research*. It seemed that this space of autobiographical expression in which memories could be accessed and subjective experiences spoken of was functioning as a creative, transitional arena:

> It's like ... helped me think about things I've not thought about before ... and yeah, I get upset sometimes ... but that's better than it happening in public ... there's no rush, neither ... then I can go and get on with the writing which I find really hard, but at least then I've got something to say, cause I've already thought about it, and know that it wasn't that bad ...
> (Marian)

What was also emerging, as this extract suggests, was that there was a relationship being built up between the learner, her 'product' through which a highly personal expression was being striven for, and the space of the interviews and sessions. In Winnicottian terms, there was both transitional space and transitional object. Both of these were being used, rigorously, to work through anxiety created through the double whammy of learning (which was difficult, and provocative in challenging old notions of 'self' and 'identity') and engaging autobiographically, reflexively and creatively, for some individuals, for the first time. And, because as educators, despite government targets and policy, we don't want 'simply' for people to persist and 'achieve', but we do want them to be able to engage deeply with learning and live more expressively, critically and creatively, it's worth looking closer at what might be going on in this transitional space.

Psychoanalytic theory has long been preoccupied with both learning and creativity, linking both at different times to desire, repetition compulsion and sublimated sexuality. While these each form provocative and rich theories that have spawned a whole industry of intense epistemological and ontological speculation, it is Melanie Klein's work (Klein, 1988; Klein, 1998) which has perhaps offered a way of thinking about the confluence of both learning and creativity. Her work on reparation and loneliness (Klein, 1963), for example, presents a delicate process of unconscious rebuilding internal objects (people, real and imagined, part-memory figures, phantasised others) in our inner landscape through engaging with a literal 'building' in the external world (Sagan, 2007a). The profound sense of relief/release at both learning and creation, as well as the deadening frustration of stuckness or failure are, by any account, deeply emotional and personal experiences. These, I argue strongly, indicate the depth of the process and the density of the psycho-social knit involved in these processes. Going back to my research with mentally ill learners, briefly, it appeared that long-term engagement with an autobiographic project (one which could be regarded as an 'identity text', exploratory of self and identity through its process and content) enabled a more reflexive learning experience, which in turn gave rise to a process through which individuals could talk and think more intimately (and at times painfully) about their subjective, past experiences. This is not to suggest all teaching should encourage autobiographical excavations, but that for many learners, a period of working through identity concerns may be necessary. This need was evident in much of the narrative of the research participants; the process of rebuilding inner schemata of one's life history was, in some cases, underway:

> It's made me think of things ... oh, that I haven't thought of ... not in fifty year or more ... memories that I haven't had ... (Pauline)

Marion Milner suggests that we create and try and express ourselves when 'the conditions of our living are changing so rapidly (that) the old forms for describing our feeling experiences become no longer adequate', and that there is 'a gap between the inner reality of feeling and the available ways of communicating' (Milner, 1950, p. 132).

Both learning and creative engagement offer some form of rescue here, offering 'new forms for describing'. Both, through enriching one's internal symbolisation, reflexive engagement and overcoming of psychical barriers to change, can become a reparative project:

> Art can provide space for reparation as people project painful, confused feelings, and work on them, imaginatively and symbolically, and can create more of a good object to be re-introjected, over time. (West, 2007, p. 12)

This model of the educative/creative project, in which emotions and psychosocially constructed identities engage in a stream of negotiations between inner and outer realities, past and present, self and other, may seem perilously vulnerable and demanding. And yet psychoanalysis has also indicated the sheer resilience of the epistemological and creative drives, a *resilience* that we, as educators, will also be familiar with.

The one liner: conclusion

The transitional space is one in which the student, artwork and tutor 'play' and enable playing, in the Winnicottian sense of 'allowing' risk taking and co-construction of identity and ideas. It is superbly akin to the space of the desk crit, where there may be a charged dynamic of play, attack, learning and creation in the triangle of tutor, student, object. This is a terrain where development of creative ideas and sensitive transformation of identity can take place, yet all too often, however, the crit, and the studio becomes a 'theatre of the repressed' (Morris, 2005, p. 147). Students project onto the teacher and the teacher in turn projects back onto the students, and transference runs a potentially harmful course (Ochsner, 2000), with ego, identities and power investments running amok. In this dynamic triangle, the psychic traffic of our unconscious desires, anxieties and fears needs to be recognised as having a profound impact on learning.

Pedagogical practice generally no longer adheres to Anna Freud's suggestion that all teachers be psychoanalysed and this paper certainly is not suggesting this. What I am suggesting, is that it is the job of educators, and art educators specifically, to engage in a reflexive understanding of the emotionality of space and the way we all, each of us, bring our psychosocially constructed identities, desires, fears and power-games into this space. Britzman and Pitt (1966, pp. 117–118) go further, maintaining:

> ... [it] is the ethical obligation teachers have to learn about their own conflicts and to control the re-enactment of old conflicts that appear in the guise of new pedagogical encounters.

However, this is acknowledged as asking a lot of an increasingly overburdened workforce:

> Such reflexive and emotionally attuned capacities are not easily won and ask a great deal of educators: including knowledge of self and self in action as well as an auto/biographical sensitivity to the emotional dimensions of the struggle to learn ...
> (West, 2007, p. 12)

This overburdening may, however, be at least in part a result of a particular set of priorities in a given institution, priorities which may be at odds with the need to allow *space* for reflexivity. So it is also, as indicated earlier, the job of the art *institution*, within which I include its curriculum, evaluation, research and assessment procedures, to offer a model of a thinking apparatus – one

> ... with sufficient psychological resilience and consistency ... to cope with the ambivalence, rejections and projections that are part of change.
> (West, 2007, p. 12)

Yet there is an inherent difficulty here, as education is increasingly subject to the instrumentalism and performativity rife in a Third Way reconfiguration of public services, in which certain provision is under attack as a result of social anxiety (Cooper, 2001). This tension means education is, arguably, less and less able to allow breathing space, let alone creative, transitional space 'in which profoundly different positions, practices and values can be voiced and realised' (Danvers, 2003, p. 50). Despite this, we seem set on a course of continued fragmentation and atomisation of experience, with a greater 'dispersal' of emotion rather than containment (French & Simpson, 2001). This, in the teaching and learning space, contributes, I suspect, to a more depleted or threatened sense of identity, and subsequent anxiety. This may well contribute to dropout rates among those less able to manage this.

To develop a holistic view of the individual learner (and teacher) as embodied, socially and psychologically constructed, emotional, and situated in space, is, I argue, a more challenging but authentic way towards a student centeredness based on actual diversity. This means inviting and taking risks with emotional interactions. It means questioning ownership (and indeed non-ownership) of creative learning spaces. It means asking whose emotional interactions are being foregrounded and whose denied by our traditional structuring of spaces. But surely risk taking, emotional connectedness and a questioning of traditional structure are at the very heart of any creative project.

Note

[1] Pilot interviews I recently ran in which students were asked to talk about studio space became focused on how they felt; interactions, memories, and so on.

References

Atkinson, D. (2002), *Art in Education, Identity and Practice* (London: Kluwer Academic Publishers)

Austerlitz, N. & Aravot, I. (2002) 'Emotions in the design studio', in Davis, A. (ed.) *Enhancing Curricula: Exploring Effective Curriculum Practices in Design and Communication in HE, 1st international conference* (London: cltad)

Bion, W.R. (1984), *Attention and Interpretation* (London: Karnac)

Bourdieu, P. (1989), 'Social space and symbolic power', *Sociological Theory*, **7**, pp. 14–25

Bourdieu, P. & Passeron, J. (1977), *Reproduction in Education, Society and Culture*, 2nd edition (London: Sage Publications)

Britzman, D.P. (1998), *Lost Subjects, Contested Objects: Toward a Psychoanalytic Study of Learning* (Albany, NY: State University of New York)

Britzman, D.P. & Pitt, A.J. (1996), 'Pedagogy and transference: casting the past of learning into the presence of teaching', *Theory into Practice*, **35** (2), pp. 117–123

Brown, T., Atkinson, D. & England, J. (2005), *Regulatory Discourses in Education: A Lacanian Perspective* (London: Peter Lang)

Carlyle, D.E.E. & Woods, P. (2002), *The Emotions of Teacher Stress* (Stoke-on-Trent: Trentham Press)

Cooper, A. (2001), 'The state of mind we're in: social anxiety, governance and the audit society', *Psychoanalytic Studies*, **3**, pp. 349–362

Coren, A. (1997), *A Psychodynamic Approach to Education* (London: Sheldon Press)

Danvers, J. (2003), 'Towards a radical pedagogy: provisional notes on learning and teaching in art & design', *International Journal of Art & Design Education*, **22** (1), pp. 47–57

Davies, B. & Harre, R. (1990), 'Positioning: the discursive production of selves', *Journal for the Theory of Social Behaviour*, **20**, pp. 43–63

Day-Sclater, S. (2003), 'What is the subject?' *Narrative Inquiry*, **13,** pp. 317–330

De Beauvoir, S. (1949/1972), *The Second Sex* (London: Penguin Modern Classics)

Dirkx, J.M. (2001), 'The power of feelings: emotion, imagination and the *construction of meaning in adult learning', New Directions for Adult and Continuing Education*, **89**, pp. 63–72

Fonagy, P. (2003), 'The violence in our schools: what can a psychoanalytically informed approach contribute?' *Journal of Applied Psychoanalytic Studies*, **5** (2), pp. 223–237

Foucault, M. (1977), *Discipline and Punish: The Birth of the Prison* (London: Allen Lane)

Foucault, M. (1986), 'Of other spaces', *Diacrits*, **16** (1), pp. 22–27

French, R. (2000), 'Negative capability, dispersal and the containment of emotion', *Bristol Business School Teaching and Research Review* **3**

French, R.B. (1997), 'The teacher as container of anxiety: psychoanalysis and the role of the teacher', *Journal of Management Education*, **21** (4), pp. 483–495

French, R. & Simpson, P. (2001), 'Learning at the edges between knowing and not-knowing: "translating" Bion', *Organisational and Social Dynamics*, **1** (1), pp. 54–77

Frosh, S. (2003), 'Psychosocial studies and psychology: is a critical approach emerging?' *Human Relations*, **56** (12), pp. 1545–1567

Gosso, S. (ed.) (2004), *Psychoanalysis and Art: Kleinian Perspectives* (London: Karnac)

HEFCE (2006), *Designing Spaces for Effective Learning: A Guide to 21st Century Learning Space Design*, report for the JISC Development Group

Hollway, W. & Jefferson, T. (2000), *Doing Qualitative Research Differently: Free Association, Narrative and the Interview Method* (London: Sage)

Hollway, W. & Jefferson, T. (2001), 'Free association, narrative analysis and the defended subject: the case of ivy', *Narrative Inquiry*, **11** (1), pp. 103–122

Klein, M. (1963), 'On the sense of loneliness', *Envy and Gratitude and Other Works 1946–1963*, pp. 300–313 (London: The Hogarth Press & The Institute of Psychoanalysis)

Klein, M. (1988), *Envy and Gratitude and Other Works 1946–1963* (London: Virago)

Klein, M. (1998) *Love, Guilt and Reparation and Other Works 1921–1945* (London: Vintage)

Lave, J. & Wenger, E. (1991), *Situated Learning: Legitimate Peripheral Participation* (Cambridge: University of Cambridge Press)

Merrill, B. (2004), 'Biographies, class and learning: the experiences of adult learners', *Pedagogy, Culture and Society*, **12** (1), pp. 73–94

Milner, M. (1950), *On Not Being Able to Paint* (Heinnemann)

Morris, M. (2005), 'After-education: Anna Freud, Melanie Klein, and psychoanalytic histories of learning', *Journal of the Canadian Association for Curriculum Studies*, **3** (1), pp. 139–156

Obholzer, A. & Zagier-Roberts, V. (eds.) (1994), *The Unconscious at Work: Individual and Organizational Stress in the Human Services* (London: Routledge)

Ochsner, J.K. (2000), 'Behind the mask: a psychoanalytic perspective on interaction in the design studio', *Journal of Architectural Education*, **53** (4), pp. 194–206

Ogden, T.H. (1992), *The Matrix of the Mind: Object Relations and the Psychoanalytic Dialogue* (London: Maresfield Library)

Paechter, C. (2004), 'Metaphors of space in educational theory and practice', *Pedagogy, Culture and Society*, **12** (3), pp. 449–465

Richards, V. (2002), 'Winnicott and education', in Barford, D. (ed.) *The Ship of Thought: Essays on Psychoanalysis and Learning*, pp. 192–211 (London: Karnac)

Rustin, M. (2001), *Reason and Unreason: Psychoanalysis, Science and Politics* (London, Continuum)

Sagan, O. (2002) 'Teaching psychiatric patients: a psychoanalytic study', *Psychoanalytic Psychotherapy*, **16** (1), pp. 58–73

Sagan, O. (2007a), 'Consonance and dissonance in narratives: thick, mad, white trash', paper presented at the Oxford Ethnography and Education Conference, St Hilda's, Oxford, September

Sagan, O. (2007b), 'Research with rawness: the remembering and repeating of auto/biographical ethnographic research processes', *Ethnography and Education*, **2** (3), pp. 349–364

Said, E. (1978), *Orientalism: Western Conceptions of the Orient* (Routledge & Kegan Paul)

Salzberger-Wittenberg, I., Henry, G. & Osborne, E. (1983), *The Emotional Experience of Learning and Teaching* (London: Routledge)

Shulman, L. (1987), 'Knowledge and teaching: foundations of the new reform', *Harvard Educational Review of Educational Research*, **57**, pp. 1–22

Sibbett, C. (2003), 'Liminality: living and practising at the threshold', paper presented at the XVII International Congress of Psychopathology of Expression and Art Therapy, City

Skeggs, B. (1999), 'Matter out of place: visibility and sexualities in leisure spaces', *Leisure Studies,* **18** (3), pp. 213–232

Tanesini, A. (1999), *An Introduction to Feminist Epistemologies* (London: Blackwell Publishing)

Taylor, Y. (2004), 'Negotiation and navigation: an exploration of the space/places of working class lesbians', *Sociological Research Online*, **9**

Todd, S. (ed.) (1997), *Learning Desire: Perspectives on Pedagogy, Culture, and the Unsaid* (London: Routledge

Troman, G. & Woods, P. (2001), *Primary Teachers' Stress* (London: Routledge/Falmer)

Turner, V. (1997) *The Ritual Process: Structure and Anti-Structure* (Chicago: Aldine Publishing Co.

Vygotsky, L.S. (1962), *Thought and Language* (Cambridge, M.A.: Harvard University Press)

West, L. (2007), 'The radical challenge of family learning: perspectives from auto/biographical research', in Alheit, P., Andersen, A.S., Merrill, B. & West, L. (eds.) *Using Biographical and Life History Approaches in the Study of Adult and Lifelong Learning: European Perspectives* (Berne: Peter Lang)

Winnicott, D.W. (1971), *Playing and Reality* (London: Tavistock/Routledge)

Woods, P. & Carlyle, D. (2002), 'Teacher identities under stress: the emotions of separation and renewal', *International Studies in Sociology of Education*, **12** (2), pp. 169–189

This paper was first published in Art, Design and Communication for Higher Education, pp173–186, Volume 6, number 3, June 2008. Reprinted by permission of Intellect Books, The Mill, Parnall Road, Bristol BS16 3JG, UK, © 2008.

Geoffrey Makstutis

In this paper, Sagan takes on some of the most highly charged issues in education and particularly those within art and design education. On the one hand, here is a call for an acceptance and embracing of the reality that emotion *is* present within the learning space (whether physical or conceptual) and that denial of this reality has implications across a range of educational activities and imperatives. On the other, is the articulation of the challenge that practitioners within HE (particularly in art and design) are caught in a double-bind of seeking to address the massification of the HE sector while implicitly recognising the role that emotion plays in the production of art/design work.

In taking up the Winnicottian conception of the 'transitional space', Sagan provides some clues as to the value of accepting emotion into the learning environment. Where we often seek to marginalise or isolate emotion (and certainly *problematic* emotion) from the studio environment (making it the responsibility of other institutional structures), Sagan suggests that, in effect, we are removing the 'culture' from studio culture. In fact, her own research shows us that students, particularly vulnerable students, relish the opportunity to use the studio and the learning space to explore emotions and share in anxieties. This is not to suggest that the studio becomes 'group therapy', but that where there are shared anxieties *about* learning and teaching that the students *and* the teachers may benefit from the exploration. Where we have, for many years, accepted a constructivist view of education from Vygotsky and others, wherein the context of the learner is established in order for effective learning to take place, we have yet to accept that emotion plays a crucial role in that context.

Sagan has also pointed to the dichotomy that such isolation from emotion is created in relation to the widening participation agenda. While on the one hand we seek to open HE to groups who may not have had the opportunity to engage in the past, we do them no favours in not developing a space in which we are able to engage and *contain* (in the Bionian sense of *containment*) the potentially negative prior experiences that these new entrants to higher education may bring with them. One must wonder whether the government drive toward a skills agenda (Leitch Report, 2006) and employability is equally creating further opportunities for anxiety in which entrants to HE, and perhaps uniquely in the arts, are continually reminded of the overriding importance of the employment market. Additionally, the challenge that teachers face in reconciling the seemingly divergent views of creativity and risk taking (cognitive, creative, challenging) with the apparently pragmatic and professional, may further charge the learning space.

While Sagan does not suggest that teachers seek to become Winnicot's 'good enough mother', there is a clear sense in which responding to the students' needs in a manner that builds toward independence is what we have been working towards for some time. The next step may be to accept that emotions play a part in this and that the 'good enough teacher' would see teaching and learning as coupled with emotional development as well as critical, cognitive and creative development.

This is not a paper that offers answers – and perhaps, in regard to the subject matter, that is not possible. It is, however, a clarion call for a reconsideration and exploration of the constructed learning spaces that we create and inhabit with our students. If we are to be able to engage diversity and divergence, then surely we must also engage in the emotions that shape the experience of learning and teaching.

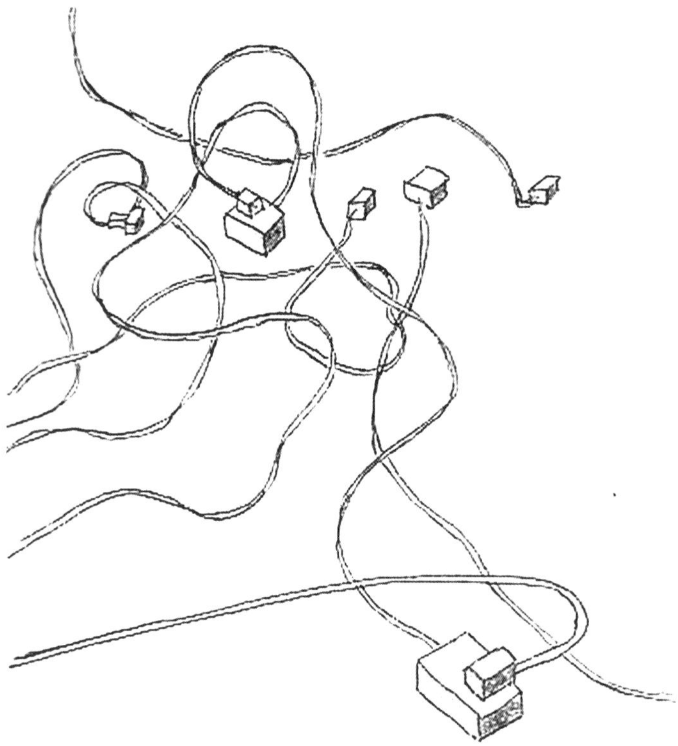

Cables Ben Jonson

Reproduced by permission of the artist

2

Experiencing emotions in design education: a studio perspective

Author: Ben Jonson

Commentary: Antony Johnston

Keywords

studio experience,
emotional intelligence,
learning theories,
assessment

Ben Jonson

Introduction

> Crucial to how we feel is being aware of how we are feeling in the moment. The sine qua non of that is to realize that you are being emotional in the first place. The earlier you recognize an emotion, the more choice you will have in dealing with it.
> (Ekman, 2003)

While some common human expressions of emotion have been identified, viz. anger, sadness, fear, surprise, disgust, contempt and happiness, many others are neither innate nor universal but complex cognitive constructs influenced and mediated by social and cultural factors (Ekman, op. cit.). The degree to which, say, culture exerts a causal influence, however, can be difficult to determine.

The difficulty in determining causal influence also raises methodological issues particular to emotion research in design. For example, how to evaluate the impact of computer technology on emotion in tutor-student interactions. Such matters of concern, however, would go beyond the scope of this essay, which, moreover, addresses face-to-face, not virtual interaction, such as e-learning.

Emotion, then, is a complex phenomenon of both learned and innate expressive displays and physical responses that can be verbal as well as non-verbal, including body postures, attitudes and paralanguage, for example, hesitation and gesture. Further, emotional responses may vary from total 'openness' to 'concealment', for example, genuine versus social ('fake') smiles, and can be very subtle, such as 'micro expressions'. Ekman says: 'These expressions tend to be very extreme and very fast. Eighty to 90 per cent of people we tested don't see them' (op. cit.). Against such complexity, I take the view that the role of emotion in tutor-student interactions is intrinsically linked with the studio experience, a form of learning that is personal and social, experiential and situated, arguing that emotion is a critical design skill.

This essay looks at the role of emotion in tutor-student interactions in the context of design education and the studio experience in particular, from both a practical and theoretical perspective, including assessment, tutor-student power relationships, theories of learning, and emotional intelligence. It draws on the author's experience of studio teaching and pedagogic research across a broad spectrum of design disciplines in London design schools. It argues that the studio experience, in integrating thinking, making and doing, is both personal and professional, where emotion cannot be separated from design processes and, in the end, becomes embedded in the design. It concludes that better awareness of emotional issues may help enhance tutor-student interaction and therefore ought to be part of tutors' continuing professional development.

The studio experience, emotion and learning

It is widely held that central to design education is the studio experience, which involves inquiry- or problem-based activities where students engage in problem identification, problem definition, problem solving, and method, in a learning environment that encourages exploration and experimentation. In this, the studio experience embodies both experiential learning (thinking *and* doing) and situated learning (function of the activity, context and culture, Lave & Wenger, 1990), serving as an educational model that recognises the need for artistry in professional education (Schön, 1987). As a form of learning that is both personal and social, the studio model offers substantial pedagogic freedom, including play, providing for rich and authentic emotional experiences that reflect how followers in art and design education have 'an intensely personal relationship with their subject' (Micklethwaite, 2005, p. 92).

The intensely personal relationship resonates with personalised learning, or constructivism, a learning theory pioneered by Jean Piaget whereby learning is understood as a very personal endeavour actively constructed by the learner (Piaget, 1969). But the studio model also reflects Leo Vygotsky's understanding of learning, also known as activity theory, as something that occurs through social interaction and language, where the role of the teacher is that of providing scaffolding to assist student learning (Vygotsky, 1962). Both theories, then, may help us better understand the role of emotion in tutor-student interactions.

The intense student-subject relationship ('doing your own thing'), however, can, in my experience, result in students developing an overly emotional attachment to their own work. Better then, I would argue, to balance personalised learning with social interaction, including peer learning, to help students stand back and take a critical view of their own work as a means to change. Such reflective practice can help students become more conscious managers of their thought processes and emotional energies.

The studio experience, then, consists of both intellectual and emotional challenges where students encounter constraints and ambiguities inherent in the processes of design as well as adversarial interpersonal episodes with tutors, for example, fear of embarrassment or failure. Tutor-student interaction, then, I would argue, includes necessarily uncomfortable or unsettling questions, although tutors also need to be aware of learners' fears (Sappington, 1984). The studio model can thus be seen as representing a cultural practice where emotion cannot be separated from learning and, ultimately, becomes embedded in the design, as exemplified by the attention given to styling or consumer branding, also described as 'designing emotion' (Desmet 2002). Design, then, I would argue, is affective both in process and outcome.

Teaching and learning styles: the studio versus the lecture model

The relocation of design education to the university sector in recent times has introduced design to the pedagogy of the university. What, then, are the pedagogic differences between the studio model and the university lecture model in terms of teaching and learning styles, and therefore tutor-student interactions?

Comparing the two models, it is notable that the lecture model has a different philosophical tradition, where faculty, through reading and writing academic texts, is focusing on intellectual development rather than the social and emotional aspects of learning. In the university, where teaching spaces (classrooms and lecture halls) are considered interchangeable with no hints at the subject matter, needs and resources are also very different from practice-based design, where designers' interests are things rather than abstracts.

This is not to say that histories and theories are unimportant in practice-based design education. Generic university courses, however, rely on intellectual discourse and have been criticised for not making more of the links between intellectual, social and emotional processes – for example, that learning is facilitated or hampered by emotions (Goleman, 1995), or that emotions drive learning and memory (Sylvester, 1994). Universities, then, have been slow to make use of social and emotional influences on learning (Love & Goodsell Love,

1995), or, when addressing emotion in educational theory, have failed to show how far the theory is actually practised (Tenenbaum et al., 2001).

But although I am arguing that emotion is intrinsic to the studio experience, the actual influence of emotion on practice-based learning is not well documented, and the same could be said about the relationship between the studio and lecture models in the new, or hybrid, university environment. Yet despite lack of systematic empirical research in this field, it might be useful to try to find a theoretical framework for describing the pedagogic differences between the two models. Such a framework, I would suggest, can be found in the variety of teaching and learning styles, as illustrated by the visual-auditory-kinesthetic learning model, VAK.

The VAK model

The VAK model, which emphasises individual learning preferences, relates to experiential learning theory, a theory representing a learning cycle of experiencing, reflecting, thinking and acting (Kolb, 1984). In his writings, Kolb acknowledges the early work on experiential learning by others, including Rogers, Jung and Piaget, for example Jung's assertion that learning styles result from people's preferred ways of adapting in the world (Jung, 1933). According to the VAK model, there are three learning styles:

- visual (seeing and reading);
- auditory (listening and speaking);
- kinesthetic (touching and doing).

That is, the visual learning style, which involves the use of seen and observed things (for example, pictures, video, and demonstrations); the auditory, which involves listening (words, music, and sounds); and the kinesthetic, which involves physical experience (making, touching, and moving).

But whereas both the studio and lecture models include visual and auditory learning styles, the studio model adds the third – kinesthetic. It is kinesthetic learning, then, and notably its 'hands-on' and 'touchy-feely' qualities ('learning by doing'), that sets the studio experience apart from learning in the classroom or the lecture hall. Kinesthetic learning, moreover, is a working style for designers, reinforcing the argument that the studio model is the preferred learning style of designers.

Emotion and assessment

Although individual learning preferences figure prominently in the studio model, the model also emphasises design as 'process'. The notion of process, however, may, in some design procedures, suggest privileging rationality above emotion. For example, in my research on conceptual tools in a digital age, the issue of sketching touched a raw nerve, or 'Why sketching?' (Jonson, 2005). Emotions, then, can be messy, unpredictable or inconvenient. How much easier it seems to 'play safe' and downplay or suppress emotions in favour of logic and reason.

Tutor-student interaction, however, is both informational and expressive. But whereas information involves transmission of facts, the action of expressing something face-to-face conveys a certain emotion. It is here, then, when speaking conveys emotion rather than mere facts that, I would argue, tutor-student interaction is at its most vulnerable. This is particularly so in the studio critique ('the crit'), or similar forms of task-, portfolio-, project- or performance-based assessments, where emotions, in my experience, oscillate between hope and fear, and every emotion in between.

For example, I was juror in a final review where a student was failed because his design solution, although technically adequate, was found lacking in imagination ('this is construction, not architecture', as one tutor put it). It emerged, then, that the student had been focusing on narrow, material problem solving ('hard facts') at the expense of 'softer', contextual issues, such as social performance or emotional effect. Moreover, when the personal tutors had questioned the student's, in their mind, negative attitude to risk taking and change, in individual tutorials and group critiques prior to the final review, the student had not raised to the challenge but responded by 'playing safe'. Unsettling questions by the tutors seemed to have triggered fear of failure in the student (hence playing safe), while the tutors seemed unaware of the student's fear.

Critiques and assessment, then, impact emotions in tutor-student interactions. The impact is particularly critical, I would argue, where assessment is the tipping point between pass and fail, also implicit in the role of external examiners, who are invited to judge final portfolios because they, unlike personal course tutors, take a disinterested view of students' work. Asking informally colleagues and students why students fail in final reviews, their responses were not just expressed in 'objective' terms, such as poor visualisation skills, inadequate research or inappropriate design solutions (as in written student feedback), but invariably included the 'messy stuff' of inarticulate or unresolved emotions in tutor-student interactions. I was left with the impression that the role of emotion was not sufficiently recognised or dealt with in tutor-student interactions, learning outcomes or assessments.

Emotion and learning theory

In the particular assessment referred to above, however, the personal tutors were not unaware of the impact assessment could have on emotion. In fact, a member of the institution's student service was on stand-by in the final reviews to offer pastoral help to failed students, who, understandably, were aggrieved or distressed by the negative outcome. However, the tutors who appeared distinctly 'cool' during the assessment viewed the 'harsh' critique as part of a student's maturing process; students had to learn to take full responsibility for their own work ('swim or sink').

Interestingly, the tutors' view, from a theoretical assumption, seems compatible with constructivism, where responsibility of learning should reside with the learner (Piaget, op. cit.), but less so with activity theory, where the role of the teacher is that of providing scaffolding to assist student learning (Vygotsky, op. cit.).

Paradoxically, then, the two learning theories may offer different perspectives on the reality of the harsh critique and its impact on emotion. Or, rather, the perceived reality: 'A paradox is not a conflict with a reality. It is a conflict between reality and your feeling of what reality should be like' (Marshall & zoner, 1997, p. 387).

Did the tutors, then, control or manipulate the assessment situation in favour of their sense of reality vis-à-vis that of the student? Or, did they privilege rationality over emotion, in which case I would argue they ignored another reality, that is, that face-to-face assessment is a mix of rational and emotional responses. At any rate, the outcome resonated with the assertion that assessment and learning are inextricably linked and not separate processes (Holt & Willard-Holt, 2000).

Tutor-student power relationships

Reflecting on human interaction through language, Hospers asserts: 'We don't so much give information, or receive it from what others say, as express our feelings and attitudes and try, through our language, to work on people's feelings and attitudes in order to change or control them' (Hospers, 1990, p. 33).

'Change' and 'control', then, seem key words in the context of emotion in tutor-student interactions. But whereas change suggests positive emotion, control is, arguably, more likely to carry negative emotion in interactions. This is so, because change is implicit in creative practices, whereas control reveals the asymmetry of knowledge and power in tutor-student interactions, where tutors hold sway by virtue of their expertise and authority, as exemplified by tutors' ultimate right to pass or fail students.

To reduce asymmetry, Munger suggests that tutors develop a more egalitarian conversational approach to tutor-student interactions (Munger, 1996). That is, rather than presenting themselves as 'expert' and working in didactic and controlling ways with students, Munger suggests tutors speak with a personal, rather than a teacher's voice. The principle of equality in conversation, however, is something of an ideal, and in practice tutors and students are aware of imbalances in the learning conversation and the special conditions under which it takes place (Rowsell, 2006). In practice, then, the studio experience highlights tutor-student power relationships where tutors might use emotions, consciously or not, to control or manipulate students. Students, however, may also seek control or resort to manipulative behaviour. But when this happens, it is, I would argue, more often than not symptomatic of an imbalance in the tutor-student power relationship.

Where asymmetry exists, Munger argues that tutor-student interaction can be focused on the effect of questions, because questions are one such speech choice that reveals power relationships (Munger, op. cit.). Illustrating this point is the personal reflection of a graphic design student:

> 'I was not alone in experiencing rudeness, sarcasm and unprofessional behaviour from some tutors and technicians. I am a confident person, but even I felt intimidated and would often withhold questions' (CLIP CETL 2007).

Questions, then, Munger continues, can play an important role in reducing asymmetry where tutors and students agree to try to reduce this asymmetry. To this, I would add that students should have a choice of personal tutors, including the right to change tutor if the tutor-student relationship should turn incompatible. Change, moreover, aligns with the view that tutors in creative practices develop a conceptual change/student-focused approach, rather than an information transmission/teacher-focused approach (Trigwell & Prosser, 1996). Further, the conceptual change approach to teaching, I would suggest, points to the studio model as a social and practice-based learning environment resembling a 'community of practice' (Wenger, 1998). That is, a social entity where members (here tutors, students and practitioners) share concerns with identity, with learning to speak, act and improvise in ways that make sense in the community. As a community of practice, then, the studio model provides opportunities for members to develop their interpersonal (social) and intra-personal (self-reflection) skills, skills that are also embedded in the notion of emotional intelligence.

Emotional intelligence

The term emotional intelligence, EI, was coined by Salovey and Mayer, who describe it as the ability to perceive, understand, manage and use emotions to facilitate thinking (Salovey & Mayer, 1990). EI also relates to 'multiple intelligence' (Gardner, 1983), and other behavioural and psychological theories. Several theories, then, make up EI. The EI concept has been used by Goleman to illuminate the importance of social and emotional abilities for personal success in the domain of work performance (Goleman, 1995, & 1998). Central to Goleman's argument is that emotional competencies are linked to and based on emotional intelligence, while recognising that individuals are a complex combination of emotion and reason (Emmerling & Goleman, 2003).

What constitutes intelligence, however, is controversial. Goleman, for example, argues that the concept of IQ, or conventional intelligence, is too narrow because it ignores essential behavioural and character elements (Goleman, op. cit.). Similarly, Bar-On asserts that, 'it is emotional-social intelligence much more than cognitive intelligence that influences one's ability to do one's best, to accomplish goals and to actualize one's potential to its fullest' (Bar-On, 2006). But Goleman and Bar-On also differ in their views on IQ. Thus Bar-On holds that: 'Evidently a high IQ does not guarantee that one will actualize one's potential, but a high EQ [EI] is definitely more important in this respect' (Bar-On, op. cit.). In contrast, Goleman acknowledges that: 'The notion of IQ as a threshold competence is an important distinction', and 'that genetics likely play an important role in the development of emotional intelligence' (Emmerling & Goleman, op. cit.). Goleman also quotes Van Rooy and Viswesvaran, who found IQ to be a better predictor of work and academic performance than EI (Van Rooy & Viswesvaran, 2004).

Emotion, however, is not universally accepted as being an element of intelligence. For example, '... existing research does not yet show that EI exists as a well-defined psychometric and theoretical construct, let alone that it is critical for adaptation for real-world challenges' (Matthews et al., 2002, p. 547). Despite their criticism, however, Matthews et al. recognise the potential of the emotional intelligence construct to educate, to stimulate thought and action and to spur further study: 'The benefits of EI appear to reside mainly in raising awareness of emotional issues and motivating educators and managers to take emotional issues seriously' (Matthews, op. cit. p. 543).

Goleman draws on Gardner's seven intelligence types:

1. Linguistic;
2. Logical-Mathematical;
3. Musical;
4. Bodily-Kinesthetic;
5. Spatial Visual;
6. Interpersonal;
7. Intrapersonal (Gardner op. cit.).

Of these, Goleman emphasises the interpersonal, or cooperation and teamwork, and the intrapersonal, or self-reflection and self-discovery, also relating the two types to preferred working and learning styles (Goleman, op. cit.). The interpersonal aspect, then, has to do with understanding others and their feelings, whereas the intrapersonal aspect relates to understanding yourself, your goals, intentions, responses and behaviour.

Further, in expanding on the interpersonal and intrapersonal aspects of intelligence, Goleman identifies five 'domains' of emotional intelligence:

1. Knowing your emotions;
2. Managing your own emotions;
3. Motivating yourself;
4. Recognising and understanding other people's emotions;
5. Managing relationships, that is, managing the emotions of others (Goleman, op. cit.).

These domains I find particularly helpful in illuminating the role of emotion in tutor-student interactions.

Emotional intelligence as teaching aid

Whereas Goleman focuses on emotional intelligence in relation to work performance, Mortiboys has applied EI directly to the teaching situation with adult learners. Mortiboys, in arguing for deliberate, and not just intuitive use of emotional intelligence in teaching, suggests that teachers should recognise and respond to their feelings as well as the feelings of their learners, and encourage a positive emotional state in teacher-student interaction that is conducive to learning (Mortiboys, 2005).

Mortiboys' approach to teaching with emotional intelligence makes common sense. This is not unlike the case of medical students, who, by observing experienced doctors, learn to adjust their feelings while dealing with patients (Smith & Kleinman, 1989). Similarly, as a teaching aid, I find Goleman's five domains a practical tool for building trust and mutual respect in tutor-student interactions. For each domain, then, I would suggest affirmative actions to developing EI competencies for both tutors and students.

So for example:

Self-awareness

Knowing your emotions is key to emotional intelligence – a capacity to recognise your feelings as they occur.

Affirmative action: Develop your emotional awareness through extracurricula activities such as music, drama or competitive games.

Emotional control

Managing your emotions is the ability to manage your emotional reactions, control impulses and to recover from life's upsets.

Affirmative action: Keep track of your emotions in the form of, say, a reflective studio diary to help manage emotional demands in different design situations and under various conditions.

Self-motivation

Motivating yourself is the skill at using your emotions in the service of a goal, staying hopeful despite setbacks.

Affirmative action: When stuck, get in touch with your emotions and remind yourself why you wanted to learn/teach design in the first place.

Empathy

Emotional sensitivity to others is the ability to recognise and understand other people's emotions, a talent for tuning into others' feelings and reading their unspoken messages.

Affirmative action: Dare to discuss emotional issues openly and honestly, both in and outside the studio environment.

Handling relationships

Grace in dealing with others – strong social skills are key to popularity, leadership and interpersonal effectiveness.

Affirmative action: Develop an authentic, unconstrained conversational style in tutor-student interactions.

Discussion

Recent years have seen considerable growth, and change, in tertiary design education in England, with young people looking for more rewarding creative challenges and opportunities. Growing student numbers, however, have not been matched with resources, notably studio space and tutor-student contact hours, resulting in fragmentation of the traditional studio experience. But in the face of fragmentation, accelerated by the use of digital and mobile technologies, what happens to the role of emotion in tutor-student interactions? Will technology, rather than face-to-face emotional engagement, act as a leveller towards symmetry in tutor-student interactions, particularly as students are often much closer to technological change and therefore might challenge tutors' expertise and authority?

If assessment and learning is one, is there a case to be made for shifting teacher-centered adversarial assessments to a student-centered approach, including peer- or self-assessment, that would encourage self-reflection and self-correction (change)?

What constitutes best pedagogic practice for nurturing emotion in tutor-student interactions?

Can EI competencies, used as teaching aid, help tutors ask better questions, particularly in assessment situations?

Summary and conclusion

The initial quote – 'The earlier you recognize an emotion, the more choice you will have in dealing with it' (Ekman, op. cit.) – suggests that tutors and students alike need to be better prepared to deal with emotions, notably in crits and assessments. A starting point, then, would be to take emotional issues seriously, to stimulate thought and action, and to spur further study (Matthews et al., op. cit.) because 'without sustained effort and attention, individuals are unlikely to improve greatly a given aspect of their emotional intelligence' (Emmerling & Goleman, op. cit.). Developing EI competencies, then, may help enhance the role of emotion in tutor-student interactions. Moreover, for tutors, the ultimate challenge would be to use emotion as a teaching aid. This suggests that emotional issues become part of continuing professional development.

References

Bar-On, R. (2006), 'The Bar-On model of emotional-social intelligence (ESI)', *Psicothema*, 18, supl., pp. 13–25

CLIP CETL. (2007).'Tell Us About It: Divers Voices in Creative Learning in Practice'. CLIP CETL and Diversity Unit project, University of the Arts London.London: clip cetl.

Desmet, P. (2002), *Designing Emotions* (Delft: Delft University of Technology)

Ekman, P. (2003), 'The 43 facial muscles that reveal even the most fleeting emotions', in conversation with Judy Foreman, *New York Times,* 5 August

Emmerling, R. & Goleman, D. (2003), *Emotional Intelligence: Issues and Common Misunderstandings*, Consortium for Research on Emotional Intelligence in Organizations. Retrieved February 18, 2008 from: http://www.eiconsortium.org

Goleman, D. (1995), *Emotional Intelligence* (New York: Bantam Books)

Goleman, D. (1998), *Working with Emotional Intelligence* (New York: Bantam Books)

Holt, D. & Willard-Holt, C. (2000), 'Let's get real – students solving authentic corporate problems', *Phi Delta Kappa,* **82** (3)

Hospers, J. (1990), *An Introduction to Philosophical Analysis* (London: Routledge)

Jonson, B. (2005), 'Design ideation: the conceptual sketch in the digital age', *Design Studies,* **26** (6), pp. 613–624

Jung, C.G. (1933), *Psychological Types* (New York: Harcourt, Brace)

Kolb, D.A. (1984), *Experiential Learning: Experience as the Source of Learning and Development* (Englewood Cliffs, NJ: Prentice-Hall)

Lave, J. & Wenger, E. (1990), *Situated Learning: Legitimate Peripheral Participation* (Cambridge, UK: Cambridge University Press)

Love, P. & Goodsell Love, A. (1995) 'Enhancing student learning: intellectual, social and emotional integration', *ASHE-ERIC Higher Education Report series 95–4, (Volume 24–4)*

Marshall, I. & zoner, D. (1997), *Who's Afraid of Schrödinger's Cat?* (London: Bloomsbury)

Matthews, G., Zeidner, M. & Robert, R. (2002), Emotional Intelligence: Science and Myth (Cambridge, MA: The M.I.T.)

Micklethwaite, P. (2005), 'Discussing art and design education: themes from interviews with UK design stakeholders', *The International Journal of Art & Design Education*, **24** (1), pp. 84–92

Mortiboys, A. (2005), *Teaching with Emotional Intelligence* (London: Routledge)

Piaget, J. (1969), *Mechanisms of Perception*, translated by G.N. Seagrim (New York: Basic Books)

Van Rooy, D.L. & Viswesvaran, C. (2004), 'Emotional intelligence: a meta-analytic investigation of predictive validity and nomological net', *Journal of Vocational Behavior,* **65**, pp. 71–95

Rowsell, D. (2006), 'Conversation revisited: the application of conversational models to the patterning of e-learning', in Davies, A. (ed.) *Enhancing Curricula: Contributing to the Future, Meeting the Challenges of the 21st Century in the Disciplines of Art, Design and Communication*, pp. 615–634 (London: cltad)

Salovey, P. & Mayer, J. (1990), 'Emotional intelligence', *Imagination, Cognition, and Personality*, **9** (3), pp. 185–211.

Sappington, T. (1984), 'Creating learning environments conducive to change: the role of fear/safety in the adult learning process', *Innovative Higher Education*, **9** (1), pp. 19–29

Schön, D. (1983), *The Reflective Practitioner. How Professionals Think in Action* (London: Temple Smith)

Schön, D. (1987), *Educating the Reflective Practitioner* (San Francisco: Jossey-Bass)

Smith, A. & Kleinman, S. (1989), 'Managing emotion in medical school: students' contacts with the living and the dead', *Social Psychology Quarterly*, **52**, pp. 56–69

Sylvester, R. (1994), 'How emotions affect learning', *Educational Leadership,* **52** (2), 60–65--

Tenenbaum, G., Naidu, S., Jegede, O. & Austin, J. (2001), 'Constructivist pedagogy in conventional on-campus and distance learning practice: an exploratory investigation', *Learning and Instruction*, **11**, pp. 87–111

Trigwell, K. & Prosser, M. (1996), 'Changing approaches to teaching: a relational perspective', *Studies in Higher Education*, **37**, pp. 275–84

Tschimmel, K. (2006), 'Let students think about their thinking in design: a constructivist approach', in Davies, A. (ed.) *Enhancing Curricula: Contributing to the Future, Meeting the Challenges of the 21st Century in the Disciplines of Art, Design and Communication*, pp. 655–668 (London: cltad)

Vygotsky, L. (1962), *Thought and Language* (Cambridge, MA: The M.I.T.)

Wenger, E. (1998), *Communication of Practice. Learning Meaning and Identity* (Cambridge: Cambridge University Press)

Antony Johnston

> All men [sic] by nature desire to know.
> (Aristotle, Metaphysica, 980a)

Learning as fundamental ontology has been taken up more recently, in particular by Barnett, who considers the being of the student and what it means to be a student (2007). Within such a context, learning becomes a vital human activity and as such inevitably leads to an emotional engagement with learning and hence becoming. Often the focus on emotions in education is upon negative constructions such as anxiety and stress, whereas positive emotional responses become embedded and perhaps obscured within notions of motivation.

Jonson asks us to consider both the positive and the negative within student-tutor interactions, powerfully calling for a greater reflexivity on behalf of the tutor and posing important questions relating to assessment and how to develop emotional awareness in tutors.

Sites of learning are sites of emotion regardless of what disciplines exist. Despite this, art and design is often perceived as occupying a unique disciplinary position in relation to the studio experience and the 'crit' as a form of assessment. Furthermore, the stakes in art and design are seen as higher, as students inscribe into a piece of work their very selves: 'You are showing your portfolio, you are bearing your soul' (student interview, 2008).

Such tensions are most salient at stressful times such as assessment or during a long period of supervision where the empathy of the tutor along with the emotional response of the student can prove an important tipping point for a student's success or failure. Within the staff room and through the observation of student teachers (many not new to teaching) in art and design, I've sometimes been shocked and surprised by the nature of engagements with students, which on the surface do not always seem supportive, constructive or 'intelligent'. Such experiences have emphasised the importance of context and intersubjectivity within such interactions and recognition that what may be appropriate for one tutor and/or student is not necessarily appropriate for all.

The question then becomes how best to support and develop emotional knowledge? Like Jonson, I too see the importance and relevance of the reflective practitioner; however, I am wary of the efficacy of normative constructions of emotional intelligence that lean on the notion of an objectifiable and measurable set of intelligences (see Nash, 2005, for a discussion/critique of IQ). Such notions are socially constructed and so we must be wary of symbolic violence (Bourdieu & Passeron, 1990), especially when considering the complexities of widening participation.

While supporting students through both studio practice and assessment, we must clearly develop 'safe' environments in which students can develop, but at the same time we must celebrate the diversity of approaches and engagements, which such activities engender.

References

Barnett, R. (2007), *A Will To Learn: Being a Student in an Age of Uncertainty* (Maidenhead: McGraw Hill/Open University Press/SRHE)

Bourdieu, P. & Passeron, C. (1990), *Reproduction in Education, Society and Culture*, 2nd edition (London: Sage Publications)

McKeon, R. (2001), *The Basic Works of Aritstotle* (New York: The Modern Library)

Nash, R. (2005), 'The cognitive habitus and collective intelligence: concepts for the explanation of inequality of educational opportunity', *Journal of Education Policy*, 20 (1), pp. 3–21

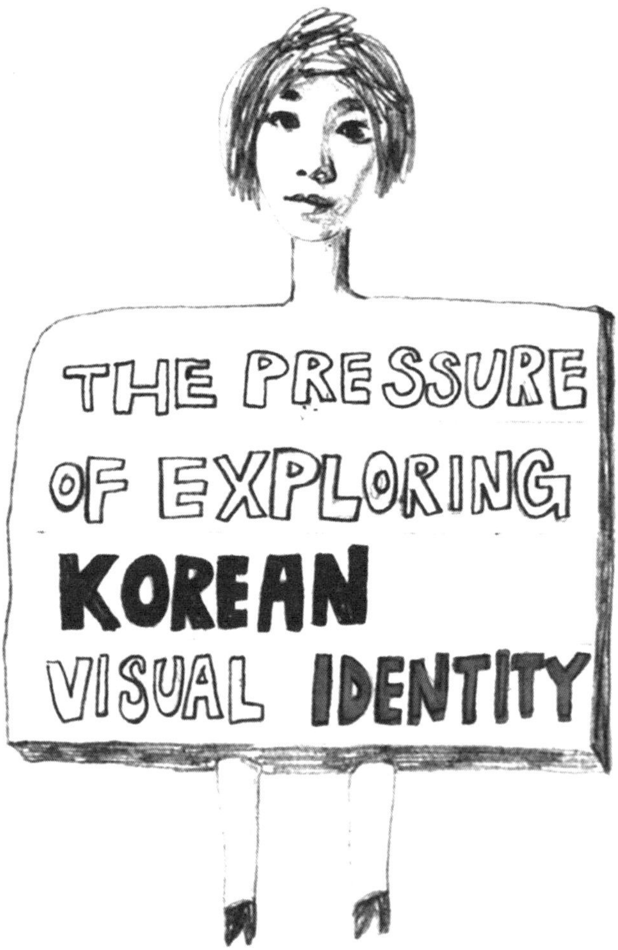

Image A4 Gwen Goeun Lee

Reproduced by permission of AREA-D, Action Research in Art & Design Limited

3

Coping with stress: the perspective of international students

Author: Silvia Sovic

Commentary: Tony Sullivan

Keywords

stress,
creative arts,
international students,
learning strategies

Silvia Sovic

This contribution explores the impact of stress on teaching and learning among first-year BA and foundation degree international students in the creative arts at the University of the Arts, London. It is based on the findings of a project, *The Experience of First-Year International Students* at UAL, commissioned by the Creative Learning in Practice Centre for Excellence in Teaching and Learning (CLIP CETL). The aims of the project were:

- to assess the extent to which international students integrate and adapt to a different teaching and learning environment;
- to identify the causes of obstacles to such integration and adaptation;
- to propose ways in which these can be remedied.

141 students from six geographical areas were interviewed in their native languages, along with a benchmark group of 21 home students. The participants ranged across the whole spectrum of creative arts disciplines taught at the six constituent colleges of the university.

The research context

The study took place within the framework of a rich literature on international students, much of which has drawn on research on the psychological effects of cross-cultural migration. In this context, a first point to be emphasised concerns the dangers of stereotyping. The students involved in this project came from a range of different backgrounds and different educational histories. While their responses show that they have many experiences in common, they are not so homogenous as to allow grand generalisations across the spectrum. It would be equally mistaken to attempt firm conclusions by nation or regional grouping (Kember & Gow, 1991; Watkins, Reghi & Astilla, 1991; Chalmers & Volet, 1997).

For example, much cross-cultural research, on emotions as on so many other subjects, has assumed a dichotomy between cultures that emphasise individualism and those that emphasise collectivism. This has rightly been challenged by more recent work, which has shown the dangers of attempting to view these individuals as representatives of homogenous, stereotyped groups (Shore, 1996; Lazarus, 1991 and 1999).

A good explanation of why this should be is found in the literature on stress. The notion, put forward especially by cultural psychologists and anthropologists, that people within specific cultures share the same values, beliefs etc., and therefore feel and react in the same way when it comes to emotions and stress, has been challenged by Lazarus (1997, 1999). He argues that the evidence on which these concepts are based is insufficient, and that data

> … have been interpreted with too much sanguinity by the protagonists of cultural differences in emotion. Most of the data seems to restate the cultural values of countries and ethnic groups. Much of it is based on reports by people who may be just restating their culture's formal values rather than portraying the actual dynamics of their stressful and emotional transactions.
> (Lazarus, 1999, p. 65)

Various studies have already demonstrated that the experiences of stress should not be perceived as something that is 'culturally specific', but, on the contrary, stress is felt on an individual basis: 'each person sees the world "through stress-coloured glasses"' (Sarros & Densten, 1989, p. 48, quoting Veninga & Spradley, 1981, p. 29). Coping strategies for dealing with stress thus vary from person to person; what one student treats as a challenge, another might see as a threat (Sarros & Densten, loc. cit.). Burns states that 'stress occurs when the individual believes that they cannot meet the demand being made on them by the environment, i.e. it is a subjective self evaluation of not being able to cope, of feeling overwhelmed to some degree' (Burns, 1991, p. 67).

Burns's description of stress follows the classic definition by Lazarus and Folkman, which is the one adopted here. They defined psychological stress as 'a particular relationship between the person and the environment that is appraised by the person as taxing or exceeding his or her resources and endangering his or her well-being' (Lazarus & Folkman, 1984, p. 19). International students are subjected to many stresses during their time at university. Although it is common knowledge that there are many factors that cause stress, this topic is relatively unexplored when it comes to international students, especially those studying creative arts.

It is widely accepted that the transition of students from one country to another is accompanied by various emotions, positive and negative. Many aspects of the process of adaptation that students have to experience –cultural, social and academic – have a significant impact on their achievements. Students are confronted with many stressful situations, of which 'culture shock' is just one. Oberg, who coined the term, describes culture shock as 'precipitated by the anxiety that results from losing all our familiar signs and symbols of social intercourse' (Oberg, 1960). He proposed four stages of this phenomenon: honeymoon, crisis, recovery and adjustment. Studies have questioned the construct of culture shock. Searle and Ward argued that it 'has been utilized both as a descriptive and an explanatory term … As a descriptor, however, it is largely inadequate to define the nature of the psychological and emotional difficulties or the adjustment demands faced by sojourners, and as an explanatory concept it becomes tautological and constrains the worthwhile investigation of variables that predict adaptation during the transition process' (Searle & Ward, 1990, p. 450; and cf. Ward & Kennedy, 1993, p. 221). In their alternative view, these scholars placed greater emphasis on two types of adjustment during cross-cultural transition: psychological adjustment, which is 'primarily affected by personality, life changes, and social support variables', and sociocultural adaptation, which is 'primarily affected by amount of time spent in a new culture, cultural similarity-dissimilarity, host-guest relations, and acculturation strategies' (op. cit. p. 241).

'Culture shock' is certainly not dead. Lago and Shipton (1994) proposed a model of culture shock specifically for international students, in which they identified five transitional stages. These are: a 'honeymoon' period; disorientation; reintegration; autonomy and independence; and finally, a 'bicultural competence' phase, which enables students to absorb both cultures. When students go through these phases their sense of identity is of critical importance; students often feel that they have lost their identity, or that their 'normal' identity had been disrupted and replaced by another due to study abroad. In his study of the relationship between identity and stress, Burke argued that this disruption can cause lower self-esteem, stress and even depression (Burke, 1991). Perrucci and Hu believe that the focus of research should not be placed on students' capacity for adaptation but rather on 'their feelings of satisfaction with their academic program, their academic appointment, and their social and community relations'.

They proposed a 'general theoretical model of satisfaction among graduate international students' (Perrucci & Hu, 1995, p. 497).

Student transition involves separation and loss, leaving family, relatives, friends and other social support networks behind (Walton, 1990, p. 509; Werkman, 1980). It is also closely associated with the influential attachment theory advanced by John Bowlby (1973). He and others argued that a child's separation from its mother results in anxiety, and that this experience can be observed later in the adult's life. Many studies have demonstrated that the influences of maternal attachment on individuals are closely related to the later development of teacher-child relationships, and remain throughout the course of life, able to be unconsciously re-awakened in any new situations that remind them of their past experiences. Melanie Klein (1959) called this phenomenon 'memory in feeling'. Recent research has also suggested that gender and different ethnic backgrounds influence the quality of the teacher-child relationship: 'ethnic differences between teachers and child may be an issue if the cultural norms of each are in conflict' (Kesner, 2000, p. 136; cf. p. 139). International students invariably encounter several new situations by coming to study in the UK and, in comparison with home students, they face additional problems that relate to unfamiliar ways of thinking and behaving. The interaction with their tutors evokes many emotions that relate to their infantile hopes and fears. Salzberger-Wittenberg, Henry and Osborne (1983) argued that the teacher can play an essential role in the mental and emotional life of students, managing their expectations and relationships, and in due course enabling them to succeed. With temporary support right from the beginning, the student will achieve an easy transition into university life and avoid further disappointments that might easily turn into anger and other negative emotions.

Looking at these issues specifically in arts and design, Austerlitz and Aravot explored the complex set of emotions in the tutor-student relationship in the architectural design studio (Austerlitz & Aravot, 2006, 2007). Communication between student and tutor is 'a central vehicle for education as it includes more than transference of professional knowledge'. They found that all participants, but students in particular, 'may experience a high level of cognitive stress and a tendency to emotionality' (Austerlitz & Aravot, 2007). The relationship between emotions and educational processes is perhaps even more complex when dealing with international students, who bring with them their own sets of values and norms. Memories of their previous experiences with tutors, communication difficulties and past learning experiences can build up into a stronger set of emotions than were experienced by those who never attempted such a transition.

Methodology

The University of the Arts, London has a high proportion of international students. According to UKCOSA, the University of the Arts was ranked 15th in the list of recruiters of international students in the UK for 2005–6;[1] international students were 17% of the total students. If undergraduates from the European Union are included, the proportions are even higher – 32%.[2] The research focused on six geographical areas that supply high numbers of students: Japan, South Korea, Hong Kong, Taiwan, India and the USA. Some UK students were also included for comparative purposes. A key feature of the project was that the students were interviewed in their own languages, by their co-nationals.[3] 14 social science postgraduates were hired from outside the University of the Arts, mainly from the School of Oriental and African Studies, the London School of Economics and the Institute of Education. The interviews were recorded and subsequently transcribed/translated.

Before being interviewed, students filled in a short written questionnaire, giving basic details about their educational backgrounds, time spent in England before studying at UAL, some demographic information, how they heard of the institution etc. Interviews were semi-structured, consisting of 16 questions. The questions covered topics such as reasons for studying abroad, expectations, cultural and educational differences in art and design, friendship, gender issues, stress, support services etc. The interviewers were consulted during the process of finalising the questions, to ensure that there were no ambiguities or culturally inappropriate questions. The interview lasted between 20 and 30 minutes. 141 international students were interviewed. 21 home students were also interviewed, for purposes of comparison, by a native English speaker. The approach of the analysis was both qualitative and quantitative. NVivo and Excel were used as the main tools for analysis, together permitting connections to be made between the interviews and the written questionnaires.

The decision to conduct interviews in the students' own languages had both positive and negative implications. The interviews provided rich insights precisely because the language barrier had been eliminated; students could express their thoughts more easily in their native languages, and to their co-nationals. The fact that the interviewers were international students themselves also helped; many of them reported that the interviewees saw them as an 'older brother or sister'. The danger, of course, was that a high degree of empathy between interviewer and interviewee might lead to unconscious distortions. Moreover, having such a large multinational team of interviewers also brought with it problems. There were some differences in their interviewing techniques, especially at the beginning, and for most of them English was not their first language. Students' views were thus filtered by the translation process, and some information may have been either misinterpreted or got 'lost in translation'. The fact that the interviewers were not creative artists may also have affected the outcome of the exercise, as they may have been less instinctively insightful of the subject. (On the other hand, they might also have been less likely to lead their interviewees in this respect.) To an extent, these potential problems were dealt with by intensive management of the interviewing process. Weaknesses remain, but have to an extent been offset by the scale of the response, which went well over the original target of 60–100 interviews. This was a conscious decision; given the nature of the responses it was felt that volume should be prioritised. If it is not always possible to be sure exactly what a student meant by a particular remark, the frequent recurrence of the same points over a substantial number of interviews allow some clear conclusions to be drawn.

One of the 16 questions put to the students at the interviews was specifically on stress. It asked: 'What, if anything, do you find stressful on this course?' Unsurprisingly, however, stress featured prominently in answers to almost all the questions. Since all the data was extensively coded, it was possible to evaluate what students said on the subject in a wide range of contexts (and of course to relate this to the data they supplied on their gender, age, nationality and linguistic competence).

Findings

Of the many findings of this survey, the following will focus mainly on those that related to academic issues. The problems students experience with language, adaptation to the English academic system, relationships to tutors, classroom participation, group work and assessment are all foregrounded in their responses. A focus on academic issues suggests that it might be useful to consider not just 'culture shock' – the features of which are well known – but actually also 'academic shock', which is composed of some less obvious elements. Some of these might also be considered as 'social shock'.

The range and extent of stress that international students experience depend on a number of factors, including linguistic proficiency, degree of familiarity with the system and the length of time the student has spent in the UK before enrolling. There are some less obvious factors as well. One is gender; it appears that, while the great majority of the international students who were interviewed said that they had experienced stress, female students tended to deal with it better than male students, either talking about it to their friends or using the counselling services.[4] Another is the age of the students:

> The students are generally very young. I am 24. I feel like an idiot in front of younger people. Well ... I don't know what they think about me.
>
> (South Korean student)

The ages of these students, and their previous educational backgrounds, are of profound significance. Many international students already have degrees from their home country and are slightly older than home students; many also have previous work experience. The analysis suggests that it is precisely these students who experience greater levels of anxiety and stress, because they come from different teaching and learning environments, and thus have, in many respects, a more fixed set of expectations.

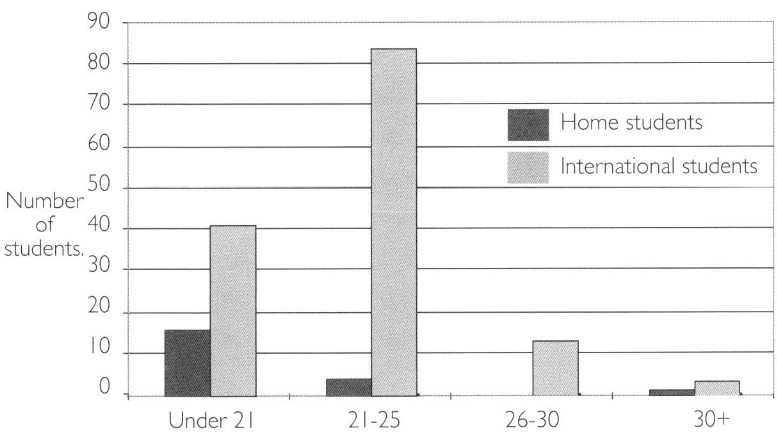

Figure 1: Age profile of first-year international and home students interviewed

Language

The most visible and obvious area of stress for the majority of international students is language. For those whose first language is not English this is usually singled out as the biggest obstacle to their adaptation to the educational setting at UAL. The study has identified the concern of international students that high IELTS test scores do not guarantee success with study. It is perceived that students are taught 'how to pass the test' rather than how to understand and communicate in 'real life' situations with fast-talking native speakers. Many students acknowledge that they had never been exposed to anything like these situations before, and stated that they consequently found it extremely hard to understand what was expected of them in their new environment.

Although the basic problem of language can appear monolithic, it is in fact complex and can impinge on all aspects of teaching and learning. Some students say that they cannot speak, others that they cannot understand, or answer questions, or read at the speed required if they are to keep up with the coursework (and they consequently need a lot of time for essay-writing). Students who are technically qualified and even fluent in a non-UK version of English (Hong Kong, Indian and even American students) can also have significant problems with the demotic London version of the language, delivered at speed and without restraint, in class or outside it. An additional problem is tacit knowledge; much that is communicated to them appears to them to be indirect, so they often cannot understand what is expected of them. They can be left out if they feel that tutors do not explain concepts or references that local students would grasp immediately, while the speed at which native speakers talk leaves them further at a loss:

> When I give a presentation, other students ask me about my work and I have to answer immediately. But if I don't understand, I cannot answer properly. It's particularly difficult to understand young students who speak very fast. I cannot catch their accent. Then, I miss a lot for my study ...
> Language is an obstacle not only for my learning but also for my social life. I'm really scared to speak to English students. I'm too shy ...
> (South Korean students)

The English system of teaching and learning in art and design

The distinctive system of teaching and learning in English universities, and specifically that of UAL, forms the main element of 'academic shock' that affects most international students, whatever their mother tongue. These students come with different expectations of what it is like to study at university, and neither descriptions of what it is going to be like nor experience of university in their home country prepare them adequately for the transition, which is a major cause of stress.

> The process that I have been through is: (1) I had high expectations about liberal teaching and learning approach in the UK; (2) I was shocked and lost; (3) I gradually learned to

> accommodate and to accept this approach, after doing so many projects. I can see my improvement, but it is a bit slow.
> (Taiwanese student)

The degree of emphasis on independent study, obviously well known to practitioners, has of course to be rediscovered by individual students for themselves:

> The system is very different here. In India, you are literally told what to do. Here you are on your own. You have to make your own decisions. In a way it is very good that it makes you independent. But at times you are so lost because when you come here initially you want someone to tell you what to do ...
> (Indian student)

In the creative arts, there are additional differences. Many students did not expect the strong theoretical slant of their course, and were surprised that (as they saw it) skills are not valued more. Several were equally surprised that the process of creative design was given such importance relative to the product

> ... in Korea, you just have to turn in the final project and there is no emphasis on the process. But here in the UK, you have to put more emphasis on the process of the project, which makes it more difficult and something I definitely had to adapt to.
> (South Korean student)

Others found that the emphasis on originality, and what they perceived as the constant demand to be original, were particular causes of stress, again because this was so different from what they were used to from home. Closely related to this is the difficulty referred to above, namely the students' feeling that it has not been made clear what is expected of them:

> I am not sure what [tutors'] expectations are. So it stresses me; I don't know how can I work harder ...
> (Indian student)

The system of independent study also leads to stress over time management, the indispensable skill that students have to acquire in the English system. This affects all international students:

> In the States, I wouldn't stress this much about my work, because the teacher would be stressing for me, saying 'you have to get this done', and I'm like 'okay, okay!,' but here I have

> no one saying that to me, so I have to say it to myself. That's stressful!
> (American student)

It places particular burdens on those students who have to contend with language problems as well:

> Of course English is stressful, as I told you. That is the most difficult thing ... ... When I have a project, I cannot do anything else. The task is so tough, so I cannot spend my time on practice such as speaking English with others or watching TV to improve my English. I've got a deadline, and it's not easy to have an idea and finish the work in a good time.
> (South Korean student)

The use of student support (in the form of an essay checking service) can undoubtedly help, but it also adds to the pressure on students who wish to use it, as they have to hand in their work well in advance of the coursework deadlines.

Interaction with teachers and students

All the stresses connected with comprehension and social integration come to the fore in the many situations in which students have to communicate and work together with teachers and with their peers. Many of the international students interviewed in this project stated that they were naturally shy, even before the stresses of difference, language and adaptation were factored in. Natural reluctance to speak, combined with the difficulty of doing so in another language in front of a mixed audience, usually with a predominance of native speakers, makes class discussion and group work immensely stressful situations:

> If the tutor points at me, I will speak. I will hide if nobody asks me to speak because my English is not good and I can't speak fluently. I feel shame to speak in front of 20, 30 something people as they are local and their mother tongue is English.
> (Hong Kong student)

> Asian students are less likely to participate in this kind of discussion. UK students would not really give many chances to us to speak ...
> (Taiwanese student)

> Also, when there is a classroom discussion, if you don't know something about it, then you feel left out because since you are

> not born here or have not spent a lot of time here, you don't know a lot of things that have already happened ... If I don't know that, I feel like I am on the moon or something like that.
> (Indian student)

The overall consequence of such stresses is that it is all too easy to opt out of interaction. But the consequence of that is isolation, failure to form bonds or friendships with fellow students, and failure to establish a communicative relationship with teachers as well. Such isolation in turn makes progress with study even harder than before:

> Sometimes when I get really stuck on something and I can't talk to anyone, like talk to a tutor, that's the most stressful thing for me.
> (South Korean student)

Isolation, in the form of retreat into individual study, is ultimately not an option in the creative arts as taught in most courses at UAL. Participation is critical, be it in group projects or in formal presentations in class. Group work can be even more stressful because a silent student is effectively excluded, whether voluntarily or not. It is also something that many international students have not really encountered before. Students were eloquent to their compatriot interviewers about the dynamics involved:

> It was difficult for me. One of the reasons was my English, but another reason would be the characters of students in my group. My students have strong characters and they tend to be uncompromising to others so it was difficult to produce an outcome as a result of group work.
> (Japanese student)

> Firstly, it is English. Secondly, UK students don't understand why Asian students spend so much time on thinking. And the ways that these two groups of students work are so different. Sometimes, some Asian students try to explain what they think. These UK students just are unwilling to listen. Third, these UK students believe that they are entitled to dominate and to lead where our discussion should go, simply they are Westerners.
> (Taiwanese student)

Presentations in class entail similar stresses; again because they may be new to the student, because of language and differences of cultural perspective, and because, in the creative arts, students are offering up so much of their own personality in the work that they do. Peer opinion is thus critical, and can be much feared:

> To me, the stress comes from my peer group. When I see others work, it is a kind of competition ... As a result, I need to push myself forward as well.
> (Taiwanese student)

The 'presentation culture' can also appear alien:

> I feel it stressful that the teachers value the presentations more than the work. I think that the practical skills are not respected enough, and it's more like philosophy than fine arts.
> (Japanese student)

> I don't like that students often cover their poor job with their fluent presentation. Everybody does that. Presentation is considered the most important thing. I am not happy with that at all. However, I think this attitude is normal in the British art scene nowadays.
> (South Korean student)

In the teaching of the creative arts, the student's confidence appears to be highly prized. Participation in class, giving presentations and working together in groups can all be immensely stressful for international students, and are often completely new experiences for them. Many Hong Kong students, whose English was very good, found it hard to adapt to these activities. Classroom situations are precisely where international students are at the greatest disadvantage – culturally, linguistically and socially. For many, these situations are exacerbated by the difficulty of transferring from a system in which standing out in class is not encouraged, to one in which self-confidence is everything. Many of the students whose overall verdict on their experience was positive said that this was the hardest part of adaptation, a stage that they had to pass through in order to progress.

An illustration of how stressful this could be was what was learned about the 'crit', where students offer their work up for discussion in a group critique. Students who commented on this practice do not appear to have enjoyed the experience:

> We present [our work] in a group crit. If my work is not good, then people look at you differently. People may say, 'oh him, I

> saw his work, it's not that good.' The stress comes from worrying that my image to others will be damaged.
> (Hong Kong student)

In fact, very few of the international students had anything to say about this (unlike the 'benchmark' home students, many of whom also found crits daunting). Yet a tutor who participated in the 'Unspoken Interactions' symposium at which these issues were aired pointed out that international students rarely came to crits, perhaps precisely because they found the exercise so stressful.[5]

Assessment

A final area to be discussed here is assessment. Almost by definition, the UAL system will be different from those to which international students are accustomed. In addition to the by now familiar issues of adaptation and comprehension, international students get stressed about their grades for other reasons. Because the students interviewed tended to be older, and thus more aware of the effects of the march of time on their career prospects – and given the substantial fees they have paid in order to study at UAL – they are very anxious to achieve, and that anxiety is easily compounded if they are unclear about, or distrustful of, the grading system.

> I feel stressed when I came all the way to UAL to study, and all I get is a C0. I want to get better grades. In Korea, there is a lot of emphasis on good grades and an impressive transcript.
> (South Korean student)

Difficulties in understanding a new or foreign grading system are perhaps inevitable, and the solution is comparatively obvious. For the students interviewed, however, the problem is deeper. Many expressed frustration at not being able to understand how they could improve their grades. The feedback that they are given is often not perceived as helpful. Some students are upset by very negative comments; others find flattering remarks too superficial. What both groups have in common is a feeling that the feedback is insufficiently detailed and specific.[6] Yet again, the linguistic and cultural barriers between international students and their teachers appear to aggravate the problem, which is felt deeply by some students. The danger of misunderstandings is ever-present, and some of the reasons for this are systemic. While the specific terminologies used in the creative arts can be an obstacle for all students, this obstacle is harder for non-native speakers to surmount. The widespread practice in these disciplines of giving verbal feedback disadvantages non-native speakers yet further (Blair, 2004). Ultimately, assessment too is a cultural issue (MacKinnon & Manathunga, 2003).

Conclusion

International students do not face a completely different set of problems from their 'home' student counterparts. Many of the most common causes of stress among students are experienced by home students as well. Group work, presentations and the 'crit' are singled out in particular by the 'benchmark' group of UK students interviewed. Yet international students are more likely to be confronted by an accumulation of these problems and, at the same time, have greater difficulty in dealing with them, precisely because lack of integration is one of them; they find it harder to develop social networks, to communicate effectively with their tutors and peers, and to articulate their concerns to the host community that is providing the support services – issues that the home students interviewed did not see as problematic.

What can be done to mitigate these problems? There are no instant or magical solutions. One way of alleviating stress must be assisting with cross-cultural communication and integration, by increasing opportunities for social integration both inside and outside the classroom. The most important key to progress, however, can be summed up in a word – understanding. International students badly need to be given full initial and ongoing explanations of what is expected of them, how the system works and where to get help (be it from tutors, peers or support staff). But such information and support can only be effective if, as well as being organised and sustained, it is based on better insight, by both staff and home students, into what international students are up against.

Notes

[1] http://www.ukcosa.org.uk/about/statistics_he.php

[2] http://www.hesa.ac.uk/index.php/content/view/600/239/

[3] Or in English, if they preferred. Only a few bilingual students took up this option.

[4] This is in line with the findings of Chang (2007).

[5] Blair (2006) p. 88 points out that the 'crit' is stressful even where tutors have gone to considerable lengths to provide a supportive environment for students, in smaller groups.

[6] This echoes the findings of Blair (2006) p. 86.

References

Austerlitz, N. & Aravot, I. (2006), 'The emotional structure of student-tutor relationships in the design studio', in Davies, A. (ed.) *Enhancing Curricula: Contributing to the Future, Meeting the Challenges of the 21st Century in the Disciplines of Art, Design and Communication*, proceedings of the 3rd international conference, pp. 79–94 (London: cltad)

Austerlitz, N. & Aravot, I. (2007), 'Emotions of architecture students: a new perspective for the design studio', in Salama, A. & Wilkinson, N. (eds.), *Design Studio Pedagogy: Horizons for the Future*, pp. 233–46 (Urban International Press)

Blair, B. (2004), 'Interpretations of assessment: a study of students' understanding of the assessment criteria through the practice of formative feedback', in Davies, A. (ed.) *Enhancing Curricula: Towards the Scholarship of Teaching in Art, Design and Communication in Higher Education*, proceedings of the 2nd international conference, pp. 74–90 (London: cltad)

Blair, B. (2006), 'At the end of a huge crit in the summer, it was "crap" – I'd worked really hard but all she said was "fine" and I was gutted', *Art, Design & Communication in Higher Education*, **5** (2), pp. 83–95

Bowlby, J. (1973), *Attachment and Loss, Volume II: Separation: Anxiety and Anger* (London: Hogarth)

Burke, P.J. (1991), 'Identity process and social stress', *American Sociological Review*, 56, pp. 836–49

Burns, R.D. (1991), 'Study and stress among first year overseas students in an Australian university', *Higher Education Research and Development*, 10, pp. 61–77

Carroll, J. & Ryan, J. (2005), *Teaching International Students* (Routledge: London and New York)

Chalmers, D. & Volet, S. (1997), 'Common misconceptions about students from South-East Asia studying in Australia', *Higher Education Research and Development*, 16, pp. 87–89

Chang, H. (2007), 'Psychological distress and help-seeking among Taiwanese college students: role of gender and student status', *Journal of Guidance and Counselling*, **35** (3), pp. 347–55

Chung, Y.B. (1993), 'The education of international counseling psychology students in the United States', *Asian Journal of Counselling*, **11** (2), pp. 55–9

Coates, N.J. (2004), 'The "stranger", the "sojourner" and the international student', paper presented at the 2nd Education in a Changing Environment conference at the University of Salford, 12–13 September

Gill, S. (2007), 'Overseas students' intercultural adaptation as intercultural learning: a transformative framework', *Compare*, **37** (2), pp. 167–83

Jones, A. (2005), 'Culture and context: critical thinking and student learning in introductory macroeconomics', *Studies in Higher Education*, **30** (3), pp. 339–354

Kember, D. & Gow, L. (1991), 'A challenge to the anecdotal stereotype of the Asian student', *Studies in Higher Education*, **16** (2), pp. 117–28

Kesner, J.E. (2000), 'Teacher characteristics and the quality of child-teacher relationships', *Journal for School Psychology*, **28** (2), pp. 133–49

Klein, M. (1959), *Our Adult World and its Roots in Infancy, II* (London: Hogarth and the Institute of Psychoanalysis)

Lago, C. & Shipton, G. (1994), *On Listening and Learning; Student Counselling in Further and Higher Education* (London: Central Book Publishing Ltd)

Lazarus, R.S. (1991), 'Emotional theory and psychotherapy', in Safran, J.D. & Greenberg, L.S. (eds.) *Affective Change Events in Psychotherapy*, pp. 290–301 (New York: Academic Press)

Lazarus, R.S. (1997), 'How we cope with stress', *Mental Health Research*, **16** pp. 1–24

Lazarus, R.S. (1999), *Stress and Emotion; A New Synthesis* (New York: Springer)

Lazarus, R.S. & Folkman, S. (1984), *Stress, Appraisal and Coping* (New York: Springer)

MacKinnon, D. & Manathunga, C. (2003), 'Going global with assessment: what to do when the dominant culture's literacy drives assessment', *Higher Education Research and Development*, **22** (2), pp. 131–144

Oberg, K. (1960), 'Culture shock: adjustment to new cultural environments', *Practical Anthropology*, 7, pp. 177–82

Perrucci, R. & Hu, H. (1995), 'Satisfaction with social and educational experiences among international graduate students', *Research in Higher Education*, **36** (4), pp. 490–508.

Pope, N.K.Ll. (2005), 'The impact of stress in self-and peer assessment', *Assessment and Evaluation in Higher Education*, **30** (1), pp. 51–63

Salzberger-Wittenberg, I., Henry, G. & Osborne, E. (1983), *The Emotional Experience of Learning and Teaching* (London: Routledge & Kegan Paul)

Sarros, J.C. & Densten, I.L. (1989), 'Undergraduate student stress and coping strategies', *Higher Education Research and Development*, **8** (1), pp. 47–57

Searle, W. & Ward, C. (1990), 'The prediction of psychological and sociocultural adjustment during cross-cultural transitions', *International Journal of Intercultural Relations*, 14, pp. 449–64

Shore, B. (1996), *Culture in Mind: Cognition, Culture, and the Problem of Meaning* (New York: Oxford University Press)

Veninga, R.L. & Spradley, J.P. (1981), *The Work/Stress Connections: How to Cope with Job Burnout* (Boston: Little, Brown)

Walton, S.J. (1990), 'Stress management training for overseas effectiveness', *International Journal of Intercultural Relations*, **14** pp. 507–24

Ward, C. & Kennedy, A. (1993), 'Where's the "culture" in cross-cultural transition? Comparative studies of sojourner adjustment', *Journal of Cross-Cultural Psychology*, **24** (2), pp. 221–49

Watkins, D. & Biggs, J. (eds.) (1996), *The Chinese Learner: Cultural, Psychological and Contextual Influences* (Hong Kong: Comparative Education Research Centre and the Australian Council for Educational Research)

Watkins, D., Reghi, M., & Astilla, E. (1991), 'The Asian learner as a rote learner stereotype: myth or reality?' *Educational Psychology*, **11** (1), pp. 21–34

Werkman, S.L. (1980), 'Adjustment of Americans after living abroad', in Coelho, G.V. & Ahmed, P.I. (eds.), *Uprooting and Development: Dilemmas of Coping with Modernization*, pp. 233–47 (New York: Plenum Press)

This paper was first published in Art, Design and Communication for Higher Education, pp145–158, Volume 6, number 3, June 2008. Reprinted by permission of Intellect Books, The Mill, Parnall Road, Bristol BS16 3JG, UK, © 2008.

Tony Sullivan

The series of 'cultural', 'academic' and 'social' shocks faced by international students and the defensive strategies they employ to overcome the stress they experience as learners is the focus of Silvia Sovic's study. Reflecting on their fears and tribulations left me considering two things. Is the emotional economy they describe a particularly intense manifestation of the wider psychic defences common to all learners? Moreover, is it a product of the pedagogical practices pursued within British HEIs that have to operate in a specific global cultural and economic context?

The words of one Taiwanese student – 'shocked and lost' – are typical of the comments made in the structured interviews. Having taught in the post-compulsory sector for many years, I'm struck by the suggestion that 'social integration both in and outside the classroom' between lecturers and students with the aim of developing 'understanding' is the key to progress. As a doctoral researcher I undertook work on the emotional terrain engendered by young people's consumption of brands. There, as here, in addition to the psychodynamic work foregrounded by the author, I turned to social constructionist and critical psychology for answers.

If, as Vinciane Despret argues, our emotions are the product of our practices so that, 'emotions so obvious, so natural so biological … the very authenticity of which fascinates us' are in fact 'cultivated',[1] then, can our pedagogical practices encourage the cultivation of 'fear, shame and feeling left out' to the exclusion of that other emotion, so vital to the process of successful learning, 'hope'? Given the demands of delivering critical creative education to increasing numbers of students in an era of flexible specialisation and neo-liberalism,[2] what can be done? How can a learning institution be both competitive and more supportive? How can we engender the triumph of 'hope' over 'fear' in the learner?

Here, Lev Vygotsky's pedagogy of supported learning[3] remains apposite. Commenting on this, Margaret Wetherell and Janet Maybin argue, 'the scaffolding provided by teacher-pupil dialogue is a centrally important part of teaching'[4] (1996, p. 251). If 'avoidance', 'magical thinking' and other defensive psychic behaviour is not to produce educational failure, then, given the deeper experience of detachment and shock felt by overseas students, that scaffolding surely needs extending. As Clive Carswell has argued, all learners need to develop the 'capacity to tolerate and work with anxiety' if they are to nurture the 'hope' which is so vital to success in the struggle to learn, and, for 'survival itself'.[5] Among no group is the opportunity to develop this capacity more important than international students.

Notes

1 Despret, V. ([2001] 2004), Our Emotional Make Up: Ethnopsychology and Self-Hood, p. 2 (New York: Other Press)

2 Bourdieu, P. (1998), Acts of Resistance: Against The New Myths Of Our Time, pp. 94–99 (Cambridge: Polity)

3 In particular his concept of the 'zone of proximal development' in Vygotsky, L.S. ([1934] 1986) Thought and Language (Cambridge Massachusetts: The MIT Press)

4 Wetherell, M. & Maybin, J. (1996), 'The distributed self: a social constructionist perspective', in Stevens, R. (ed.) Understanding The Self (Oxford: OUP/Sage)

5 Carswell, C. (2007), 'On struggle, study and success' Therapy, 18 (10), p

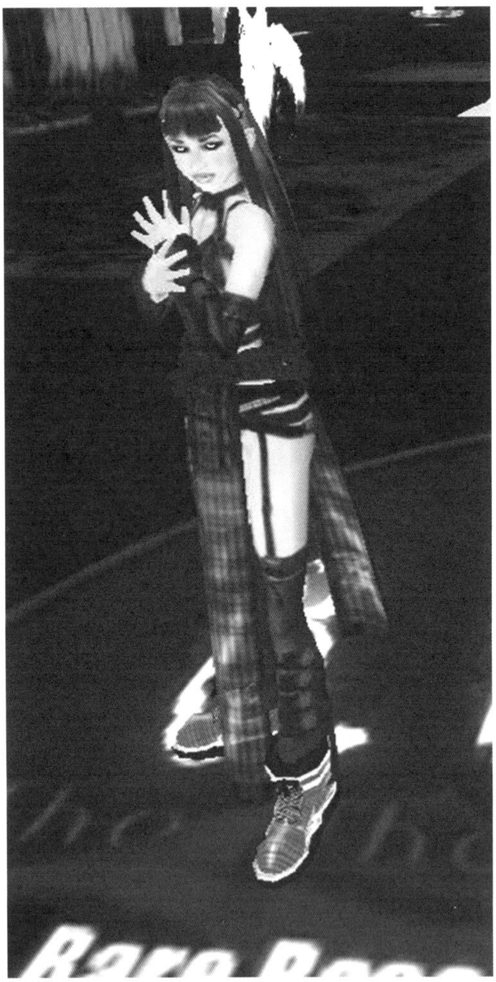

Twilight market Julia Gaimster

Reproduced by permission of the author

4

Reflections on interactions in virtual worlds and their implication for learning art and design

Author: Julia Gaimster

Commentary: Teal Triggs

Keywords

virtual worlds,
art and design learning,
on-line interactions

Julia Gaimster

Introduction

3D virtual learning environments such as Second Life are being promoted as the future of e-learning in education. However, there are many questions to be asked about the nature of interactions in these environments and how teaching and learning in art and design translates from the real to the virtual world. For example:

- What is the emotional impact of engaging in learning in a virtual space?
- What are the issues that educators need to consider when venturing into this new territory?
- What impact does it have on the teacher/learner dynamic?

Although there is little research in this specific area, there is however a body of literature that has investigated computer mediated communication and the impact of emotions in educational environments. Although, much of this work was carried out before rich 3D virtual environments such as Second Life became a reality, there are parallels to be drawn and lessons to be learnt from this literature. This paper explores existing literature to reflect on the nature of the advantages and risks of learning in art and design through virtual reality.

Real-life student student-tutor interactions

In recent years, the value of emotions in the learning process has begun to be recognised (Spendlove, 2007) (Spendlove, 2007). Educators increasingly talk about emotional literacy and the need for learners to have emotional intelligence. Spendlove claims that emotions play a particularly important role in art and design education and that critical emotional literacy is a "prerequisite of creative educational practices" (Spendlove, 2007, p. 157)(Spendlove 2007, p157).

He also points to the emotional dependency that students have on their teachers and the power of the teacher to determine the types of interaction that are allowed within the classroom and to adjust the environment. The Tutors is are 'de facto' - in a position of power, and what they say and how they interact with a students can have a major impact on a student's sense of value and well-being. (Cotton & Wilson, , 2006). Positive social and academic interactions can have a strong impact on a student's confidence and academic performance. However, as Cotton & and Wilson have noted, the amount of interaction between students and tutors can be limited to the classroom or lecture space. Austerlitz and Aravot (2006) note that student-tutor interactions are an important aspect of the studio method of teaching in art and design. They state that the tutor's character, verbal and non-verbal behaviour can generate different and quite intense emotions in students and these can have a lasting effect.

Thus key questions relating to delivery of art and design in virtual worlds would be:

- Is the same intensity of emotion generated when students and tutors are interacting with each other's avatars (visual representations standing for the person behind the keyboard)?
- Does the studio approach to teaching translate to a virtual environment?
- If body language and other cues are missing, will students still connect with tutors and have the same emotional responses?

One of the central issues in art and design education – and which requires examination in relation to learning in virtual worlds – is exposure and critical assessment of students' work. This aspect of studio learning, where students and tutors interact in fairly informal ways as work is being produced, is highlighted by the formality of the crit (Blair, 2006; Orr, 2007). The critique is a particular and well-used form of interaction in art and design education. Handled properly, the 'crit' can be a creative and inspiring experience but it can also be an occasion in which students feel demeaned and embarrassed by a tutor who may or may not be aware of the emotions that their words are eliciting. One theme that may be explored in a virtual setting is whether a mediated 'crit' elicits the same emotional responses as a real real-life version. Does the crit transfer to a virtual space and how is this best done? Does it add distance between the student and the tutor, the student and the work or are the emotions just as powerful?

The ability of the student to become self-critical is essential to their that student's development as a reflective practitioner. In order to achieve this, they he or she also needs to learn to cope with the emotions which that are elicited by critical reflections. The tutor also needs to apply emotional intelligence to facilitate a learning environment which that supports such processes. Goleman (1998) describes one of the aspects of emotional intelligence as "managing feelings so that they are expressed appropriately and effectively, enabling people to work together smoothly and toward their common goals." (p. 7). Mortiboys (2005) suggests that teaching with emotional intelligence enables the tutor to be more flexible, ; that if you can use emotional intelligence to build a relationship of trust with your learners that they will respond more positively to new activities and methods of teaching. Building this trust will be a key factor in enabling students to engage in meaningful learning in an unfamiliar environment.

In virtual worlds, too, where interaction is between avatars, visual representations standing for the person behind the keyboard, trust is a key element in building relationships, because one cannot see the real person behind the avatar, you have no visual and sometimes no auditory clues as to their real identity. There have been reported cases of deception in virtual worlds, ; however, keeping up a deception is a fairly complex process that requires a great deal of determination and a good memory. The number of people engaged in this, particularly in an educational environment, is probably minimal, but one needs to be aware of the potential of the environment to support this kind of behaviour.

However, educators have the tools to create protected environments where the participants are known to each other and outsiders can be excluded. This helps to form a sense of community with the associated social benefits. As well as trust in the tutor, students also need to develop their self-esteem.

Spendlove (2007) points to the fact that students are more likely to be successful and to develop critical emotional literacy if they have a high level of self-esteem. This self-esteem needs to be nurtured and developed through the pedagogical process and is especially important in an area such as art and design where:

> … the outcome of the learning process is not predetermined in terms of the precise, tangible outcome as in the execution of a creative and learning orientated challenge …
> (p. 157)

Negative emotions and low self-esteem are usually not conducive to learning; creative people often have a very personal involvement with their work that needs to be nurtured in a supportively critical environment. Students also want to hear their tutor's opinions about their work and often they want this to be in a one-to-one rather than a group situation, possibly to avoid the embarrassment of public humiliation if the work does not meet expectations (Blair, 2006). The communication tools in virtual worlds enable a private exchange within a public forum and this could be a valuable addition to the critique scenario, enabling the tutor to provide the student with individual attention within a group activity.

It is clear therefore that communication in virtual worlds is not just a technical issue but also involves an understanding of the social context in which the communication is taking place. However, before moving real real-life activities into virtual environments it is important that students and tutors understand the social rules.

Rules and conventions in virtual worlds

A 'newbie' (newcomer) entering a virtual world for the first time can be easily confused by the social conventions. These can range from the use of acronyms – LOL (laughs out loud), BRB (be right back) and to other issues around codes of behaviour, whether it is appropriate to ask questions about an avatar's real-life persona etc. This is often described as 'netiquette'.

Many sites post frequently asked questions (FAQs) dealing with these issues and some, like for example Second Life, have rules about what is acceptable in areas that are PG (Parental Guidance) rather than mature. Even with these guidelines to help, the first time you enter a virtual world can be daunting, a little like arriving at a party where you don't know anyone.

Participation is the key to becoming part of an online community, and indeed in any community (Wenger, 1998), and as Markham (1998) points out, you need to know the rules in order to participate. Moving around in Second Life is an art that takes practice if you are not going to crash into walls or commit the taboo of invading an avatar's personal space.

In order to fully engage in the experience, students will need to understand the norms in this environment, to build confidence with the tools for participation, and to feel that they are in a non-threatening environment and are part of a supportive learning community. This mirrors the ideal function of a tutor working in any learning environment, but there are differences between virtual and real teaching and learning worlds.

Computer-mediated communication

This paper aims to identify what the differences are between teaching and learning in a virtual world and the real world. Will the current pedagogies transfer? Will students and tutors experience the same emotions when interacting through avatars? Is it possible to elicit strong emotional responses when there are limited non-verbal cues? A partial answer to these questions can be found in the literature on computer-mediated communication (CMC).

Much of the literature argues that computer-mediated communication (CMC) is not as rich as face-to-face communication and that it also can be more liberating. Joinson (2003) argues that 'over time the amount of social information communicated using CMC converges with the amount sent verbally face to face' (p. 36). The reason for this is that typing is slower than talking and people need time to understand the particular nuances of the medium such as the use of acronyms and emoticons, visual indicators of how people feel. He calls this 'paralanguage' and stresses its importance in the social aspects of communication where body language and facial expressions are missing.

Joinson (2003) states that 'when our communication is mediated [by computers] it is possible that the outcomes are likely to be quite different than in a similar encounter face to face. This is the crux of cyberpsychology' (p. 3.). Certainly, email in particular has been accused of being lacking in emotion, hence the development of emoticons and smiley faces to help the writer convey the emotional intention of their communication. This practice has extended to virtual worlds where the uses of acronyms such as LOL (laughs out loud) are used to convey humour or emotion where the main tool for communication is text.

Markham (1998) points out that one of the positive aspects of CMC (computer mediated communication) is that of control, that users can 'limit the extent to which others can view or touch them, physically and, presumably, psychologically' (p. 124). This may enable introverted personalities to become more extrovert and to participate more easily in communication, participants have more time to consider what they are saying and how they are presenting themselves (Markham, 1998).

What is clear therefore is that many people see CMC (computer-mediated communication) as a positive way of engaging in communities, networking and socialising, as Rheingold states:

> People in virtual communities use words on screens to exchange pleasantries and argue, engage in intellectual discourse, conduct commerce, exchange knowledge, share emotional support, make plans, brainstorm, gossip, feud, fall in love, find friends and lose them, play games, flirt, create a little high art and a lot of idle talk. People

> in virtual communities do just about everything people do in real life, but we leave our bodies behind. You can't kiss anybody and nobody can punch you in the nose, but a lot can happen within those boundaries.
> (Rheingold, 2000, p. xvii)

There are however powerful differences between communication in virtual worlds and other forms of computer-mediated communication. Users of 3D virtual worlds report that it is the sense of presence, of feeling as if you are actually within the world that sets these environments apart from other web-based forms of communication. Companies like IBM use them extensively for meetings because, unlike a videoconference, where users disappear once the call is finished, in virtual worlds people break into smaller groups at the end of the meeting, they socialise and create new networks (Metz, 2007).

Ellie Brewster (her Second Life name) of Ohio State University teaches an introductory course in women's studies in Second Life. She finds that students communicate within Second Life on three levels, using voice, via the chat window and on a one one-to to-one basis using the instant messaging system. She has discovered that the students still like to have a structure to their in-world activities and that discussions still require guidance from the tutor. The main difference she says is that "you are no longer the expert on the stage, you are working beside your students and the group are finding things out together". She has found that teaching in Second Life is very much a communal activity.

The potential of virtual worlds to create a sense of community is also noted by Jensen (1999):

> ... the encounter with the computer is transformed from an experience of a two-dimensional interface, which can be clicked on, to the experience of a space in which the user feels a presence and a community with other people; and correspondingly, that the encounter with the Internet tends to change from an experience of a web of linked 2D-documents, to and experience of a galaxy of interconnected 3-dimensional Virtual Worlds.
> (page p. 26)

This sense of community can be so strong that relationships can be formed in similar ways to those in face face-to to-face encounters (Turkle, 1995, ; Rheingold, 2000, ; Joinson, 2003). Indeed there are examples of these relationships moving into the physical domain and resulting in real real-life friendships and even marriage (Turkle, 1995).

The evidence in the literature on CMC (computer-mediated communication) suggests that the norms of social interaction and the powerful emotions generated by social interaction in the real world are also evident in the virtual worlds. We should expect therefore that this would also be true for interaction between students and tutors in virtual worlds. Tutors engaging in virtual worlds should expect to experience a wide range of emotional responses from their learners and indeed to have their own emotional response to the learners and the environment. It is also important to understand that whilst while it is the avatar that one is engaging with in the virtual world, it is the identity of the avatar's human driver that is important (Meadows, 2008), even though that driver may choose to represent themselves himself/herself in a form that is at variance with his/her real real-life persona.

Identity and anonymity

In virtual worlds it is possible to create any number of avatars and each of these may have a different persona. The avatar's persona may reflect or exaggerate that of its real real-life owner but can also be quite different. Avatars can adopt different roles and enable their owners to experience situations that would be impossible or uncomfortable in real life. In virtual worlds you can be yourself or live out your wildest fantasies.

The ability to be anonymous and to try out new identities is a key component of life in virtual worlds. Anonymity carries with it both advantages and disadvantages. You are never totally sure whom you are conversing with. The natural instinct in the real world is to believe what people tell you and to check this against their facial expressions and body language. In virtual worlds these cues are either absent or can be controlled and therefore falsified by the participants.

It has been noted that anonymity can have a strong impact on people's behaviour and in particular the degree with which they conform to social norms. Joinson (2003) points to the context in determining the level to which people either conform to social norms or set their own personal norms and standards:

> … whether or not people conform when interacting on the Internet depends on two factors: whether they are visually anonymous or not, and whether there is a shared social identity or personal identity salient at the time.
> (p. 45)

It appears that the screen provides a barrier that enables people to act or communicate in a way that they would not do otherwise. It has been noted that when people are lacking the usual 'social context cues' that their behaviour can become more self self-centred and less regulated. (Sproull and & Kiesler, 1986, p. 159).

The impact of anonymity can also sometimes lead to aggressive behaviour, known as flaming or griefing, harassment or other behaviours which the perpetrators would probably not engage in if their identity was known or they did not have visual anonymity.

One avatar described how he had been 'shot, caged, insulted and orbited' but that it did not bother him as he had developed the ability to 'retaliate in like manner'. For a newbie entering a world for the first time this can be an upsetting and unsettling experience and can feel very personal.

The issue for teaching in virtual worlds is that, depending upon the set of circumstances, it may not be possible or desirable for people to remain anonymous; this then creates a new set of dilemmas. It may be necessary for the tutor to know the identities of the students in order to assess the learning or confirm participation.

These are issues that are not unique to virtual worlds but are amplified by the open-ended possibilities presented by the environment and they raise a lot of questions. Is it acceptable for students to turn up to virtual lectures dressed in fetish wear? How do you control a teaching space where people can suddenly materialise, change shape completely or introduce a pet dragon? Artists and designers are renowned for their idiosyncratic dress in real life so perhaps having a fire-breathing alien in your 'crit' will not be too much of a distraction. These issues point to the need for an agreed virtual classroom etiquette to be devised at the start of the proceedings. Acceptable standards of behaviour within the learning area need to be discussed and agreed to ensure that appropriate boundaries are maintained.

This will have particular relevance in the context of the critique. It has been noted that when online interaction is not moderated it can descend into flaming and inappropriate comments (Markham, 1998; Sprull & Keisler, 1986). If critiques in a virtual world are anonymous, this behaviour may transfer, however, allowing students to comment on each other's work anonymously may lead to a more honest and reflective approach, though this has yet to be tested. The important issue is that the tutor must be aware of the impact that negative comments can have on the a student's' emotions and sense of self-esteem. It has been shown that when used effectively virtual environments can offer a nurturing space in which confidence can be built, new relationships can be developed and learning can be a creative experience. As in the real world, criticism – whether from the tutor or the peer group – needs to be framed constructively and appropriately to support learning.

Relationships between the real and virtual worlds

The social and immersive aspects of virtual worlds are among their key attractions (Pursel, 2007). The richness of 3D environments seems to stimulate a more realistic and immersive experience that can enhance the learning experience. However, the divisions between the real and the virtual, the authentic and the synthetic, are becoming blurred. People can become lost in the virtual world and feel more of a sense of presence there than they do in the real world. In extreme cases, some people come to identify more closely with their avatar or become deeply involved with their in-world personas to the point where the boundaries between the real and the virtual become indistinct (Meadows, 2008).

This sense of presence seems to be intensified in 3D worlds although it has also been noted in purely text-based environments. One of the attractions of being in the virtual world is the ability to suspend reality and to control the way in which one is represented (Markham, 1998). For students in art and design, it also provides a unique opportunity to become emotionally engaged with a creative process that transcends the laws of physics and enables collaboration on a global scale. The ability to suspend disbelief and to engage in the experience requires one to not question the notion of reality. As Markham (1998) noted, to many users of virtual space "everything that is experienced is real" (p. 20) and in this reality the student would need to develop a new or different facet of his/her identity. Guest (2007) states that "virtual worlds aren't just a window into another world; they become an instinctive extension of the self" (p. 68). Turkle (1995) also raises the notion of the computer as a virtual extension of the physical self; she identifies the need to question the limits of our responsibilities in these new environments.

The literature (Sanders, 2005; Buscher et al., 2001) also debates the importance of metaphors in virtual worlds where the line is drawn between real and virtual and whether the virtual world needs real-world metaphors and symbols in order that users are able to situate themselves. Buscher et al. (2001) argue that straightforward reproduction of the real-world environment may not be helpful because it does not take advantage of the capacities of the virtual environment.

For practitioners in art and design, this raises questions about whether it is appropriate to try and create the traditional studio environment and its interactions within virtual worlds or whether a completely different approach should be identified. This is an area the author has identified as requiring a detailed empirical study.

Clearly there are areas of good practice in art and design teaching that could easily be transferred to a virtual environment. Educators in art and design are aiming to develop students who can engage in critical thinking, and reflection. They are also preparing students to enter a community of practice. Virtual environments offer opportunities for students to engage in work-based learning (developing an e-business, putting on an exhibition, working on a live brief), to work collaboratively to solve problems and manage projects, to reflect upon the strengths and weaknesses of their solutions and to engage with practitioners from the wider art and design community. The technology can facilitate engagement with others on a national and global level, giving students access to experts who might otherwise be unavailable to them.

Building communities and relationships in virtual space

The actual design of the world may be less important than the nature of the interactions happening there. A virtual world without people to interact with is not engaging, no matter how realistic or fantastical it may be.

The potential for building communities of art and design in virtual worlds is vast; the technology supports a wide range of media traditionally used by artists and designers and enables them to easily create environments in which to display, share and discuss their work. Virtual environments offer the opportunity to incorporate the design and functionality of the environment into the activity. The global accessibility of these environments creates unique opportunities for cross-cultural engagement and interaction, but also plenty of scope for cultural misunderstanding, generating possibly negative emotions and poor communication. These aspects need to be considered when designing collaborative learning activities using this technology. As in any other learning environment, the relationships and communities that are formed can be an important aspect of the learning process. This is reflected in the experiences of Michael Wright from Otis College of Art and Design who has conducted projects in Second Life with his digital media students. He found that:

> … the students found working in teams on a group project a great icebreaker in getting to know one another. They enjoyed the social interaction from the class brainstorming to learning to work with each other as avatars in world. Deeper friendships were developed

> and a joy of seeing what each one would come up with in a creative manner. This project could not have been successful without the social interaction and teamwork.
> (Wright, 2007)

The comments from his students describe the power of the environment to develop positive team working that reflects working practice in the industry.

> Having to work in large groups to achieve a common goal was a great way to prepare us for future work situations. While it was not easy, it did make for a unique view on producing something as large as what we had to do. In the end it feels good to be a part of creating something as a group and seeing it through to the end.
> Art Lopez (Wright, 2007)

The experiences of Wright, other educators and people working in other communities point to the potential of virtual worlds to support a wide range of educational and social activities. Indeed, many people use the Internet as a support tool, seeking advice on medical conditions or as a release from social isolation brought about by physical or psychological conditions. For these people, virtual communities are an important part of their lives and provide the kind of support that is lacking in much of modern society, for example, a group of physically disabled people in Boston, USA, have found a new form of freedom through an avatar named Wilde Cunningham. This avatar enabled them to make friends, build an online gift shop and, according to their care worker, enriched their lives and made them more confident in the real world (Jones, 2007).

There is great potential for educators to use virtual worlds to engage with disparate and disadvantaged groups of learners. The interesting thing about online communities is that we may be alone and isolated in real life but we can still participate in the new public forum that has been created by the Internet (Jones, 1997) and we can participate in a creative way made possible by tools that do not require the user to engage in complex scripting or necessarily to understand how they work. There are however some downsides to being in a virtual community, for example, if you spend too long there, it is possible to become isolated from the real world.

Engagement, addiction and flow

There is a great deal of debate about the addictive nature of the Internet in general and computer games in particular. However, the research to back up the notion of extensive Internet addiction is somewhat thin. Joinson (2003) points to a number of flawed studies where the criteria (e.g. the number of hours spent on the Internet that qualify you as an addict) have been placed too low, leading to overestimates of the number of people affected.

However, there are clearly some cases of extreme addiction. Joinson claims that the factors that make the Internet so attractive are its ability to provide 'an escape from everyday problems' and that the anonymity on the Internet makes it particularly attractive (or addictive). Users of virtual worlds have been known to spend as long as 80 hours a week online (Guest, 2007).

These same elements that can create problems can be used to advantage in engaging students; immersive environments promote the notion of 'flow', the term coined by Mihály Csíkszentmihályi to describe:

> … the state of total engagement. In order to allow users to achieve flow, an activity should strive to absorb all of their attention, give them control, allow them to lose self-consciousness and distort time. A person has attained the flow state when she/he has no conscious awareness of time passing.
> (Metros, 1999, p. 284)

There is a fine balance between flow and addiction that tutors need to be aware of, however a certain element of engagement is vital to the learning process and promotes a 'deep approach' to learning (Marton & Säljö, 1976).

Educators can utilise the immersive elements of virtual worlds to create dynamic interactive learning environments but only if they adopt new pedagogies; simply holding a lecture in Second Life is not going to transform the student experience, though getting them involved in an authentic learning situation that is emotionally engaging might. Providing students with the appropriate structure and boundaries to their learning will help to ensure the appropriate level of engagement, flow without addiction.

Conclusion

A survey of the available literature that has informed this paper found that virtual worlds are powerful tools that can be used to develop creative approaches to learning and provide different ways for tutors to interact and engage with students.

The key questions were:

- Is the same intensity of emotion generated when students and tutors are interacting with each other's avatars?

- Does the studio approach to teaching translate to a virtual environment?
- If the body language and other clues are missing, will students still connect with tutors and have the same emotional responses?

The literature review indicates that emotions in the real world are transferred to the virtual world. Even when body language and other signifiers are missing, people manage to connect through their avatars and have deep and meaningful social experiences. This bodes well for the studio method of teaching, which depends upon an open critical dialogue between tutor and student. There is no technical reason why this should not be possible within a virtual environment. However, it seems that in order for this to happen the tutor may have to work a little harder at building the necessary levels of trust, as without the non-verbal cues there is greater potential for confusion and misreading of a situation.

In order to engage effectively in these worlds, both students and tutors will need time to experiment and adapt to the environment, to discover the social norms and to work out how to manoeuvre and express themselves through their avatars. The nature of the communication can be as rich as face-to-face communication, but this is dependent upon the extent to which the users are willing to suspend disbelief and immerse themselves in the environment.

Educators already working in this environment have identified the need for guidance and structure, as one would expect in real-world studios and classrooms. Students need to know what is expected of them in terms of behaviour and the activities they need to engage in.

The advantages are that the technology enables people to express themselves and to create alternative personas in which they may feel more comfortable and engaged. It is an immersive experience that encourages engagement on the part of the learner and creates opportunities for developing new kinds of extended communities. In terms of art and design, virtual worlds offer an environment that supports a wide range of creative media and can be applied to most disciplines in art and design from architecture to cultural studies, fashion to product design, graphics to filmmaking.

It is clear that there is the need for more empirical research into how educators and students interact in virtual worlds and how this impacts upon the educational process. This will increase our understanding of virtual interactions, help us to gain a deeper understanding of the mediated learning process and apply this knowledge in the context of art and design.

References

Austerlitz, N. & Aravot, I. (2006), "'The emotional structure of the student-tutor relationship in the design studio"', in Davies, A. (ed) *Enhancing Curricula: Contributing to the Future, Meeting the Challenges of the 21st Century in the Disciplines of Art, Design and Communication*, proceedings of the 3rd cltad international conference, pp. 91–106 (London: cltad)

Blair, B. (2006) Does the studio crit still have a role to play in 21st century design education and student learning? in Davies, A. (ed) *Enhancing Curricula: Contributing to the Future, Meeting the Challenges of the 21st Century in the Disciplines of Art, Design and Communication*, proceedings of the 3rd cltad international conference, pp. 107–120 (London: cltad)

Büscher, M., Mogensen, P. & Shapiro, D. (2001), *Spaces of Practice*, proceedings of the 7th European conference on computer supported cooperative, pp. 139–158 (Bonn, Germany)

Cotten, S.R. & Wilson, B. (2006), 'Student-faculty interactions: dynamics and determinants', *Higher Education*, **51** pp. 487–519

Goleman, D. (1998), *Working with Emotional Intelligence* (London: Bloomsbury Publishing)

Guest, T. (2007), *Second Lives: A Journey Through Virtual Worlds* (London: Hutchinson)

Jensen, J.F. "'3D inhabited virtual worlds: interactivity and interaction between avatars, autonomous agents, and users'," WEBNET 999 conference proceedings, available online (accessed 15 September 2007) at: http;//www.editlib.org/

Joinson, A.N. (2003), *Understanding the Psychology of Internet Behaviour* (New York: Palgrave Macmillan)

Jones, S.G. (1997), *Virtual Culture: Identity and Communication in Cybersociety* (London: Sage)

Markham, A.N. (1998), *Life Online* (Walnut Creek: Alta Mira Press)

Marton, F. & Säljö, R. (1976), 'On qualitative differences in learning', *British Journal of Educational Psychology*, **46** pp. 4–11

Mckenna, K.Y., Green, A.S. & Gleason, M.E. (2002), 'Relationship formation on the Internet: what's the big attraction', *Journal of Social Issues,* **58** (1), pp. 9–31

Meadows, M.S. (2008), *I, Avatar: The Culture and Consequences of Having a Second Life* (Berkeley, CA: New Riders)

Metros, S.E. (1999), 'Making connections: a model for on-line interaction'. *Leonardo*, **32** (4), pp. 281–291

Metz, C. (2007), 'The emperor's new web', *PC Magazine*, 24 April, pp. 70–77

Mortiboys, A. (2005), *Teaching with Emotional Intelligence* (London: Routledge)

Pivec, M., Baumann, K. & Gütl, C. (2004), 'Everything virtual – virtual classes, virtual tutors, virtual students, virtual emotions – but the knowledge', in Cantoni, L. & McLoughlin, C. (eds.) *Proceedings of World Conference on Educational Multimedia, Hypermedia and Telecommunications 2004*, pp. 4009–4015 (Chesapeake, VA: AACE)

Postmes, T., Spears, R. & Lea, M. 'The formation of groups in computer-mediated communication', *Human Communication Research*, **26**, pp. 341–371, retrieved 2000

Pursel, B.K. & Bailey, K.D. (2007), 'Establishing virtual learning worlds', VirtualLearningWorlds.com, available online (accessed 10 October 2007) at: http://www.virtuallearningworlds.com/vlw_working.pdf

Rheingold, H. (2000), *The Virtual Community*, revised edition (Cambridge, Massachusetts: MIT Press)

Sanders, R. & Tashner, J. (2005), 'Metaphorical design of virtual learning environments', in Crawford, C. et al. (eds.) *Proceedings of Society for Information Technology and Teacher Education International Conference 2005*, pp. 2326–2331 (Chesapeake, VA: AACE)

Spendlove, D. (2007), 'A conceptualisation of emotion within art and design education: a creative, learning and product-orientated triadic schema', *International Journal of Art & Design Education*, **26** (2), pp. 155–166

Sproull, L. & Kiesler, S. (1986), 'Reducing social context cues: electronic mail in organizational communication', *Management Science*, **32** pp. 1492–1512

Turkle, S. (1995), *Life on Screen* (New York: Simon & Schuster)

Wright, M. (2007), Virtual World Project, available online (accessed 17 February 2008) at: http://tlc.otis.edu/Faculty%20Development/wrighttech.htm

This paper was first published in Art, Design and Communication for Higher Education, pp 187–199, Volume 6, number 3, June 2008. Reprinted by permission of Intellect Books, The Mill, Parnall Road, Bristol BS16 3JG, UK, © 2008.

Teal Triggs

When Second Life is the plot device in an episode of *CSI: New York* you know it has hit the mainstream. A cross between computer and online gaming, Second Life creates a virtual world to be engaged with through interaction rather than passive viewing. *CSI* fans can even log in to Second Life as avatars plying their trade as investigators in a virtual New York City. Perhaps, as art and design educators, we should take this up as a clue. Of course, bad things happen in cop shows and there is lots of virtual blood spilling. But, for educators, Second Life provides the potential to explore how the environment of virtual spaces might be used to enhance the student learning experience. And it is through the blurring of boundaries between the virtual and the physical teaching environments where the potential for a new type of leaning may be situated.

Julia Gaimster, in her insightful overview of computer-mediated communication, advocates Second Life as a 'dynamic learning environment'. She remarks on the positive aspects of what this means in terms of online communities, networking and socialising. However, she cautions as to the set of emotions attached to taking on alternative personas (human avatars) and 'bots' (programmed avatars) – including anxieties about deception and trust. It must be said that such fears are nothing new. Science fiction filmmakers and writers have long examined life in virtual worlds and the emotional dangers inherent in the relationships between androids, robots and humans. The 1973 film *Westworld*, for example, promised holidaymakers the 'ultimate resort' where androids help humans act out their holiday fantasies. On the other hand, Ridley Scott's film *Bladerunner* (1982), based on Philip K. Dick's *Do Androids Dream of Electric Sheep?*, explored the complexity behind the replicants' struggle with human emotions. Cyberpunk writers in the 80s and 90s took these ideas further, speculating on a future in which the virtual is real enough to be a viable environment for interaction. Now, with Second Life, that future is more or less here.

Second Life is an opportunity for developing learning environments that engage with the 'imaginary' and work both within and between the virtual space and its physical counterparts. Ken A. Graetz, drawing on the work of Jane Bennett (2001) for example, observes the potential benefits of responding to the concept of 'enchantment' in relationship to learning strategies. That is, applying knowledge of the way in which students could be 'caught up and carried away' by innovative uses of virtual and physical learning environments. Enchantment is thus a learning 'hook', and one emotion which provides a positive experience and may be used to great effect. It is insights such as these that are worth exploring further.

References

Bennett, J. (2001), *The Enchantment of Modern Life: Attachments, Crossings and Ethics* (Princeton: Princeton University Press)

Graetz, K. (2006), 'Chapter 6. The psychology of learning environments', in Oblinger, D.G. (ed.) *Learning Spaces* (Washington D.C.: Educause)

Section 2

The emotional landscape in practice

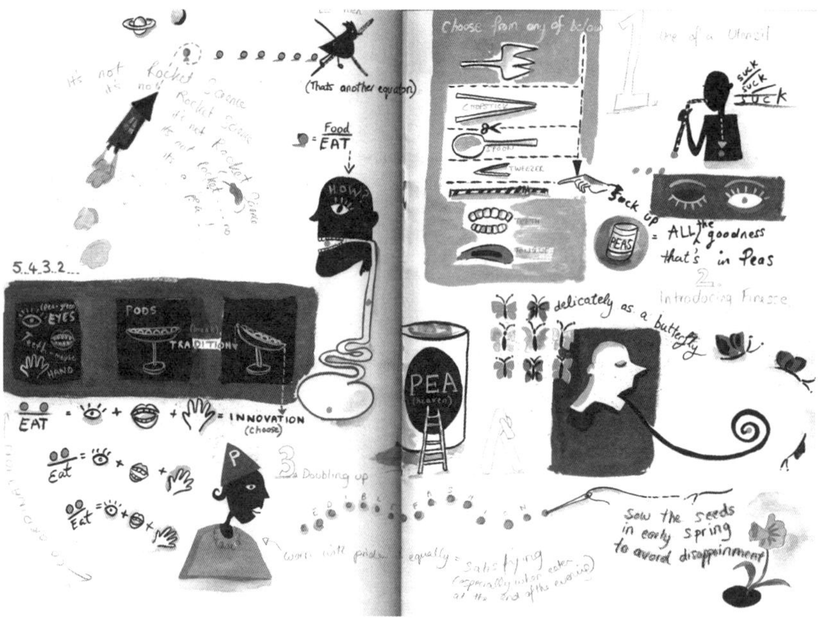

Pea eating

Su-Lynn Tan

Reproduced by permission of the artist

5

Emotions and interactions around sketchbooks

Author: Su-Lynn Tan

Commentary: Sarah Atkinson

Keywords

sketchbooks,
feelings,
space,
emotional behaviours,
interaction

Su-Lynn Tan

Introduction

The sketchbook still dominates as an integral part in teaching research methods on higher education (HE) courses in art and design, and its use is expected and actively encouraged throughout the art student experience in colleges and universities. The diversity in the student population, including international students, the differences in educational backgrounds and the post-internet generations may lead us to question if sketchbooks are still relevant to student learning or whether their importance has diminished with new technologies, new generations of students and evolving student culture. With the traditional 'art school' method of sketchbooks constant and pervasive on art and design courses it is appropriate to examine if sketchbooks really are effective in teaching students how to research within their educational development. This article takes a holistic viewpoint on student responses to the experience of using a sketchbook. It will examine the emerging emotions that affect the prolific or random entries that are made and the role emotions play in making decisions on how to research.

The sketchbook is a common link to developing artists and designers across all practices in the studio environment, and perhaps it could be considered the first step we take in communicating ideas in experiential learning. Hence, sketchbooks have the potential, if there is an emergence of emotions experienced by the user, to elicit complex feelings within our interior and exterior worlds. In the former, the sketchbook functions at a highly personal level as a tool to express our innermost thoughts and record ideas of how we experience life. It has a practical function in the exterior world, or external experience, as a key element in the unspoken and spoken interaction between student and tutor in the design studio. Moon (2004) describes this metacognitive functioning as the network of knowledge and understanding and associated feeling or emotion – 'what is known' by the learner at a particular time. Austerlitz and Aravot (2007) argue that students' emotions play a major role in design students' learning, including their learning approaches and interactions with tutors. Thus it is argued here that the emotions that are involved while students use sketchbooks in the HE context should be further explored.

This article is based on my experience as a former design student and presently as a design tutor. It employs insights gained through an action research process where my objective was to explore how students perceive, use and feel about sketchbooks, the importance of sketchbooks in their learning, interactions with the studio audience and how the experience impacts on their interior worlds.

Envy

My own experience of using sketchbooks is linked to many emotions in the context of a student of art and design in London, as a professional artist working as an illustrator and art director, to my present situation as a practitioner and lecturer in animation.

As an infrequent sketchbook user myself, I place a personal view on the love/hate feelings of the sketchbook user. As a student, I was always made aware by the tutors of the merits of sketchbook work. Yet, what I recall mostly are feelings of envy towards my peers who could fill the pages with effortless creativity, and I admit that I had little interest in 'working' in my sketchbook when I was studying for my BA degree at Camberwell College of Art and Design. 'Working' rather than enjoying the creative freedom of expression was how I remember feeling about it. Those memories fuel this research paper.

Research method

McNiff, McGeady and Elliott (2001) point to the option of using self-reflection as a research method:

> Although self reflection is essentially an individual activity, it can also be participatory, because we tend to share our ideas with others and they can help us find new ways forward that we might not have thought of ourselves.

This article uses epistemology to look at the way foundation degree students perceive, use and feel about sketchbooks. In particular, I was interested in the kinds of emotions that occurred in student learning around sketchbooks and the differences between the first- and second-year students. The article also investigates how technology has impacted on sketchbooks. Finally, the research looks at how the expectations of the university and assessment (pleasing tutors) affect emotions and interactions around sketchbooks

Five Foundation Degree Animation (FDA) students and one tutor agreed to be interviewed informally in the studio environment. The soft data was used to shape the research method. This data indicated:

- Tutors regularly have to coerce students to do sketchbook work.
- It is made explicit in project briefs that sketchbooks are part of the assessment criteria at the summative assessment stage.
- Preconceptions are formed on further education (FE) courses at foundation level when the importance of sketchbooks as an integral part of portfolio submissions for application to HE courses is stressed.
- One notion is that students save their sketchbook for 'best' work; they use it to repeat illustrative styles they are already proficient in and feel confident to practise, with little evidence of risk-taking, subconscious ideas or letting the mind wander.
- One student indicated that he didn't allocate much time to sketchbook work but thought it was 'good for him'. The immediacy and ease with which new media can aid creativity was seen as being an easier and quicker route to achieving an outcome. He felt deleting mistakes in Photoshop was easier than making them on paper.

I found the last comment particularly interesting because the very nature of a sketchbook will show 'mistakes' that can be considered evidence of development and self-evaluation.

Further insight was gained through informal discussions with an animation tutor who uses sketchbooks as part of his praxis. He talked about how, before he became a professional animator, he used it as a way of formulating the ideas that often came to him when he was working in a bookshop. He felt the bookshop environment inspired many ideas and reflected how his latest sketchbooks showed much less spontaneity in his drawing. He talked about how someone looking through his sketchbook would 'dry up' his ideas and block his creativity. He stated: 'You can't succeed as an artist without using one.'

The initial findings as a result of a number of naturalistic inquiries helped to gain further insight into students' emotions and interactions around sketchbooks, which influenced the design of a set of questions (see Appendix).

The study focuses on the views and experiences of two groups of mixed-gender animation students at London College of Communication (LCC) with diverse ethnicity, ages and cultural and social backgrounds: twelve year-one students and nine year-two students. The participants were part of the Foundation Degree Award (FDA) in animation during the summer term, 2007. The qualitative data was collected on two separate days: the first focus group had only first-year (Y1) students and the second focus group second years (Y2) only. Both focus groups lasted approximately one hour. An impartial senior staff member at LCC who was not part of the animation team led the focus groups.

In the next section I explore the key themes that came out of this inquiry.

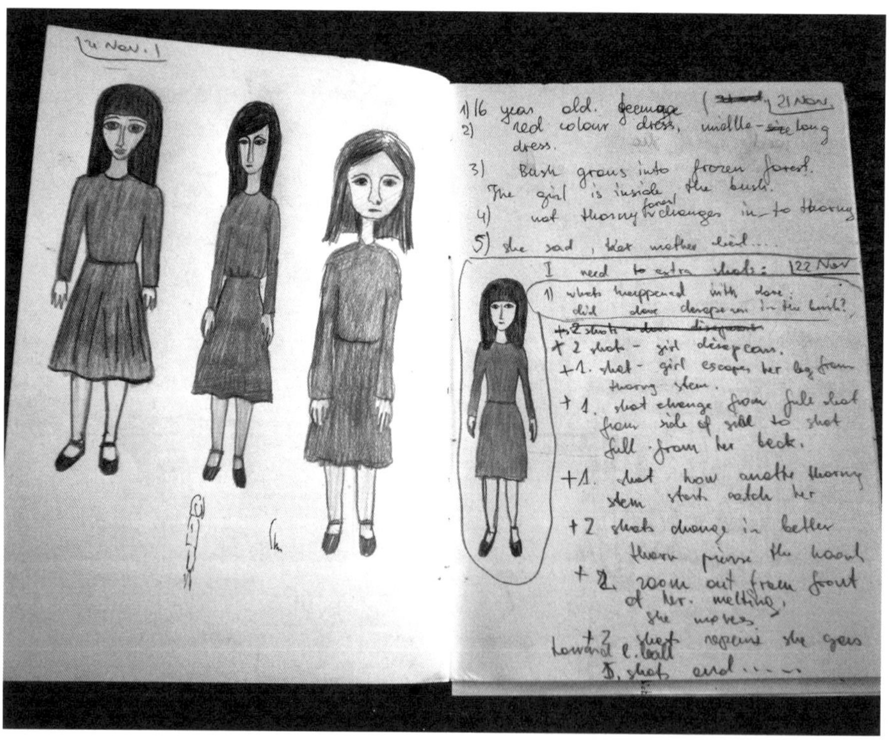

Sketchbook Character Design
Reproduced by permission of the artist

Salomeja Marcauskaite

Research results

Learning to expose

Negative feelings towards studio activities involving sketchbooks could lead to creative blockages and the student feeling uncertainty about the learning potential of sketchbooks. It is often the earlier experiences of sketchbook work that are loaded with emotional responses such as feeling shy, as one student recounts:

> **Q: How often and when do you use sketchbooks?**
>
> I use an A5 one it's less intimidating for you if you are in a bar, for example. If you have a large one you feel shy people around you are going to notice what you're doing. (Student Y1)
>
> **Q: Does the knowledge that people will see it affect what you put in it?**
>
> It makes me conscious. (Student Y1)
> I don't naturally write what I want to. (Student Y2)

Both groups were conscious of the fact there is an external audience. It was felt that their perception of sketchbooks as tools for self-expression and the studio audience (tutors and peer group) did not 'mix that well'.

When asked how they would feel if it was not seen, most replied that they would feel freedom to express themselves. 'Things' that they would not 'normally' do would be added. They would not be conscious of how their thoughts and drawings would be interpreted by tutors. However, first-year students commented that in animation you always think about 'who your audience is' and making yourself understood. Lawson (1990) talks about a generation of design problems originating not in the designer's mind, but with a client. While the artist deals with problems that are important or are more fascinating to him at that particular time.

The findings indicated that students like owning multiple sketchbooks to serve different purposes, such as separate personal and coursework-orientated sketchbooks. The personal sketchbook was likened to a diary for documenting 'memories'; this was not shown to tutors.

The student responses implied that over time they felt using sketchbooks was a rewarding process after progressing from the initial feelings of dread and resistance that exposing oneself can manifest.

A sense of personal and artistic growth

Q: How do you see sketchbooks? Is it a chore? Or inspirational?

> Depends … if it's something that's set for you yes it's a chore. (Student Y2)
> When you look back and see how crap you were and how much you've got better you realise that obviously it's for my own good and made me a better artist for it I guess. (Student Y2)
> It made me do stuff I didn't want to do … like avoiding colours … like I actually put paint and started painting inside my sketchbook … that was cool. (Student Y2)

Second-year students indicated that if they were comfortable with sketchbooks it was not a chore. They felt there was value in being able to look back at work to see improvements. It has echoes of ipsative assessment as students evaluate their progress against their past performances and begin to establish autonomy. The realisation of the 'good' that sketchbooks can bring to learning was through self-discovery.

Emotional behaviours and creative blockages

Austerlitz and Aravot (2007) concluded that 'design students' emotions are not random phenomena, but rather a cognitive mode of interpretation of their environment, and a response which obeys a "logical" pattern.'

One supposition for creative blockages could be that this is contributed by risk-avoidance and creative unrest manifesting in procrastination or activities to avoid committing to making a mark on a blank page.

Q: Does it suit your style of learning?

> Too controlled … every page looks the same, I like it a bit different … I like to have a huge piece of paper and draw …that's what I enjoy doing …sketchbooks are too confined. (Student Y2)
> I don't like drawing … I think sketchbooks is about drawing otherwise it would be lined paper. (Student Y2)
> For me I completely seize up in a sketchbook … so I will always have pieces of paper that I'll sketch on and I'll keep them if I like them or chuck them … whereas if I've done something wrong or something looks bad then it's in my sketchbook and I go, 'Oh god now I have to stick something over it.' (Student Y2)

Responses from second-year students indicated they felt pressurised to produce work that they perceived was worthy of a sketchbook. Some factors that they considered were the high monetary cost and aesthetic of a perfectly bound book. Loose paper seemed to be a preferred option for some students to help the flow of ideas and not worry about 'mistakes'.

Q: How often and when do you use sketchbooks?

> Sometimes I look through it and think I better quickly draw something in it because the tutors are going to look … you used to get your sketchbook out like every couple of days and everyone would look through it but it made me think it had to be finished you know … and the drawing had to be really good. (Student Y2)

They felt there was an artificial element (like filling up the sketchbook two days before assessment) and the content was about making their research explicit to the reader rather than for self-gratification.

Q: Do you see it as part of your assessment?

> Yes they are when they tell you the criteria for the hand in … and you know you haven't done one and panic for the next five days … and quickly fill one up. (Student Y2)
> It's part of the research … however you collect it … so it would be a sketchbook I guess. (Student Y2)
> We haven't ever had a solid sketchbook grade have we? It's part of the grade we get. (Student Y2)

There was no consensus about whether or not sketchbooks formed part of assessment. Morrison (1990) cited in Moon (2006) advises students not to try to leave writing up their journals 'at the last moment' before they are handed in. Not taking the advice of Morrison (1990) seemed to have an emotional impact on several participants of the focus group, mainly the feeling of stress from pressure to meet the assessment criteria.

Pragmatism

> It is a well known fact that all inventors get their first ideas on the back of an envelope. I take slight exception to this, I use the front so that I can include the stamp and then the design is already half done. (Roland Emett, cited in Lawson, 1990)

Q: Where would you put your gathered information down?

Sketchbooks. (Student Y1)
I collect things from different sources … yes, separate pieces of paper. (Student Y1)
I've got a notice board in my room I just pin up things. (Student Y1)
I quite disorganised … I mean I take the notes, I take the pictures, I take bits of paper but then it's hard to keep them all together but what I found really inspirational to be working with is the mood board. (Student Y1)
Do sketching on wacom tablets … digital tablets … but it's not as easy to save and stuff … it's not like a sketchbook you can't just flick back through it. (Student Y1)
I have some on my computer … some are books, photocopies, drawings … I keep sketches and stuff … when I'm gathering information it's like one giant scrapbook … a metaphorical scrapbook. (Student Y2)

Both groups talked about using sketchbooks to store gathered information but there were quite a few popular alternatives as well, such as mood boards, plastic folders and digital storage. Students liked multiple ways of capturing and storing ideas. One student talked about the limitation of a sketchbook because 'it's still' and 'animation is a moving art form'. He took much of his research and inspiration from scenes from 'movies'.

Q: How often and when do you use sketchbooks?

I tend to use it more when I'm working on a project. (Student Y1)
I tend to just really carry it about like if I've got a bag … I don't like to carry it in my hands. (Student Y1)
I used to walk around with an A3 one … I went down to A4 … then I realised it's so much easier to carry about one smaller … you look forward more to sketching if it's easier to access. (Student Y1)
I used to carry two, a bigger one and a smaller one I'd put in my pocket but I've kind of slacked off because we're busy working on our final project. (Student Y2)

Students from both groups owned more than one sketchbook and felt the size of their sketchbook was significant and had different functions; a smaller one that they would carry about for sketches, doodles and observation drawings (e.g. on trains and in bars) and a large one for 'better' and more 'important' drawings. Male students from both groups stated that they only carry a sketchbook if they have a bag or a jacket pocket because they would not carry it by hand.

The frequency and occasions when the sketchbook is used seemed to be determined by the course curriculum, for example if they had a project to begin or complete. Some students did not use sketchbooks all the time, 'only when I need to'. Lawson (1990) writes that after a period of hard work in the preparation period there follows a period of 'incubation' where little work is achieved but which is often terminated by the sudden emergence of an idea ('illumination').

The second-year students felt there was a pragmatic cut-off point to research because it consumed too much time that they felt needed to be scheduled for making an end product. Feelings were expressed with comments such as, 'research slows you down' and 'you don't keep researching'.

Feelings about technology

In the past decade, the extent to which technological advancements have penetrated society makes it impossible to separate Internet culture from the way students choose to research. 'Google' and 'Youtube', for their speed and efficiency, have to some extent replaced looking through the humble library book. Students are now confronted with so many choices to make and collect research that the priority that was once placed on sketchbooks might be under threat.

Q: What does research mean to you?

Gathering information … from archives, from documentaries, people. (Student Y1)
To try out stuff … experiment with ideas. (Student Y1)
Taking a lot of photos. (Student Y1)
Look up images and things that have been written about. (Student Y2)

Q: Where?

On the Internet. (Student Y2)
TV, films. (Student Y2)
Library. (Student Y2)

Q: Is it usually Internet first then library?

I would probably go to library first because the books are in front of me … it's much easier to make photocopies … usually you find something you wouldn't expect. (Student Y2)

Answers from both groups indicated they understood research as a gathering of information as text and pictures. Only the second-year students talked about using the Internet and the library as resources.

Q: What's the balance between doing things digitally and the old-fashioned way (sketchbooks)? How dependent are you on the Internet?

I do the work faster on computers … at the same time if I use it for a long time I miss the old way of doing things. (Student Y1)

It depends where I get the information from … like if I find it in newspapers it will go in my sketchbook if I'm looking at the Internet I just save it to my USB stick. (Student Y1)

My generation is that the Internet wasn't always there … so I never always had it when I studied before … so like we used videos and stuff. (Student Y2)

It's easier to be creative in a sketchbook. (Student Y2)

Yeah you can flick through … and might find something that gives you an idea. (Student Y2)

I don't really like doodling and stuff … I just research and look at stuff and store them in my head. (Student Y2)

Dependence on the Internet varied to some extent with age and access to computers. The first-year students tended to see computers and the Internet as 'quicker and easier' to do research; however, there was a move to using both computers and sketchbooks according to where information was found. The tactile nature of the latter and the act of making was preferred by both groups. The second-year students saw sketchbooks as a creative medium. Two students from the second year did not feel that sketchbooks fitted into their research methods and preferred to go straight into the making.

The research findings indicated a definite emotional response to sketchbooks in the conversational analysis of the focus group, a significant portion of this related to how students interpreted tutors' responses to sketchbook work.

The role of tutors in activities around sketchbooks

> Self-initiated learning which involves the whole person, feelings as well as intellect, is most lasting and pervasive.
> (Carl Rogers, cited in Brockbank & McGill, 1998)

Sketchbooks by nature are a method of self-directed learning. Tutors facilitate this activity within the course content at the beginning of a project, with intervals of evaluation at tutorials throughout the project duration and, finally, at the project assessment stage. Students are left to decide when and where they use their sketchbooks. There is little directed study for using them so there is a notion that learning to take ownership of work begins here.

The design tutors' prescriptive assumptions lead them to believe that sketchbooks play an important role in developing conceptual and analytical skills especially in problem-based learning. The message is passed on to students who start to form perceptions of what the tutor thinks is a good sketchbook.

> **Q: How do you see the tutors' role in helping you use sketchbooks?**
> Push us into doing more drawing. (Student Y1)

There was a general feeling that tutors coerce students to do more drawing and encourage experimenting with new techniques. However, they appreciated that tutors are trying to improve drawing skills.

Both groups commented there was no structured tuition in techniques or time allocated to using sketchbooks; they understood that tutors expected sketchbook work to be done independently. They felt tutors made general comments but no personal feedback about individuals' sketchbooks. Students recognised the importance of sketchbooks from experiencing the tutors' pressure to use them in studio activities. It was felt there was a lack of divergent thinking on the course and that tutors should show flexibility according to the individual's preferred way of research. The second-year students who did not use sketchbooks reflected that perhaps, if they had used them, they might get better results from their finished animation.

There was a notion amongst the second-year students that tutors liked to see sketches because this was evidence of development and a thought process. Students commented, 'tutors like proper evidence'. They described the tutor's ideal sketchbook, 'all sorts of pieces of paper coming out, like you live in it'.

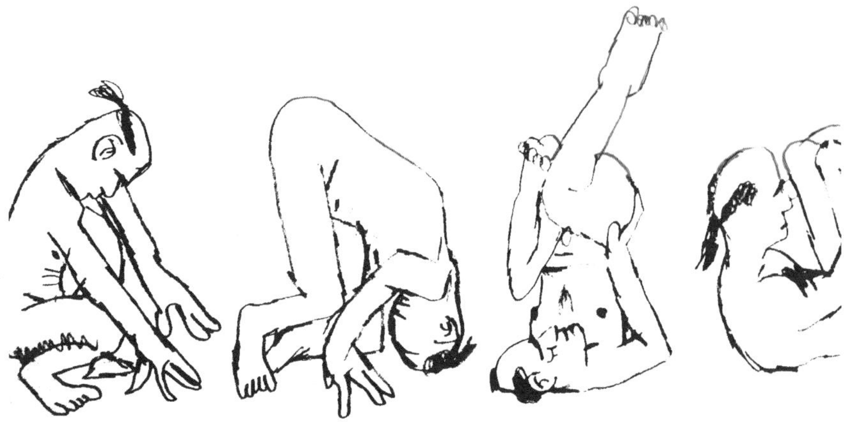

Sketchbook life drawing Andrei Thomas
Reproduced by permission of the artist

Conclusion

In this book I have examined how students perceive, use and feel about sketchbooks, the importance of sketchbooks in their learning and the relevance of emotions to student's learning from the experience of using a sketchbook on an animation course.

Students tended to fall into one of three categories: those who didn't like to use sketchbooks at all; those who put research straight into their sketchbook; those who sometimes did research in another medium and used sketchbooks for storage.

When developing students into designers, growth can be thought of as how the student learns to master their situation as a designer. Learning to expose or reveal themselves in sketchbooks is part of this growth, where emotions are intrinsically linked.

The emotional responses that rose from the research were confirmation of the argument Austerlitz and Aravot (2007) posed, that emotions have a significant role in students' learning.

Many students seem to have difficulties with expressing ideas 'freely' in their sketchbooks, that is to say in loose sketches or scribbled thoughts and ideas. There was a tendency to reserve entries to only planned art-worked designs with no risk-taking and using only practised styles of drawing. This suggests the following emotional responses:

- The fear of making a mistake that may be linked to 'perfectionist thinking'.
- Anxiety created by forced entries (or 'last minute' sketches). Morrison (1990, cited in Moon, 2006) advises students to try not to leave writing up their journals 'at the last moment' before they are handed in.
- The feelings of pressure and frustration from unsuitable ways of learning.

This could be an explanation for creative blockages as well as other phenomena that relate to pragmatism and choices that are made according to different learner styles.

Students talked about feeling forced by tutors to use a sketchbook and the feeling of being conscious and pressured to please their studio audience (Moon, 2006). Students talked about a degree of artificial work that is produced for assessment purposes (formative and summative) and the preference for owning multiple sketchbooks. Lawson's theories on generators of design problems and the difficulty sometimes in separating art and design highlighted the role of the sketchbook within design-based learning. The research showed students found that design problems in project work and solving artistic problems in sketchbooks had conflicting roles.

Tutors teach students that sketchbooks are an expressive and autonomous research component, however the creative process does sometimes cause confusion resulting in student's thinking that there needs to be an end product. This confusion can create positive and negative emotions. Every individual is different so students will have their own experiences, however the research suggests there are some common cognitive patterns. Students experience the emotions of fear and pressure because each time their sketchbook is seen they are exposing their work and what is intrinsically linked to sketchbooks – their thoughts. The knowledge of this affects how they cope with future situations and, eventually, they learn to be pragmatic perfectionists. After receiving tutors' feedback in the first year, the second-year students talked about not worrying so much about making the sketchbook look 'pretty' and concentrating more on putting down thoughts. The feeling of fear of exposure they experienced in the past moved to emotional detachment with the knowledge that the work was done for an audience, and depersonalising the object. Lawson (1990) tells us the product itself rarely tells us much about how it came to be. The students appreciated and recognised that sketchbooks can document the process to get to the product. Hence, the focus is changed from object to process.

This research offers insights into how a particular group of students experience sketchbooks and indicates the pressure students feel to fit sketchbooks into their learning.

I hope my research will encourage more investigation into the role of emotions in student learning to help students use sketchbooks and help tutors understand how they map on to different learner styles with the possibility of new definitions of sketchbooks and terminology (i.e. the limitations of the term 'sketchbook'). Perhaps as teacher-practitioners we should introduce allocated time for sketchbooks within the course structure, especially early on in student learning where we could show methods and give specific direction to demystify sketchbooks across all levels and disciplines.

As we uncover how students really feel about sketchbooks and how they incorporate these emotions into their cognitive structures we need to help them learn how to function in the studio environment. More emphasis on and a better understanding of the role of emotions in creative spaces such as the sketchbook will support student learning.

References

Austerlitz N., Aravot I. (2007). Emotions of Design Students: A New Perspective for the Design Studio, in Salama A. and Wilkinson, N. (Eds.), *Design Studio Pedagogy: Horizons for the Future*. (Chap. 3: Teaching Styles in the Studio) U.K.: Urban International Press pp. 233-246

Brockbank A. & McGill, I. (1998), *Facilitating Reflective Learning in Higher Education* (Buckingham: SRHE and Open University Press)

Lawson, B. (1990), *How Designers Think: The Design Process Demystified*, (second edition) (Oxford: Butterworth Architecture)

McNiff, J., McGeady, L. & Elliot, R. (2001), *Time to Listen: An Evaluation Project* (Magee: University of Ulster)

Moon, J.A. (2004), *A Handbook of Reflective and Experiential Learning* (Oxon: RoutledgeFalmer)

Moon, J.A. (2006), *Learning Journals* (Oxon: Routledge)

Appendix

Data: 2 focus groups (21 students) fully transcribed.

Analysis: conversation analysis.

Students participating in the focus group sessions were encouraged to discuss around the following.

The first set of questions asks if the sketchbook is outdated:

- What does research mean to you?
- How does research start?
- Where do you put ideas down?
- What would you like to use instead of a sketchbook?
- What other mediums do you use for research?
- How have the Internet and computers helped with research? Could you work without it? Does it outdate working in sketchbooks?
- How often and when do you use the sketchbook? (Project work? Only when asked to by tutors?)

The second set of questions asks how they perceive sketchbooks:

- How do you see sketchbooks? Is it a chore? Or a moment for inspiration?
- Do you see it as part of your assessment?
- Does it suit your style of learning?
- Does the knowledge that others will see it affect what you put into a sketchbook?
- How much of the work is in your comfort zone and how much of it are things you think you should be doing?
- How would you feel if it was never seen?
- Would that affect the way you work in it?
- How do you see the tutor's role in using your sketchbook?

Sarah Atkinson

The emotional responses to the sketchbook studied in this paper highlight the inhibitions students feel about being judged in this most sensitive of areas. Revealing, as it does, thoughts at a formative stage, the sketchbook raises issues of huge sensitivity and vulnerability for students. Su-Lynn Tan explores how students perceive, use and feel about sketchbooks and how this most fundamental of art and design tools can impede and inhibit the student's creative potential.

Experience as a teacher in both further and higher education has given me a particular perspective. In my own research, the loss of playful experiment in students, as a result of an over-prescriptive and over-assessed curriculum has a particular resonance with feelings expressed by these students in discussing their work. The students here talk about the artificiality of filling in pages because the project demands a completed sketchbook. The necessity to display to an audience causes the student to configure their thoughts to please others. There is a fear of failure inherent in a student's approach to any form of assessment, whether formal or informal. The result is often a presentation that seeks acceptance and affirmation rather than a true revealing of early thought processes and discarded ideas.

The sketchbook is, as Tan demonstrates, a place where the private and the public space meet. It is also the focal point of the move from internal imaginary ideas to the realisation of those ideas to an audience and to critical observation. With that initial reluctance to express an idea on paper, revealing as it does ideas that may not be fully formed, creative blockages occur specific to the development of ideas in a sketchbook. This leads to an overuse of found imagery – other people's work, Internet downloads and magazine tears – as a substitute for drawing. We need to introduce a terminology to the problem of sketchbook freeze and seek better solutions for overcoming it.

There is a universal understanding of the need to induct students into the use and value of sketchbooks as part of their studio practice. As a student progresses through the system, the sketchbook becomes something that is required as a tool for storing information and developing ideas, but there is a difference in disciplines even within our field – the student of animation, for example, who needs a moving record of ideas, or the student of dress or textiles, who requires a tactile element that would be unnecessary for someone working in a purely two-dimensional way. As teachers, we should be able to recognise and celebrate this diversity and welcome innovation and alternatives. Are sketchbooks an essential tool for artists and designers? Perhaps not – a notebook or laptop carried around and used daily could provide more evidence of thinking than a sketchbook used sporadically and without conviction.

The students here discuss a need for a thinking space without feeling they are being judged or assessed on the content and quality of their visual records and ideas development. They talk of the private or 'personal' sketchbook that is not for external scrutiny by tutors. This personal sketchbook, if revealed, invariably contains far more of value, in terms of the creative process, than the 'presentation' sketchbook. Students are often required to answer the question:'How did you arrive at this idea?' The taking of risks and the acceptance of mistakes is a vital part of that creative process; the sketchbook remains the bridge between thoughts and substance, containing the visual evidence of evaluation and selection, proving ownership or intellectual property.

This paper opens up the discussion and poses questions of accepted practice. As teachers, we should be demystifying the sketchbook, its use and value, and encouraging students to understand that, in whatever form it takes, the sketchbook is a place where they can feel free to explore and experiment with ideas without the pressure and anxiety of assessment.

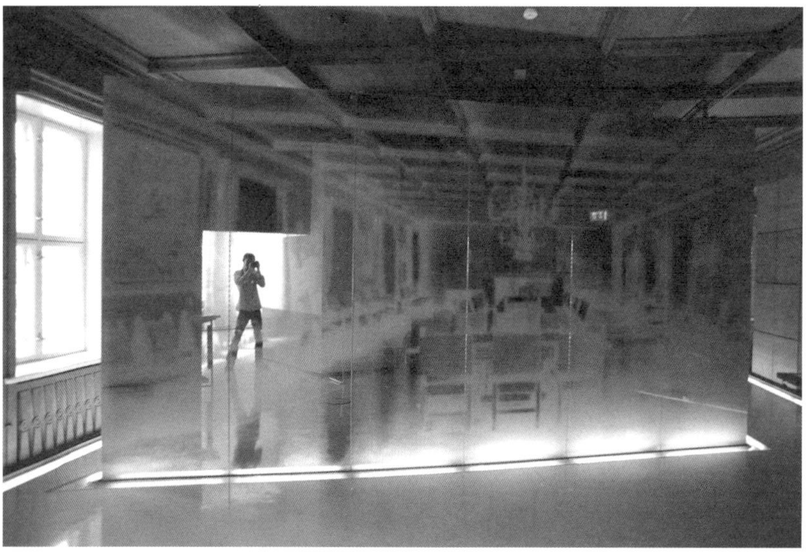

Untitled 2006 Katrine Hjelde

Two way mirror glass installation with inkjet print H288x w 450x990x1260x220cm

Permanent installation for Holocaust Museum, Villa Grande, Oslo, Norway, with b+r architects

Photo: Matthew Flintham

6

Between fine art and teaching: reflecting creative passion

Author: Katrine Hjelde

Commentary: Rebecca Fortnum

Keywords

creative passion,
fine art,
reflective teaching

Katrine Hjelde

Introduction

This paper explores the role of creative passion in relation to fine art teaching and learning on student-focused courses, where tutor-student interactions are frequently based around the students' individual practice. It will examine how the tutor-student relationship in fine art is related not only to a sharing of practice but also to a sharing of emotions about the creative act. I will focus on the emotion of creative passion, how it is both a subjective emotion and also culturally/historically produced in relation to art and the role of the artist, and I will look at some consequences this has for teaching and learning.

As part of my ongoing PhD research, I have begun to explore how tutors' art practices come into their teaching and this paper will examine how this transfer has an emotional dimension. How the tutor conceives of his/her practice in emotional terms will also be related to how it is framed by the tutor within student-tutor interaction. Emotion is also explored here in relation to theories of reflective learning and teaching and this paper will look at two typical teaching and learning situations, the one-to-one tutorial and the group seminar, with this in mind.

Creative passion

The emotion that I will focus on within these teaching and learning situations, is what we might call 'creative passion', for want of a better term, knowing full well that this emotion is what Ben Ze'ev (2000) refers to as a cluster emotion, an emotional resonance, which contains a number of related emotions like excitement, confusion, envy, etc.

Passion is defined as obsession, love, fervour and enthusiasm. Passion is the emotion of feeling very strongly about a subject or person. As a term it is mostly used in a romantic context, but equally it is a religious term denoting various forms of emotional suffering. Its etymology comes from the Latin *pati*, meaning to suffer or to endure (Oxford American Dictionary). Perhaps creative passion as a concept 'contains' both these meanings? Maybe an interesting question for art and design pedagogy is whether we can – or should – harness this dual understanding of passion?

After all, certain aspects of emotion in relation to visual art are a particular kind of historical construct, relating to the cliché of the tortured artist, in thrall of his/her emotions as a source of both aesthetic creations and experiences. This is a legacy from the Romantic era, and from this moment a cultural and hence personal and institutional expectation of passion within fine arts practice evolved. Following a constructivist approach, considering that we construct meaning from current knowledge structures, it seems necessary to mention these expectations also.

It is difficult to talk about emotion in teaching and learning. The word itself often conjures up something off-putting within the context of education, from boredom to humiliation, discomfort to despair. The educational experience is indeed emotional, and can include the emotions as listed above – but here I will focus on these and all other emotions as potentiality. Both negative and positive emotions can facilitate potentiality, meaning that not one kind of emotion is privileged in relation to learning. Thus the emotion of creative passion can be examined as a powerful tool towards facilitating a deeper experience of learning and reflective teaching and learning in fine art.

As an artist/teacher I will consider how theories associated with emotions can be interrelated to pedagogic theories of reflection, to explore one particular link between emotion and education. These theories can be used to explore emotion as a way to mobilise the potential for double loop learning that emotional involvement can facilitate. 'Double loop' is a term coined by Argyris and Shön (1973, cited in Brockbank & McGill, 2007, p. 50) to describe learning where assumptions are challenged and values can be transformed, leading to what they call potentially *paradigmatic* (2007) shifts in the learner. This builds on but leaves behind single loop learning, which although important with regards to gaining competence and confidence, leaves the underlying values of a theory unchanged. Double loop learning has been described as typical for postgraduate or mature undergraduate work. However, the critical nature of fine art practice and learning encourages students to undergo these shifts from early on in their course. As these learning shifts need emotion to enable this change, they may be unsettling and problematic for the student, and may help explain why art students are, or are perceived to be, more emotional.

Reflection in/on contemporary art practice/pedagogy

The relationship between contemporary art practice and pedagogy is not extensively written about, either with regards to emotion or in other terms. There is one exception to this, which is how fine art education is increasingly being held up as an ideal towards other kinds of education. This includes the idea of the 'art academy' being used as a model for other activities, like exhibitions and biennales (A.C.A.D.E.M.Y, Manifesta 6, Documenta 12, Frieze Art Fair) and why conferences like Summit Kein (2007) in Berlin focus on the potentiality of art schools in relation to education as a whole and as a platform for cultural actualisation and self-organisation within society. However, in these discussions any mention of an emotional aspect/dimension is largely absent, and this evasion is noteworthy. Why does even cutting-edge theory shy away from this area? The cognitive/emotional split is still underlying and informing these theoretical shifts, further entrenching the divide between what is seen as critical theory relating to education and what seems to be seen as the caretaker aspect of the role of the tutor and the institution.

Judith Carroll's research into the hidden frames of reference for artist/teachers, can be used to outline an alternative way to frame the interrelationship between practice and teaching. In her studies of *Convention and Practice* (2004), Carroll has challenged the belief that artists' practice conforms to an integrated and disciplined pattern, which can be used towards a pedagogy of fine art teaching. Instead, she believes that there are concealed frames of references, which are the artist's beliefs about art teaching, which she found to be *not* directly related to his/her own practice, but rather related to the tutor's own art education. However, Carroll did her research in Australia on teachers operating within highly structured courses.

At Chelsea, it is ideally the students' own practice that sets the parameters for the learning, (within an institutional framework of a shared curriculum in terms of modules, learning outcomes and assessment criteria). This is what the Chelsea BA Fine Art Handbook refers to as 'student focused learning'. Within this course delivery mode, I find that my teaching practice relates less to my own education and more to my art practice. It is, however, the *students' practice* that establishes the terms of engagement. But through this work on hidden frames of reference, Carroll raises very important questions with regards to *tutor predispositions* in general and I would say also with regards to what exactly is an artist practice when discussed in relation to teaching. Commonly today an arts practice is to perform different roles such as theorist/archivist/artist and to use a range of formats from exhibition to think-tank including the whole gamut of relational art practices as defined by Nicholas Bourriaud (2002). In addition, from Joseph Beuys to Copenhagen Free University, there are many artists who make work explicitly through the medium of education, however, in contemporary practice this tends to take place outside of art education institutions. Does a practice only include works *produced*, which in the context of contemporary practice could be an entirely immaterial and/or relational practice, or can practice be seen to incorporate the *performing* of all those activities that are related to or spring out of practice? In that case, one would expect that for this inclusive way of viewing the artist's *production*, different kinds of questions can be asked with regards to *arts practice* in relation to what we might call *teaching practice*?

So from this point we could tentatively say that the kind of passion held by a tutor towards his/her practice will relate to *a number of areas and activities, including teaching, and will be constantly evolving, changing and shifting. Thus in effect the same situation as the student finds himself/herself in.* The other thing we have to consider is that in teaching it is not only the teacher's practice (however this is defined) that comes into the encounter, but also the teacher's experience of having been a student and all the related emotional investment.

As previously asserted there is not much literature available within the area of emotion in teaching art, so I have also looked at studies relating emotion directly to creative production as well as mapping some myths relating to artists. This includes how artists' work/art is produced and how art is consumed. The second point is important as we also have emotional expectations of an encounter with an artwork. And perhaps this situation has some resemblances to the case when a tutor meets/encounters the work of a student.

As artists, our art practice informs our teaching in various more or less subtle ways. Therefore, the notion of a pedagogical stance that builds on or incorporates a tutor's particular sense of practice could encompass the notion of *reflective knowing*, whereby a particular idea of knowing is embraced but at the same time also queried.

The passionate art student

Avril and Nunley (1992) have written on 'living an emotionally creative life'. Their book is not about the kinds of emotions experienced by artists during the creative process, but on how we can (all) be emotionally creative, which again links us to the idea of the potentiality contained in emotion in an educational context. Also, they too emphasise that all emotions are the product of our cultural heritage, which brings us back to the cultural expectations of the perceived emotional state of artists/art students.

> To achieve our full potential, to actualise our unique and genuine selves, we must be open to discovery, exploration and challenge in the emotional as much as the in the intellectual domain.
> (1992, p. 14)

Emotion can, following Avril and Nunley, be defined as a constructivist conception – thus it is a feeling that can encompass both rationalist and romantic conceptions. Their perception of a relationship between creativity and emotion can be used also to make connections between the processes of creativity and the process of learning. So where it is perhaps most useful to talk about creative emotion or passion in their terms is actually when it is most closely aligned with concepts of learning: as acquisition, refinement and transformation. I do not believe that students on fine art courses learn very differently from students in other subjects. But as they are expected to be independent and define what they set out to learn themselves, the fine art course does require that students are willing to take this responsibility for their learning, for mapping out the area to learn within and have the maturity to structure their time and work appropriately.

According to perceptions held by art students, tutors and society, art students are more passionate about their subject, than many other undergraduates. By stepping away from beliefs and myths passed down from the Romantic era, this passion could also be partly explained because many art students have already invested in their art education through undertaking a foundation course. Generally speaking, few students will be on fine art courses due to pressure from the family or similar. They will be there because they want to be artists or at least work within the creative industries. The *Destinations and Reflections Research* (1999) into the careers of British art, craft and design graduates has found that a few years after graduation only 20% of student are in employment unrelated to art and design, which is higher than for graduates in other fields. On the whole, a lack of engagement with subject is perhaps less of an issue on a fine art course than on some other courses.

Teaching art as a reflective practice

Brockbank and McGill acknowledge the importance of emotion in their writing and state:

> We shall need those who are comfortable, and who are willing to take the risk of sometimes being uncomfortable with emotion, to handle the volatile fuel and ensure that the energy is contained for the benefit of learning.
> (Brockbank & McGill, 2007, p. 53)

They argue that as emotion is one of the three aspects of what they call the learning triangle (with knowledge and action interaction), emotion in fact 'holds the key to a higher level of learning through reflective dialogue' (2007, p. 49). This means that emotion is a necessary component to achieve double loop learning where beliefs are challenged and underlying values are changed, and this is the kind of learning that fine art students will have to engage with even on an undergraduate course, as critical reflection on their work, the context of the work and on the discipline itself is expected. This relates well to my own experience, both as a student and as a teacher.

Brockbank and McGill further outline the necessary requirements for reflective teaching and learning, and the first condition mentioned is *relationship*, thus foregrounding that interaction with learners is about forging a connection. With their focus on the relationship, Brockbank and McGill build on the work of the clinical and pedagogical psychology of Carl Rodgers (1983) who outlined the necessary qualities of a relationship between the learner and the teacher including:

- realness or genuineness;
- prizing acceptance and trust of the learners;
- empathic understanding – which must be communicated.

When I have felt that I have learned most intensely or (effectively) this has always been in some way emotional and it has (sometimes unconsciously) taken place as part of a reflective process, sometimes as or after a dialogue with an empathic teacher. I do not distinguish emotional learning from other types of learning, rather here highlight the role that emotion plays in most if not all learning.

One-to-one tutorial

The one-to-one tutorial is still a defining trait of learning and teaching in fine art. Towards facilitating a reflective dialogue, I would argue that it can be invaluable. In the one-to-one, the student has enough time to start to relax, let down his/her guard, discuss being stuck, frustrated or depressed about current work and equally able to share unselfconsciously successes, progress and joy, as well as confusion and fear of failure. It is the place where tutors can have the space to be empathic in their engagement with the student and his/her work. Again, Roger (1983) and Brockbank and McGill (2007) emphasise that this form of empathy is primary, and thus does not enter into the arena of the work of the therapist or counsellor.

Example based on own studio teaching

One-to-one with stage two student:

> Student uncommunicative and disengaging with the situation, looking away. Very little work evidenced. How do I communicate empathy through my belief in creative passion here? In a way this is not something to be switched on at the time but a fundamental approach to teaching. But faced here with a not very obviously passionate student, the tutor has to further tap into that passion for himself/herself, in order to reach out to the student, and make a connection, which will enable the student to get something from the encounter. Tutor has to believe that this student cares deeply. Tutor does and says very little, tutor waits, is friendly and makes 'small talk' in some way modelling an interest in the work of the student without questioning or pushing the student. This is as a form of 'connected knowledge' where tutor suspends judgment in an attempt to understand the student's way of making sense of their experiences (Brockbank & McGill, 2007, p. 69) Student starts to relax, looks at tutor, starts to talk about feeling very unsure about the current work, about feelings of being lost, of feelings of disengagement with process and the course. Then after an unpacking of these feelings by voicing these to an empathic listener, the student is ready to engage with the actual art work(s) and discuss this from a less emotional perspective and throughout the tutor's stance is that this work is worthwhile and important and has potential. This way the student himself/herself will do the job of the critical reflection needed to move the work forward and learn.

Group seminar

The group seminar is the area where emotion has to become more formally framed within a critical position towards the work. This is a difficult balancing act for the students. The situation itself can be fraught; students can feel very ambivalent about being 'judged' by their peers, and by their tutors, in public. The group seminar should not be about passing judgement, however this is probably the emotional response to the situation that many students feel. Some students relish the chance of multiple feedback positions and the possibility of lively debate with their work in centre. These students are the minority but in my experience there will for most be an element of excitement mixed in with the dread at the seminar situation.

In some respects it is not the student whose work is being discussed who will learn the most from the encounter, it is often more likely the other students taking part. They will also be apprehensive, as there is an expectation of being able to discuss work critically and offer constructive criticism intelligently, and thus all students who participate also feel that they may be judged in some way, particularly, perhaps, by the tutors(s) present.

However, in learning terms in relation to reflective practice, the group crit allows for dialogues, which can be reflective in the sense that as learning always takes place within a social context – the learners are also a social construct. Here there can be dialogues as forms of social engagement. This is an arena where the idea of practice in all its dimensions can be examined and explored and where the result of (often private) creative passion can be unpacked and reflected on as a group. This is where creative passion can be shared and redefined in a useful way between peers, witnessed by the tutor.

Conclusion

Passion towards art as a subject, activity and event will be part of the stance of most tutors in fine art. For tutors to examine this stance, to make it more specific, overt and transparent, can perhaps provide a productive starting point for empathy that can make reflective dialogues between tutor and student or between students facilitated by tutors more effective in terms of learning for the student.

As a tutor, the passion I have for art enables me to empathise with a student in a teaching and learning context. This helps me when I am faced with a student whose work I do not immediately understand or when I am faced with students whose work I find very problematic and/or difficult to relate to. Students often expect teachers to be able to read and decode their projects – perhaps they want us to do this job for them. I think we can get the student to do this work of analysing, describing and critically evaluating his/her practice through reflective dialogue, between tutor and student, in an empathic context. This can then form part of a discursive model that can be used between students in group crits, as well as towards informal studio discussions.

A truly reflective dialogue cannot happen without empathy, and empathy in this case is based on my passion for the subject that we are both engaged with. In the one-to-one tutorial, my practice and my other predispositions, like my own art education, do influence my engagement with the students' work, but as the one-to-one tutorial affords the time and space, this can become transparent and also be offered up and used as part of the reflective dialogue. An empathic approach in the one-to-one should include a sharing and showing of passion towards creative practice and art. By communicating passion, not only verbally but equally through body language, speech pattern and intonation, we can set up a platform for passionate belief in the importance of art in life.

References

Averill, J.R. & Nunley, E.P. (1992), *Voyages of the Heart: Living an Emotionally Creative Life* (New York: The Free Press)

Ben-Ze'ev, A. (2001), *The Subtlety of Emotions* (MIT Press)

Bourriaud, N. (2002), *Relational Aesthetics* (France: Les Presse Du Reel)

Brockbank, A. & McGill, I. (2007), *Facilitating Reflective Learning in Higher Education* (SRHE and Open University Press)

Carroll, J. (2004), *Convention and Practice: Working Papers in Art and Design 3,* ISSN 1466-4917, available online (accessed 15 January 2008) at: http://www.herts.ac.uk/artdes/research/papers/wpades/vol3/jcfull.html

Destinations and Reflections – Careers of British Art, Craft and Design Graduates (1999), available online (accessed 22 January 2008) at: http://www.shu.ac.uk/research/cre/publications/dr/drexec.html

Rogers, C.R. (1983), *Freedom to Learn for the 80s* (Columbus, OH: Charles Merrill)

Rebecca Fortnum

Alison Wilding: The next sculpture is [from] when I made all the work myself and my engagement with the objects that I made was ... very personal ... it was a really fabulous rapport with doing and making that is very unusual with me. For me a good piece of work (something that either I have made or someone else has made), is when the hair at the back of your neck stands on end when you encounter it... ... that's what I demand from the things that I do...

Maria Chevska : I'm really interested in that sort of epiphany type moment that you can have with a work that would give that visceral reaction... ... I would think they're very few and far between but an artist continues to make work and I'm interested in the sense of failure you could have by showing a body of work that you've not had that experience with.
(artists' seminar, www.visualintelligences.com)

This exchange, between two successful artist-lecturers articulates the passion (both the highs and lows) that many contemporary artists experience in their practice. As Katrine Hjelde points out, passion is a term with devotional overtones and words such as 'epiphany,' or 'belief' are quite commonly used to convey artists' deep attachment to their work. Indeed, at times, the strength of these feelings, our 'leaps of faith' as it were, seem only to be matched by our apparent inability to analyse them. And, although such scrutiny is difficult, as teachers (and probably as artists), we need to be able to examine the mechanisms of our value systems. Hjelde's important paper tackles these complex issues and demonstrates how the passion felt for fine art can become the vehicle for empathy and thus communication between artist-tutor and artist-student. More than that, much fine art teaching requires students to examine their own passions as the subject of the art-work itself. This dynamic, which makes private feelings public (in both the work and the teaching dialogue around it), requires conditions of trust. Hjelde's eloquent descriptions of her own teaching make it clear that sensitivity to the vulnerability issuing from disclosure is required from both tutor and student for successful learning. It is also interesting to note that this sense of shared passion aids artist-teachers when speaking to artist-students outside their immediate discipline areas.

One of the most interesting areas of debate the paper raises is how notions of passion might allow us to examine the flux between learning, teaching and making. Hjelde focuses on 'emotion as potentiality'; by this I understand her to mean that the powerful, complicated and possibly conflicting feelings of passion are, above all, a prompt to activity, even an agent of change. Change 'facilitated' by 'emotional involvement' can be learning of the deepest kind, engendering what Hjelde calls 'paradigmatic shift[s] in the learner'. Tutor and student's shared understanding of the struggles and the euphoria of making (the 'rapport' that Wilding and Chevska discuss above) ensures that traditional teaching hierarchies are shaken, if not removed. Thus passion becomes an important leveler. As Hjelde says:

> "... we could tentatively say that the kind of passion held by a tutor towards his/her practice will relate to a number of areas ...and will be constantly evolving, changing and shifting. Thus in effect the same situation as the students finds himself/herself in".

It is precisely because the relationship of the artist to his or her practice is so emotionally fraught that the possibilities for deep learning present themselves. Within the teaching situation, how these feelings, ideas and processes are articulated, organised and presented will not only impact directly on the art-works 'in progress' but will also affect the artist-student's whole sense of (artistic) identity.[1] As the tutor facilitates understanding of what students have made, he or she is also encouraging them to test their passions, to find the limits of their beliefs. In doing so the tutor's own emotional and passionate engagement with art practice comes into play, with potentially negative, as well as positive, results. In these circumstances, Katrine Hjelde's call on us to reflect further upon the emotional dynamics of teaching fine art seems most urgent.

Note

[1] For an in depth discussion of this please see Sandino, L. (2007), "Relating process: accounts of influence in the life history interview', *Journal of Visual Art Practice*, 6.3 pp 191-199

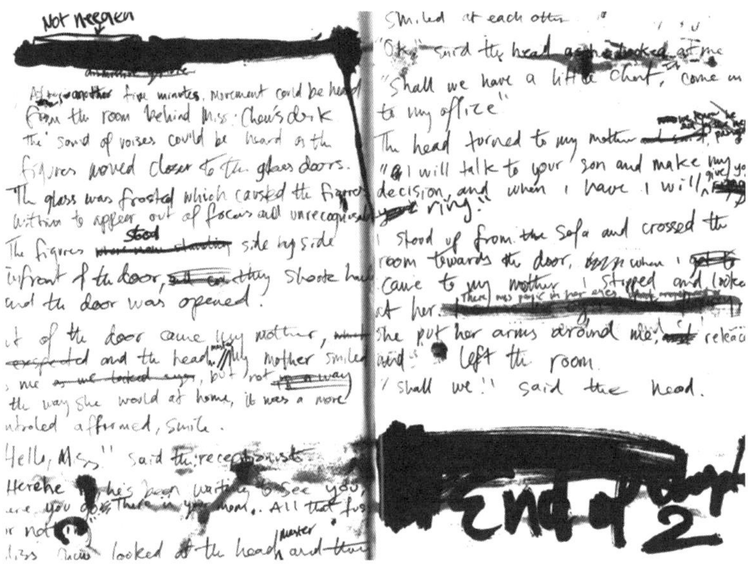

Untitled — Oliver O'Keeffe

Reproduced by permission of AREA-D, Action Research in Art & Design Limited

7

The written stuff: creative writing activities on a visual arts course

Author: Andrea Lioy

Commentary: Jane Tynan

Keywords

creative writing,
identity,
extra-curricular learning,
action research,
student centered teaching

Andrea Lioy

Introduction

This short paper concerns an extra-curricular activity devised in conjunction with students on the BA (Hons) graphic design course (BAGD) at Central Saint Martins College of Art and Design, and the curriculum-related issues that it addressed. This activity was called 'The writing workshop' and was created to support international, mostly Asian, students in writing their dissertations, a part of the course for which I am responsible. On the BAGD, the dissertation is presented to the students as an opportunity to reflect on their learning journey. Some quandaries arose due to the fact that the work on this project starts at the beginning of the second year, when the course of their learning has barely just begun.

Initially, the workshop aimed to address the students' problems by giving them an alternative space to explore their learning curve. Being extra-curricular, it ended up becoming a series of meetings with friends and so that exploration simply did not occur. However, another exploration happened, possibly more relevant to the students themselves because it happened spontaneously. This was an exploration of their own identity as students far away from home, having to cope with different curricula, different learning styles and different expectations. It also had another positive and unanticipated outcome in the fact that most of the students joined the workshop because they did not feel confident about their writing. Now they do, to the point that they are now working on a new publication.

In the following pages I will present the key dilemma and the evidence that led me to take action and create the writing workshop. I will also provide an overview of the writing workshop context and identify the main questions that it addressed and how. I will then discuss the effects of the writing workshop on students from my point of view. I will also discuss the effects this experience had on me as a teacher and how it made me more aware of my professional and personal responsibilities.

The writing workshop context

I teach on the BA graphic design course at Central Saint Martins College of Art and Design, on a programme called 'context', short for contextual studies. This is the part of the course that asks students to submit a dissertation as partial fulfilment of the requirements of their degree. The 'context project' (the course refers to the dissertation as a project because it does not only contain a 6–8,000 word dissertation but also a piece of creative work based on the research the students make while writing their theoretical text) is presented to them as an opportunity to reflect on their learning (UAL-CSM, 2006, pp. 57–64). Students are asked to be reflective practitioners. Their final work should be produced not only thanks to their artistic talent, but also through their ability to consider the wider social and political context in which their work can be situated.

A work of such depth takes almost a whole academic year to produce and therefore must be launched at the beginning of the students' second academic year. The students are asked to reflect on their learning as the learning happens. In reality, things are more complicated than this because reflections – and the production of artistic work that proves these reflections – need time, and the development of critical tools that, in this case, are supposed to be acquired through both learning and reflection. The students were aware that they were asked to manage many tasks at once. They were honestly voicing their concerns regarding their own learning.

I realised that the writing workshop could also become a good opportunity for an action research project. I hoped it would give me the possibility to reflect on my own learning as it was happening, precisely the way we brief students. I would find myself in their position, going through the same process of discovery. For this reason, I believe the students felt they could discuss ideas and concerns with me as with one another, so they opened up completely and I could do the same. Our relationship started moving towards real peer collaboration – if not friendship. This was definitely a good moment because we felt we were starting to accomplish something important together. At the same time, it opened up the danger of manipulation, a point that I will develop later.

I started implementing weekly meetings referring to the classification of educational media proposed by Laurillard (2002, pp. 83–84). I was equally interested in all of her four models:

- *Discursive*, where 'teacher's and students' conceptions are each accessible to the other and the topic goal is negotiable' (p. 83);
- *Adaptive*, where 'the student must be able to use their existing conceptual knowledge to adapt their actions in the task environment in order to achieve the task goal' (p. 84);
- *Interactive*, in which 'something in the environment must change in a meaningful way as a result of [the students'] actions' (p. 84);
- *Reflective*, by which 'the pace of the learning process must be controllable by the students, so that they can take the time needed to reflect on the task goal-action-feedback cycle in order to develop their conception in relation to the topic goal' (p. 84).

I reflected on these models in relation to my Montessori background. The ideas of the Italian educator seem to bear resemblance with all of the four models above. For her, the child is a being capable of

- learning, not as much as through direct instruction as through a collaborative adventurous exploration of the environment with their teacher – the *discursive* model (Staley, 1998);
- using their 'creativity ... to solve problems' – the *adaptive* model (Malaguzzi, 1998, in Loughran, 2001);
- changing the environment along with their perception of it in order to make it more apt to their newly learnt abilities – the *interactive* model (see Lubienski Wentworth 1999, p. 23);
- making sense of their own experiences in their own time by relating to each other – the *reflective* model (Katz & Chard, 1989, in Loughran, 2001).

This arrangement seemed to be an apt one because the group was developing characteristics from both conceptualisations of teaching. It was participatory, collaborative and creative, and students were sharing their knowledge spontaneously.

Extra-curricular experience vs. the curriculum's learning outcomes

I asked the students what they really wanted from their time with me and they said that they wanted to learn to write. The ability to synthesise ideas and concepts and to communicate them to a wider audience was relevant to them. They thought they were unable to do so and that this was keeping them apart from belonging to a larger group of students who were able to take care of their thesis writing without external help or language support.

It was clear to me that the workshop meetings needed to become more focused on the students' learning outcomes, as that was their fair request. At the same time, they also felt empowered by the fact that the activity was happening outside the curriculum, as this freed them from anxieties concerning assessment. My interpretation of the term extra-curricular acknowledges that these activities can strengthen the curriculum because they can relate to it and even propose changes to it while allowing the students to explore the same learning outcomes from a different standpoint (see Cassel, Chow & Demoulin, 2000; Demoulin, 2002, on extra-curricular activities in high-schools; also see Tierney, 1989, p. 73 on curricular changes in academic environments).

The learning outcomes, as the BAGD course handbook (UAL-CSM, 2006) states them, seem to be perfectly achievable considering Laurillard and Montessori – outcomes that 'challenge established values' (p. 57), generated through 'reflection on [the students' own] experiences' (p. 16), '[synthesising] ideas and concepts' (p. 63) in order to communicate to a 'wider audience' (p. 17), while keeping a 'spirit of adventurous enquiry' (p. 17).

In order to discuss a variety of writing contexts, we started reading. Articles from magazines and newspapers and excerpts from books were selected by the students themselves on the basis of their personal interests. I also selected something when my turn came. Speaking to the students later in the year I found that because we had decided upon choosing anything we wanted, even if not technically related to the course, everybody was interested. Not because they shared a passion for the topic but because they could feel the genuine enthusiasm of the student giving the presentation. Those presentations became the starting point for short written pieces.

I asked the students to send me some feedback emails. 'It [was] suddenly so different from the Context presentations. I felt I could do something for my friends here' wrote a student in an email to me. 'I'm learning many many things, although I'm not sure when I will use them' wrote another. And a third one: 'I wish [they] stopped going on about their personal interests, but then I also like when they listen to me. I don't think it has anything to do with writing, though.' There were mixed feelings about the topics that were on offer but generally speaking the students were happy to be part of the group. They began a series of adventurous theoretical explorations and made sense of their new environment through collaboration and reflection.

I was happy because what was happening responded to their official learning outcomes. The students were happy because they had a general feeling of emancipation when thinking about the possibility of learning while having fun and finding alternative ways of meeting the requirements for the degree.

Until that moment the workshop had asked participants to get involved with a variety of written material and to produce some of their own. However, because not everyone was attending every meeting, some of the students were not informed of what was going on. I decided to create an online space where students could upload their work for one another to observe, read and comment upon.

The writing workshop blog was successful for some time as a tool for organising meetings and sharing ideas. My posts became little briefs that the students could take in order to look for or produce the work that would be discussed during the following session. Having some sort of a little schedule online also allowed the students to be aware of what was going to be discussed in advance and prepare their contributions in advance. The group started functioning again in a slightly different way. Having the time to see some work published online before the weekly session originated more articulated feedback. Students started to collaborate more and more, even outside the workshop. At the same time, the blog created and initially fulfilled the need to make ideas available in written form. This was instrumental to the decision of publishing The Written Stuff as the record of some of the writing workshop experience.

Biggs (2003, p. 20) discusses three levels of thinking about teaching, arranged in ascending order of sophistication (p. 56):

- Level 1 teaching is dependent on student-based factors, like for instance cultural differences.
- Level 2 is dependent on the teacher's activities; Level 3 is based on the students' activities within the interactive system created by the co-presence of peers and teachers.
- Level 3 teaching depends on the communal teaching/learning environment and is vital in avoiding 'surface learning' (Biggs, 2003, p. 14) and promoting 'deep learning' (Biggs, 2003, p. 16).

Both surface and deep approaches are not fixed characteristics of students (this would be Level 1 thinking). A deep approach can be reached by anyone who feels motivated to learn and understand what improvements their learning can bring to the community in which it happens (Biggs, 2003, p. 138). I was aiming to achieve what Biggs defines as Level 3 teaching, but I felt that my presence as tutor was still too visible and that this was hindering the students from understanding their community as only theirs.

According to Freire's educational philosophy (1970, p. 33), students can motivate themselves to become critical thinkers through recognition of the creativity that allows them to transform situations. I briefly introduced Freire's approach to the students and their response was more than enthusiastic. The students recognised themselves in the idea of a kind of research that could wake them up as a collective. Three students volunteered to coordinate different focus groups about some of the problems that the students had previously discussed. They were starting to take full responsibility for their learning. At the same time, I finally had some material for my own action research (and for this paper), which:

- recognised my own responsibility in creating the problem;
- individuated at least part of the problem;
- prompted me to take action to improve the situation.

This arrangement was consistent with Level 3 teaching and at the same time I was on the route towards self-reflection and self-improvement with a coordinated action research project. However, the writing workshop experience revealed the risk of such concepts of teaching to be manipulative.

This danger was primarily recognised by Freire himself, when he wrote about the possibility of education to instate imperialistic power, 'messianism, mechanical transfer, cultural invasion, [and] manipulation' (Freire, 1973, p. 93), in the methods through which change is promoted. There was something in the way I had earned the trust of my students that I could have very easily used to enforce my own authority, or the one of the institution I represented, upon them.

Also, a more recent strand of critique is questioning whether participative learning environments, like the action research setting, have become a new form of tyranny (Cooke & Kothari, 2001). In this sense, 'programmes designed to bring the excluded in often result in forms of control that are more difficult to challenge, as they reduce spaces of conflict and are relatively benign and liberal' (Kothari, 2001, in Buehler, 2002).

The necessity for multiple approaches to research in participatory environments, in order to avoid manipulation not only of the participants but also of the collected data – distortion of which would make the research completely unreliable – had already been expressed by Guijt and Shah in the context of gender studies (1998).

The writing workshop's outcomes

Effects on the students – empowerment

When the focus groups formed, the number of students involved spontaneously fixed itself at 16. These were the students who really wanted to contribute to the project that they had helped shape from the very beginning. From this moment on attendance patterns became more regular, showing that although free exploration is an interesting avenue to walk, in this case more focus was necessary to create that feeling of belonging that the students were looking for from the beginning. The students started working unsupervised by me for longer periods of time. This cemented their friendship and created spontaneous groups, as some of them realised they could collaborate more closely. Their focus and commitment towards their studies grew as well. They stopped complaining about the course and started having a positive attitude towards their own work and its value. They realised how their presence was *actually* defining the course itself. They have already graduated from Central Saint Martins but the writing workshop is still running and their presence is still visible, both in the publication of their work and their search for external criticism.

A booklet called *The Written Stuff* was published and is now in free distribution. *The Written Stuff* is a synthesis of two different processes of thinking, writing and imaging, recreating their story of exploration on the printed page. The second issue is now well under way.

Some students organised two exhibitions for Asian students at the University of the Arts, one of them being the very successful WEMIX (West, East, Memory, Identity eXperience) at the Nolias Gallery, Islington, 31 May–13 June 2007.

Effects on me as a tutor – vision

Some of the students told me they considered the writing workshop a life-changing experience. It helped them understand their equality, through focusing on their differences and reflecting on their own roots and on their journeys until that moment. I have the feeling that I am the person who changed more through the experience.

In brief, I have now fully understood the importance of the tertiary level of teaching in supporting students through a Level 3, deep approach to teaching. I know that the workshop helped the students reach that high point in which they became aware of their knowledge and skills and also of what they did not know because they learnt how to reflect and make independent connections between ideas (see Biggs, 2003, pp. 38–43 for his SOLO taxonomy). The publication also showed that they had the capability to reflect on these gaps and to set up and employ creative strategies to bridge them in an independent way, acquiring more knowledge and generating research outputs that can in turn become learning materials for the following years.

However, I have no way of knowing if these students would have reached the same point without the workshop or if other students have not reached this outcome because they were not part of the workshop. The workshop was just one of the possible ways. It worked well with some students but, from my observations, it was not useful to the whole course, rather to a minority.

My own new realisations have provided me with the motivation to take the next step, to test whether and how this effect could be expanded.

Saying that there is always room for improvement is not just a case of commonplace, but rather the way that I have to relate to my own process of learning. Reflecting on one's own experience and improving one's course of action means to move forward – sometimes sideways, sometimes backwards – adjusting one's perspective. When one sets out saying: 'I need to improve this', one may think they are doing just what is necessary. But only when this is done and one sees things from a different position, can one recognise what else needs to be done that was just not visible earlier. I think my teaching has improved, but at the same time I am able to see more things that I want to improve in me. Furthermore, I think I will need to acknowledge the importance of approaching any development in this research from a disparity of perspectives, rather than action research alone.

Unachieved goals

As it is often the case with experiments, the workshop was not exempt from problems. In the end, its two main shortcomings were:

- failure to become a real community of practice;
- failure to find a creative approach to academic writing.

My unspoken hope was that – while recognising the organisational problems that this would imply – the workshop would have gradually involved more and more students. Instead the opposite happened. As a new item on offer, it started by making a third of the students curious. But as the work became progressively more focused, it started resembling an extension of the context unit, rather than an extra-curricular experimental space. It is still true that the work produced is very experimental and is not carried through in any other part of the course. However, in the end, the students who were part of the workshop started to feel like an elite. One of the ideas of the workshop was to establish a larger sense of community – and this happened, but only within the workshop students themselves. This was not planned, and I recognise the necessity to avoid this exclusive attitude as far as the next workshop's students are concerned.

Another idea of the workshop was to discover a workable method for the students to produce creative academic work. However, I was not able to find the right activity that could make academic writing a more accessible prospect. A lot of research was involved in what they wrote, but there is no real analysis of the findings. As a matter of fact, the visual work is in itself an analysis of the findings but the link is not yet very clear. This is another element that still requires work.

Conclusion: the role of emotional interactions in tutoring

I consider this writing workshop experience successful in terms of indicating the clear need for more student interaction on the BAGD course and demonstrating some of the possible ways in which this could be achieved. However, it also revealed the danger of manipulation that is inherent in participatory ideas of teaching.

Although the writing workshop did not fulfil the purpose for which it was initially created, there are at least four reasons, two on the side of the students and two on my side, why it can be considered an extremely positive experience:

- It supported the students in reaching the learning outcomes that are part of the context unit.
- It partially satisfied learning outcomes that are part of other units.
- It gave me the possibility to test ideas of contemporary pedagogy.
- It showed that part of my teaching method was already in line with these ideas.

This last point was made in recognition of the fact that I was taught according to these theoretical principles and so it seems I have somehow absorbed these methods and was putting them partially into practice, oblivious of their source. This action research project has become the vehicle through which my awareness of these principles has matured and I have begun to modify my teaching methods accordingly, while adapting the principles to the circumstances.

The students clearly showed me that their emotional bonding created the intellectual space for a reassessment of their position on the course. The institution that was at the beginning perceived as malevolent, an abstract entity that did not appreciate them, was personalised and further recognised as made up of all of them and their peer students and tutors together. This bonding provided them with a space outside their course that eventually made them feel more integrated into the course itself. They understood that this integration was not a simple attachment to a pre-existing unchanging reality. A course becomes reality only thanks to the students' presence. They felt and finally understood that by changing themselves they could change the course and maybe the world around them.

References

Biggs, J. (2003), *Teaching for Quality Learning at University: What the Student does, Second Edition* (Maidenhead and New York: The Society for Research into Higher Education & Open University Press)

Buehler, U. (2002), 'Participation "with justice and dignity": beyond "the new tyranny", *Peace, Conflict and Development: An Interdisciplinary Journal*, available online (accessed 10 March 2008) at:
http://www.peacestudiesjournal.org.uk/docs/Participation.PDF

Cassel, R.N., Chow, P. & Demoulin, D.F. (2000), 'Extracurricular involvement in high school produces honesty and fair play needed to prevent delinquency and crime', *Education*, **121** (2), pp. 247–252

Cooke, B. & Kothari, U. (eds.) (2001), *Participation: The New Tyranny?* (London and New York: Zed Books)

Demoulin, D.F. (2002), 'Examining the impact of extra-curricular activities on the personal development of 149 high school seniors', *Journal of Instructional Psychology*, **29** (4), pp. 297–313

Freire, P. (1970), *Pedagogy of the Oppressed* (New York: Continuum Publishing Co.)

Freire, P. (1973), *Education: The Practice of Freedom* (London: Writers and Readers Publishing Co-operative

Guijt, I. & Shah, M.K. (eds.) (1998), *The Myth of Community: Gender Issues in Participatory Development* (London: ITP)

Katz, L.G., & Chard, S.C. (1989), *Engaging Children's Minds: The Project Approach* (Norwood NJ: Ablex)

Laurillard, D. (2002), *Rethinking University Teaching*, 2nd edition (London and New York: RoutledgeFalmer)

Loughran, S. (2001), 'An artist among young artists', *Childhood Education* **77** (4), pp. 204–212

Lubienski, R.A. (1999), *Montessori for the New Millennium: Practical Guidance on the Teaching and Education of Children of All Ages, Based on a Rediscovery of the True Principles and Vision of Maria Montessori* (Mahwah NJ and London: Lawrence Erlbaum Associates)

Malaguzzi, L. (1998), 'History, ideas, and basic philosophy', in Edwards, C., Gandini, L. & Forman, G. (eds.) *The Hundred Languages of Children: The Reggio Emilia Approach – Advanced Reflections* (Greenwich, CT: Ablex)

Staley, L. (1998), 'Beginning to implement the Reggio philosophy', *Young Children*, **53** (5), pp. 20–25

Tierney, W.G. (1989), *Curricular Landscapes, Democratic Vistas: Transformative Leadership in Higher Education* (New York, Westport CT and London: Praeger Publishers)

UAL-CSM (2006), School of Graphic and Industrial Design: BA (Hons) Graphic Design Course Handbook 2006–2007

Jane Tynan

There has long been official unease with acknowledging the role of emotions in learning. As a result, it has attracted little attention in research on student learning, particularly in higher education. As one of the major institutions through which social control is exercised, education finds security in the language of formality. Those familiar with the rigid euphemistic language that characterises the managerial regime in British higher education will know it distances teachers from learners. For the French philosopher Michel Foucault, this was a question of power – the means by which 'regimes of practices' shape our experience of modern institutions (Foucault, 2004).

However, it is clear that educational experiences are profoundly affecting. Depending on student experience, cultural background, race, class, ability, sexuality and gender, learning experiences arouse a range of emotional responses. Indeed, negative formative experiences establish the most stubborn barriers to future learning. Institutional learning is fragile and complex because students find themselves submitting to power structures. Such is the context for Andrea Lioy's paper exploring unspoken aspects of the learning process, of which the most compelling is how it makes students vulnerable. Supplying a safety valve to release the pressures created by outcome-led learning gives students space to explore informal aspects of the learning experience.

This is a particularly urgent task at a time when higher education is becoming increasingly commodified. Lioy worked with students who felt these pressures, but sought a more meaningful learning experience. The result was what Paolo Friere described as the emancipatory potential in learning (Friere, 1996, p.29), which promotes freedom rather than conformity. Lioy's interventions were collaborative and reflective. Rather than focus on student deficits, he instead looked to the immediate environment to exploit the relationship aspect of learning. His workshop used peer-learning to promote in students feelings of ownership over their own learning. If, as argued by Biggs (2003), student learning is about transformation, then for students it involves a personal negotiation with past experience, rather than conformity to the educational establishment. Transformation is not transmission of knowledge, but is about subverting the dominant order (Friere, 1996). Student subjectivities, the outcome of various discursive and material practices, many extra-institutional, are often constructed in the spaces between formal and informal structures. Lioy's experiment demonstrates the role of informality in creative learning, which demands that we broaden current understanding of what happens when people learn.

References

Biggs, J. (2003), *Teaching for Quality Learning at University* (Maidenhead: Open University Press)

Foucault, M. (2004, first 1966), *The Order of Things* (London: Routledge)

Friere, P. (1996), *Pedagogy of the Oppressed* (London: Penguin)

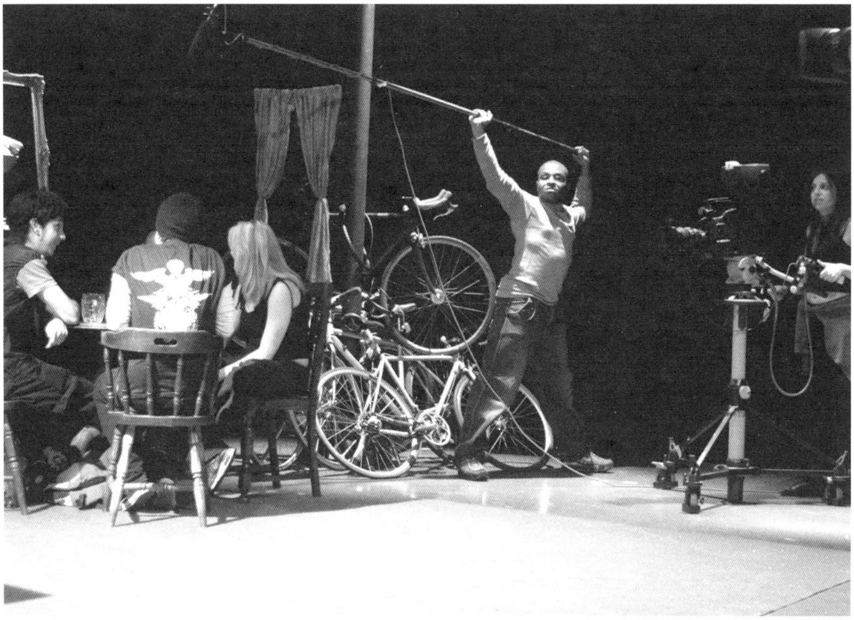

TV studio — Carlton Boulter

Reproduced by permission of the artist

8

Emotion in teaching and learning collaboration in film practice education

Author: Cathy Greenhalgh

Commentary: Alison Shreeve

Keywords

collaboration,
embodiment,
appropriation,
affect,
project-based

Cathy Greenhalgh

Emotions are commodities on a film shoot. On set, for example, there is a mood, which can be affected by the adrenalin rush and excitement of creative flow, long working hours, unforeseen delays, personalities, power relations, unusual physical conditions, cultural dissonances, etc. Health and safety combined with maximising speed and flow of work requires 'moment-by-moment planning, diplomacy, developed intuition, humour and leadership to retain any creativity'. Feelings can range from 'boredom, fear and insecurity to a sense of belonging and pride all in one day' (Greenhalgh, 2007, p. 79). Key personnel need to keep the crew constantly motivated to get the best contribution of energy, intuition and creative results on screen. The safety valves needed to cope with the stress of this are exacerbated when away on location for weeks or months on end.

LCC's BA in Film and Video encourages collaboration, viewing the course as shared practice and inter-class dialogue as resource. This is pertinent to film crews where work is collaborative, but within a strict hierarchy. Group dynamics and affective and emotional expertise are facilitated, built into learning outcomes, and assessed in the teaching programme. Students work on group projects in specialist roles. Positive interactions and solutions are explored through group tutorials and workshops. I teach cinematography and work with colleagues teaching film directing, scriptwriting, production design, editing, sound design and producing. We have frequently discussed the nature of collaboration, its fundamental place in our pedagogical approach and the emotion-coping strategies we try to develop in students.

The subject of this paper is fuelled by discoveries and observations from two sources. First, ethnographic research carried out over several years with feature film cinematographers; the configurations of agency and practice within the film industry and a creative collaborative art form. Second, data acquired during a

CLIP CETL (Centre for Learning in Practice – UK Centre for Education, Teaching and Learning) award, 'Teaching Collaboration in Film Practice Education', granted in 2006–7.

The ethnographic research reveals that the longevity of individual 'career capital' (Jones, 1996) is often bolstered by a grounded understanding of how emotion and camaraderie work within a freelance, project-based industry. In the study of students in LCC School of Media's Film and Television department (BA Hons Film and Video), it can be seen, in addition to hard work and creative talent, that affective resources are key to student success among peers, in assessment and in gaining employment. Certain stories, talk and action appear stimulated by certain emotions and are apparent, particularly in group dynamics.

CLIP CETL data included video shot during second-year student workshops and live shoots in the TV studio, student reflective writing and staff interviews. The department is one of seven UK Skillset Screen Academies (jointly with Ealing Institute of Media) and as such receives substantial extra funding to bring in industry mentors and undertake specialist workshops. These have 'upped the game' for staff and students during the period of study and perhaps highlighted more acutely the problematics of care-taking emotion involved in staff-student interactions in risk-taking and ambitious group work with the students.

The research assisted us in revealing areas where we were aware and unaware of the effects of emotion. Some of the questions posited included:

- What emotions are produced in group work and under what circumstances do they happen?
- What affective sensing and emotional controls seem present?
- How do students and staff perceive situations differently?
- What mechanisms for expression are there for staff, students and staff-student interactions?
- What stresses and advantages are evident in student learning experiences when emotion 'intervenes'?
- What types of guidance are students given and when?
- How do students reflect on emotion in their written critical reviews of practice?
- How is emotion 'included' in assessment?

This essay points up ways in which emotion can be used as a resource in teaching and how the energy produced by expressing, managing and coping with negatively or positively perceived emotion may be harnessed in creative acts and in manifesting artefacts, particularly in groups. It is suggested that physical grounding, i.e. embodied learning in groups, is one key to students gaining confidence and maturing in affective expertise directly transferable to the workplace.

Creative industries and pedagogical context

The film industry is project based, with a horizontal pattern of linked companies, rather than a vertical hierarchy (as in the old studio days). It has many service companies and corporations who bring freelance labour and expertise together for individual projects. Using the film industry as an example, Candace Jones argues that in project networks:

> … the task is complex and non-routine, which requires many individuals to join in creating the product or service; this high level of mutual responsibility is called team interdependence. For example, making a film requires coordinating the efforts and talents of hundreds of subcontractors from a variety of backgrounds … The project network usually operates in an uncertain and dynamic environment, primarily due to unpredictable and rapidly shifting consumer demands … Not only do the interpersonal networks allow skilled entrepreneurs access to exciting projects among myriad firms, but the boundaryless quality of the new career enhances both skill and reputation, due to increased experience in different work settings and exposure to a variety of tasks and people. However these boundaryless careers often make significant demands on time, energy and lifestyle … A career in the film industry is a difficult process, due to a lack of the traditional recruiting and selection practices that initiate most careers. Yet the film industry's exposure to potential recruits is pervasive, intensely competitive … those who get their foot in the door are sorted by two attributes: good interpersonal skills and being highly motivated. (Jones, in Arthur, 1997, pp. 61–62)

So, if film projects require individuals who are skilled, responsible, available, permanently motivated, well connected and good communicators, how do individuals maintain this expertise over time? New work conditions in creative industries are being created, as Hartley outlines: 'the no collar workplace … replaces traditional hierarchical systems of control with new forms of self-management, peer-recognition and pressure and intrinsic forms of motivation, which I call "soft control" (Hartley, 2005,p. 2). University of the Arts London is a mainly practice-oriented university with a long history in its separate art colleges of vocationally oriented courses. The importance of the creative industries to London means UAL has a commitment to supplying talent to these industries at the heart of its strategy.

Understanding that practice can be seen itself as 'knowing in practice', action constructed through ongoing processual physical and mental interaction, is essential. This term, posited by Sylvia Gherardi (2006) in her work on safety practices in the construction industry, explains that learning is not simply about transferring knowledge, but becoming an 'insider' during actual practice. This praxis of moving, thinking, and communicating is networked through local, national and international levels. Film industry communities of practice (Wenger, 1998), establish and market technical, logistical and creative/craft competence. Individuals are (surreptitiously for newcomers) questioned, checked and tested for reliability in 'on-set etiquette' and behaviour by local leadership and communities of practice politics to sustain employability, cohesion and transmission of knowledge. Reputations on set are discussed primarily in terms of control, flexibility, agility, timing and humour under pressure. Film production is a heightened situation, the shoot an event with no written rules and no personnel department. Misbehaviour or misunderstanding can be immediately removed.

Daskalaski and Blair (FIRG, 2002) note knowledge of work process, culture and rules of film production is 'gained and stored by individuals and semi-permanent work groups (SPWGs) outside of company structures and can eventually be lost to the industry because of this'. Employment is found through 'dense networks of contacts' and 'informal internal contracting' through these temporary project groups moving from film production to production. It is a matter of survival, and why rumours of nepotism, cronyism and long-held loyalties do have some foundation. However, colleges can also be a hotbed for the nurturing and structuring of collaborations that can foster exactly these kinds of useful alliances.

Beth Bechky, in her study of film crews, notes: 'On each film set, role expectations are communicated through practices of enthusiastic thanking, polite admonishing, and role-oriented joking, which enable crew members to learn and negotiate role structures … [the crew]face high levels of task and environmental uncertainty, they … rely on interpersonal processes rather than depend on formal structures (Bechky, 2006, pp. 1–2). The film set is an immersive, strangely scheduled and isolated temporary world in which 'role structures are provisional, influenced and maintained by participants' behaviour on each set'. Work is 'intensive and visible short-term interaction with an expectation of repeated interactions in the future … Film sets are characterised by an atmosphere of continual communication … walkie-talkies, megaphones, mobiles … but people embrace their roles, looking to capitalise on their experiences to move forward and upward in the network of career progression' (2006, pp. 6–9).

Film and TV industry career narratives reveal the complexity of incorporating constantly changing locales with management of relationships, diversity, technology and environment in working life (Greenhalgh, 2007). Understanding the immersive nature of the work is essential for students. The working environment for learning simulates the industry, where understanding of technology must become 'second nature' and health and safety issues require attention between individuals. Repeated crew collaboration across film projects maintains trust, camaraderie and career. Key to this is affective organisation as practised on set and over long periods spent on location.

Collaboration and affective expertise

In teaching film-making, it is imperative that students understand the need and acquire a talent for emotional as well as cognitive and physical skills. Film-making is a group activity as soon as a project requires any complex logistics with several cast and crew. The idea of collaboration and creativity practised within a hierarchy of crew (very strict in the industry) should be inculcated from the outset. While many film industry members love cinema or television as an art form and the camaraderie and travel possible with a freelance life, this glamorous side is often counterpointed by long hours, unemployment between jobs, time spent networking and tenuous personal relationships. This downside means that understanding that emotion is part of the organisation and can play out in particular ways for a crew and for individuals can help students to at least continuously reinvent a 'working identity' for themselves and plan a route after college.

The film industry, which has long used collaboration across projects, has been used as a model of where other industries might follow (Daskalaski & Blair, 2001; Jones, 1996). Emotions in collaborative learning are central to the drive and creative process in teams and to successful creative industries. In her study of collaborative creativity, Vera John-Steiner (2000) writes of 'felt knowledge' in 'the emotional dynamics of collaboration'. Borrowing from non-Cartesian models of the self in psychology, educational models and neuroscience, via Bakhtin, Vygotsky, Lakoff and Damasio, she states: 'Effective creative outcomes require the rigorous, sustained labour of nurturing, shaping, and developing imaginative leaps. The motivation for such discipline is strengthened through mutual support.' She posits 'affective resources' are developed 'by appropriating the consequences of shared experience'. Such a process includes 'identification, scaffolding, expansion by complementarity, and constructive criticism' (p. 123). 'Emotional scaffolding is multifaceted; it includes the gift of confidence, and the leaning on that gift by creative people during periods of self-doubt and rejection by those in power' (p. 128).

On the BA Hons Film and Video we facilitate, teach technique and take care of the collaborative process as students progress into more complex, highly technical projects. Leaning on each other also gives students confidence to question tutor models. Student colleagues create a safety zone and share risk in a bigger endeavour and shared ownership. Identity is strengthened and tested through partners. Thus, 'mutual care-taking is fundamental aspect for learning … for dialogic relationship, mentoring and collegiality' (John-Steiner, 2000, p. 159).

> Each participant's individual capacities are deepened at the same time that participants discover the benefits of reciprocity. But the achievement of productive collaborations requires sustained time and effort … shaping a shared language, the pleasures and risks of honest dialogue, and the search for a common ground. By teaching what we know, we engage in mutual appropriation … We can live better with temporary failures as we rely on our partners' strengths. By joining with others we accept the gift of confidence, and through interdependence we achieve competence and connection.
> (John-Steiner, 2000, p. 204)

Group tutorial conversation and students' written reports about embodied practice would seem to show conviction to take on challenging problem solving is increased through intense group interaction in the physical conditions of the studio set or location, and therefore the purpose of preparation, planning, script and visualisation. Accurate assessment and belief in each other's abilities is essential in collaboration. This means understanding reciprocity and appropriation, and allowing time to set up the conditions for 'rapport' between students (Murphy & Valdez, 2005).

Emotion and situation

Studies of group emotion and interaction in pedagogical research influenced by psychology and organisation studies (Goleman, 1996; Ben Ze'ev, 2001; Hochschild, 2003 (1983); Fineman, 2003; Bolton, 2005) and recent observations coming from neuroscience (Damasio, 2000) suggest dialogic ways of positioning the self-group-environment dynamic, which allow a way out of systemic approaches, which often stereotype or underplay the existence of emotion. The senses, somato-sensory dimensions of practice, affective interpretation, and emotion as learning opportunity are all coming to the fore.

Here are two descriptions that express an emotional undercurrent to the work on set:

> A crew, it's a thing that is so totally organic, like a chorus. Every film is a different way of growing, even if the same people have worked together, a different feeling, a different momentum and strength inside. You have to feel all of these tensions, the screams for help or love that go in there ... It's very physical when you are on set. You know everyone has their place where he stands and needs to be. You have to feel the space and time. Some people are never there when needed, always off for a drink, and others seem to always be there, even if they're not.
> (Eduardo Serra, cinematographer, 1999)

> Temperament usually comes from insecurity ... half my energies as a leading man in a picture go into keeping the tensions down. You set the tone on set. (p. 140) ... You aren't working on an assembly line. A stage set is more like a trampoline. (p. 128)
> (Michael Caine, actor, 1990)

These examples show pleasure in the diversity of people being worked with combined with an air of impatience with those who haven't found a way to cope and just get on with the job, despite film-making being a high-pressure situation. Language often heard on film sets and among film students, for example, 'so-and-so is a right prima donna' or 'so-and-so is a bit of drama queen' (or king), or 'they're high-maintenance' refer to individuals' handling of emotions, expectation of support and whether need is evaluated as 'true'.

Ben Ze'ev suggests affective skill is 'understanding cathexis, susceptibility, hunch, nuance, tone' (Ze'ev, 2001). Emotions are unpredictable, intense, often brief and typically occur in 'significant, changing and often unusual circumstances' (p. 167). We make emotional judgements to assess the 'praiseworthiness, desirability and appealingness of agents' (2001, p. 94). He characterises 'affectless' as negative emotion – 'unfeeling, animosity, over sentimentality, histrionics, obsessed, zealous, cloying, apathetic' etc. (Ben Ze'ev, 2001).

The intensity of interaction on film sets is such that emotional tension is likely. The film set and, indeed, the film department at college are intensely social places. Depression and tiredness are usually short circuited through camaraderie and humour. Damasio suggests the biological purpose of emotions is 'not clear, but they're not a dispensable luxury'. Emotions are 'complicated collections of chemical and neural responses, forming a pattem, all have a regulatory role to play' (Damasio, 2000 p. 145). There is 'emotion work' or expenditure of feelings in service to the job or role. Coping strategies for dealing with emotions at work have been studied in organisations for some time (Fineman, 1993, 2001; Hochschild, 1983). Goleman's term 'emotional intelligence' (Goleman, 1996) seems to have ubiquitous use now, but emotional expenditure on the part of individual freelancers has often been ignored. Fineman analyses work as an emotional arena. Hochschild presents emotions as codified by organisations for service. Emotions are deemed territory for harnessing productively by organisations. This applies to the teaching and learning environment as much as the industry we prepare students for. There are also sensuous and aesthetic aspects to embodied, located and contingent practices. There can be confusion and misunderstanding to negotiate; pain and pleasure. Groupwork, teamwork births collaboration, and possible creative partnerships. The complexity of this is difficult to teach and sometimes even to verbalise. We can only set up situations where students are likely to experience in ways that they can then incorporate and know with intuitive as well as intellectual confidence.

Groups and student-tutor strategies

Student induction to LCC's BA in Film and Video encourages embracing collaboration, viewing the course as initiation into shared practice, and inter-class dialogue as a resource equal to staff teaching and expertise (and increasingly so with larger students numbers). At interview, we look for applicants with a sense of themselves in the world, something to say and some evidence of 'people skills'.

Group tutorials monitor ideas and visualisation, planning and logistics for filming, and are primary place where the tutor helps cohere the student crew. This can be in any number of ways, but can include using problem-based learning, demonstration, setting tasks and schedules, doing visualisation exercises, sharing research materials or script reading together etc. It can also be the forum for resolving team breakdown, raising energy and commitment levels, making group agreements on role interdisciplinary knowledge needs (students are involved in radically different activities within the different jobs which make a up a crew), sudden change of plan, planning time management, coordinating individual needs with the group, incorporating disengaged members etc. Practical and theory class dialogue is sometimes recalled to reiterate experiential and propositional knowledge and aid in teaching students problem recognition.

Staff must become proficient in recognising gestures of students, power issues and discourses within groups. Feelings of pride and confidence, or envy, denial, betrayal (mild or strong), tend to be observable very quickly in student members' proactive or silent (or absent) participation in the tutorial. Behaviours appear to be as much in response to classmates as the tutor, even though students know staff glean information about the process of work, which may be used in assessment, from group tutorials. With any project brief, it is important that technical and brainstorming workshops as well as tutorials build the necessary rapport that may enable groups to collaborate.

Tutor X describes purposes and challenges of group tutorials thus:

> Group tutorials are the spine of the degree... Teaching collaboration is a weird kettle of fish. It works differently for every project and for every individual within that project group. Every project is a group project so that in that three year degree you go on a journey when you learn to collaborate, you learn to lessen your ego on important things, but you become clearer on what you want to do ... We all know it's a collaborative process. You can't be a filmmaker alone, it looms over the whole thing. Here we're shaping people as much as films. Students learn to be part of the film community. We also teach them to explore their artistic selves. The pleasures of collaboration are obvious. It pushes your idea much further than you could go on your own.

The belief expressed here is that while students can be guided and encouraged, a level of maturity is needed to make the emotional journey. While group tutorial is one instrument at the disposal of both tutor and student, individuals have to decide how far they can go, based on their own calculation of the available conditions of trust and empathy for their suggestions. What happens when students don't want or choose to participate? Here senior lecturer Y explains how students are helped to define collaboration as a growth, a propeller forward from groupworking:

> I always say this: 'A collaborator is not a lover, not a friend, not a work colleague' exactly, it's a different kind of relationship. And

> it might involve arguments ... because each person has to rise to the top of their creativity, rise to the top of their leadership in their area, but understand that the other person has a similar level of skills but in a possibly completely different area ... I positively encourage them to work with someone they haven't spoken to yet or who normally sits on the other side of the class.

Staff share workspaces at LCC and also often team-teach on this course. Stories of how well workshops and shoots are going are shared daily, as are problems and ways in which difficult group dynamics were resolved. It's a very collegiate atmosphere. We can experience the happy explosions of energy with students as much as occasional malaise. But perhaps it is because we have all worked on crews on film sets in our art practice or in industry, that we are used to qualifying gossip and riding with adrenalin or calming it down. Film-making can be very intense as it requires combinations of very different skills, and students will often make out there is a 'catastrophe' of 'life and death' proportions if the creativity of the project or their pride in their own contribution is suffering. We tell students that each film will have its emotional tone and there might be someone they don't get on with. As jobs are often short, patience is required. The film at college will not be the only thing they will make in life. It's okay if things go wrong; it's part of the learning process. While trying to create an atmosphere of support and comfort, we are also quite tough in promoting students in supporting each other.

Group tutorials happen in the pre-production, production and post-production phases, whereas whole-class presentations begin and end projects. Assessment feedback is given in writing, but verbal feedback, which includes peer review and which draws out filmmaking lessons for all, is given at whole-class sessions. The group project tutorial process ascertains what kinds of issues might come up from aesthetic to practical choices.

Embodiment and reflection

In year two, the students undertake five television drama productions in the TV studio. This is the largest collaborative project before students prepare for year three graduation projects. They also work with acting, costume and make-up students from other colleges in UAL and beyond. Later in the year, they write a critical review of the process of making the productions from the point of view of their own specialist role.

Viewing emotion as central may help us to understand how planning and manifestation, confusion and solution develop and are acted upon. For example, in the studio (as well as on location, where weather is also a consideration), the students have to learn to 'fit bodies with technology.' Organising the blocking and performance of actors for camera framing, movement and lighting is what takes the real time and energy of cast and crew. Most shots require complicated choreography within the geography of the set space. This is known in film set parlance as 'cheating'. Normal societal rules of proxemics are constrained and altered continuously. Emotional awareness and affective expertise, practised by the crew and cast in such intimate, in-your-face situations, are essential.

This expertise is not textual or verbal, but corporeal. Often, too, teaching methods proceed by creating immersion experiences rather than using too much demonstration. This can be difficult to achieve with large classes and takes time. However, it is clear that once learned physically in situ, learning is more 'implanted'. Further, students reflective writing suggests it increases their 'feel' for and 'practical faith' in film-making. They are then more likely to use their emotions as positive motivators. Tacit knowledge (such as blocking/'cheating', which is very difficult to verbalise) is often 'learned by osmosis over long periods in very particular contexts. [It]is robust, and often intuitive, habitual and reflexive. It is knowledge best acquired by doing and best communicated by example' (Leadbetter, 1999, p. 28).

Here are some year two student written responses after this project that describe on-set physical conditions and communication issues:

> I was compelled to observe the bottlenecks in the chain of command on the set, and the resulting frustration felt by some.
> (Student A)

> On the emotional side, my self-confidence increased and I learnt how to follow my gut instincts in times of indecision ... Simple rules such as confidentiality were also established and constant meetings took place so everyone from the team could express their ideas before we went into production.
> (Student C)

> In order for the production to be a success it was of paramount importance that each crew member pulled their weight, as everyone was affected the moment they didn't.
> (Student N)

> The most important thing I realised during this project and something which all of us failed at to some degree was that 'listening is paramount'. Both to your crew and the tutors and

> the technician. Without listening there can be no discourse or creative problem solving.
> (Student K)

> An important point is not to let negative energy you may be feeling be projected onto the actors and the rest of the crew. The floor manager had an exceptional ability of keeping any issues or problems I was facing (as director) between the two of us, enabling the actors to maintain their energy and the crew to remain focused.
> (Student O)

It is clear from these accounts that the students seem to equate emotional stability with good communication, and recognise that the filming can make hefty demands on these abilities. There is also a hint of humour (perhaps in hindsight), in the retelling of tales from the set in a 'war-story' like fashion. This is common in collaborative work and is part of the sense-making process. What is striking in the next account is honesty and the effects of belonging, shared skill and achievement, camaraderie and pride in a project.

> There was a point on my shoot that I was ashamed of myself. The producer accused me of something very silly and after long days of constant pressure, which is not something new to me, I actually lost my temper, which looked very unprofessional. I quickly rectified the situation by moving our misunderstanding outside.
> (Student G)

The students are also quite candid about tutor intervention:

> As floor manager I was overwhelmed by the sheer amount of information I had to process and relay. This was exacerbated by technicians and visiting tutors who felt that by shouting what I should be doing at me would somehow help me to process the already insurmountable flood of words and queries flowing into my ears.
> (Student F)

Even though staff are practised, it should be noted that it can indeed be stressful for staff to intervene and sometimes the tactics for this are discussed between staff observing behaviour on a shoot before so doing. The students appear to show confidence in their team and year, which is sometimes equal to any worry they might have about assessment criteria. The nature of film-making seems to run from smooth teamwork to emotional overwhelm, and sometimes staff have to 'ride' this along with the students. Tutor K, who specialises in TV direction, describes seeing students in the TV studio hit 'the zone', like athletes, where teamwork, delegation, creativity and kindred spirit all seem to work together. Students need to trust, analyse, re-imagine and communicate fast, in situ, in what seems like an improvised setting. Tutor K claims:

> There's moments when a group feels an energy that's informed by the feeling they are on track and contributing to the production itself. There seem to be conversations that occur, where people feel they have responsibility in the sense of hierarchy to actually keep that energy going throughout. That energy, I'd like to think in a romantic sense that it's ingredient X, it's informed by atmosphere, by mood, by using the right phrase ... a set of parameters, of influences that happen ... so if their emotional intelligence is as strong as their general intelligence they can read situations and amalgamate those ideas into every given moment, then that's I think how you get golden moments when that camera's rolling. So it's not only supporting the script ... it's an emotive expression ... If the atmosphere isn't there, then people fall back on process, on formula, on just using equipment without there being a drive. That drive can follow and if it's in your consciousness, if it's on your radar, everybody feels it. In a work context ... someone there must understand that film-making in one sense is an environmental activity, it's a climate ... that climate changes day to day and you need a good weather forecaster to be able to kind of control that, let you know what the weather's going to be.

In part, this kind of comment from a staff member reflects the complexity of filmmaking as an art form, but also of teaching and disseminating concepts such as 'energy', 'creativity', etc.

Conclusion

The CLIP CETL project concentrated on collaboration and in particular on embodied skill. While we were aware of emotional dynamics in groups and encouraging confidence in students through the practice teaching, we have become more attuned to how we guide students through the group tutorial process. We can now begin to look more closely at when this is successful and when not; i.e. how to catch the few students who still 'fall through the loop'. We can also improve how we 'monitor' emotion in group workshops, particularly with visiting tutors/mentors.

We also note that both in the explicit requirement language of learning outcomes there is inadequate language to describe emotion. Practice language, where it tries to describes affective modes, which is required in student critical review reflective writing, is also an issue, and so is how it fits with study support mechanisms and cultural diversity. We need to support ourselves as teachers, too, because collaborative learning is exciting, but demanding and on the increase.

Note

All interviews conducted and student written work collected in February 2007 and February 2008.

References

Bechky, B. (2006), 'Gaffers, gofers and grips : role-based co-ordination in temporary organizations', *Organization Science*, **17** (1), pp. 3–21

Ben-Ze'ev, A. (2000), *The Subtlety of Emotions* (Cambridge, Mass.: MIT Press)

Bolton, S.C. (2005), *Emotion Management in the Workplace* (Basingstoke, Hampshire, and New York: Palgrave Macmillan)

Caine, M. (1990), *Acting in Film – An Actor's Take on Movie Making* (New York: Applause Theatre Book Publishers)

Damasio, A.R. (1999), *The Feeling of What Happens: Body, Emotion and the Making of Concsciousness* (USA: William Heinemann Ltd.)

Daskalaski, M. & Blair, H. (2002), '"Knowing" as an activity: implications for the film industry and semi-permanent work groups', paper submitted for Organisational Knowledge, Learning and Capabilities Conference, Athens, April 2002, Royal Holloway, University of London

Fineman, S. (2003), *Understanding Emotion at Work* (London, Delhi and Thousand Oaks: Sage Publications)

Gherardi, S. (2006), *Organizational Knowledge – The Texture of Workplace Learning* (Massachusetts and Oxford: Blackwell Publishing)

Goleman, D. (1996), *Emotional Intelligence – Why it Can Matter More Than IQ* (London: Bloomsbury Publishing Ltd.)

Greenhalgh, C. (2007), 'Travelling images, lives on location – cinematographers in the film industry', in Amit, V. (ed.) *Going First Class? – New Approaches to Privileged Travel and Movement*, pp. 72–86 (New York and Oxford: Berghahn)

Hartley, J. (ed.) (2005), *Creative Industries* (Malden, Massachusetts, Carlton, Australia, and Oxford, UK: Blackwell Publishing)

Hochschild, A.R. (2003), *The Managed Heart: Commercialization of Human Feeling* (California: University of California Press)

John-Steiner, V. (2000), *Creative Collaboration* (Oxford: Oxford University Press)

Jones, C. (1996), 'Careers in project networks: the case of the film industry', in Arthur, M.B. & Rousseau, D.M. (eds.) *The Boundaryless Career: A New Employment Principle of the New Organizational Era* (New York and Oxford: Oxford University Press)

Leadbetter, C. (1999), *Living on Thin Air – The New Economy with a Blueprint for the 21st Century* (Penguin Books)

Murphy, M. & Valdez, C. (2005), 'Ravaging resistance : a model for building rapport in a collaborative learning classroom', *Radical Pedagogy*, 7.1

Serra, E. (1999), interviewed by James Emmet, LCC student Lisbon, Portugal, 12 February

Wenger, E. (2006/1998), *Communities of Practice – Learning, Meaning and Identity* (Cambridge, New York: Cambridge University Press)

Alison Shreeve

Greenhalgh's insights into the complexities of learning for the film industry provide a prism for us all to re-examine our own disciplines and the centrality of emotions and personal interactions in the learning and teaching process. For the student, becoming an 'insider' in professional practice is not solely about being competent. Competencies, whether these consist of more traditional forms of academic knowledge in written form or the procedural forms of knowledge in most art and design subjects, are only part of the picture. Competency, without a broader understanding of the social contexts of knowing, provides limited access to the practice students desire to join. As Wenger (1998) states:

> ... knowing is defined only in the context of specific practices, where it arises out of the combination of a regime of competence and an experience of meaning.
> (p. 141)

The experience of meaning, as Greenhalgh shows us, also includes a raft of affective experiences that contribute to what it is to know in this particular practice. The technical skills alone are insufficient to succeed. However, developing an awareness of those social, personal, embodied knowledges and making them explicit presents a challenge to tutors.

The affective sensitivities belong to the realm of the symbolic in Kristeva's terms (Moi, 1997). These feelings precede speech, yet are fundamental to art practice, to our relations with others and to learning to produce a skilled performance. Yet it is not sufficient to say that these emotions, feelings, awareness and understanding remain within the realm of the unspoken. It is through speech that they gain signification and through speech that we begin to move towards a common understanding, an explication of what it means to experience the unspoken aspects of knowing. Within this is embedded the challenge for tutors for structuring learning. How can we enable students to understand the unspoken components of practice and the importance of these ways of knowing?

Greenhalgh points to ways that tutors share their stories of learning. Narrative helps us to bring out aspects of experience into the open, but we need to share with students and to ensure that they share with each other. Preparing students through short exercises and through group tutorials as well as practice appears to sensitise them to the emotional work that is involved in group practices. We could learn from many other disciplines, too. Through gesture and mark-making in drawing, enhanced through performance techniques, costume students learn to understand the performance and space of the costumes they design; they are no longer static images, but part of the performance (Barbieri).

We need to 'feel the space and time' in everything that we do, because a professional performance is enacted with others, whether we are nurses, designers or mathematicians. Through touch, movement, sound, emotion we collect information and process decisions. This was brought home to me in a recent conference presentation by Fenton-O'Creevy, who demonstrated that the most successful city traders drew on all knowledge they had, including their emotions, in order to make decisions. Those who denied their emotional responses were less likely to be successful. The challenge for educators is to bring such forms of knowledge to the fore, to articulate them and to celebrate their role in successful learning.

References

Moi, T. (ed.) (1986, originally published in 1977), *The Kristeva Reader*(New York: Columbia University Press)

Fenton-O'Creevy, M. (2007), 'Trading on emotion: the role of emotion in traders' work and learning', Unspoken Interactions Symposium, University of the Arts London, 10 December

Barbieri, D (2007) 'Proposing an interdisciplinary, movement-based approach to teaching and learning as applied to design for performance related areas', Research Office, LCF, London. First presented at the Prague Quadrennial.

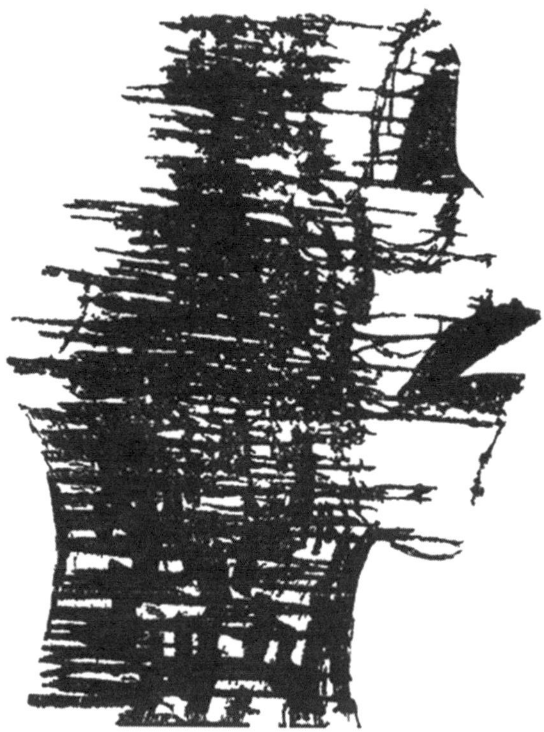

Black Skull — Yewande Okuleye

Reproduced by permission of the artist

9

Alchemy of happiness: transformative conversations in art school

Author: Yewande Okuleye

Commentary: Janice Miller

Keywords

student-tutor interactions,
reflections,
creativity,
motivation,
art tutors' role

Yewande Okuleye

Introduction

The purpose of writing this paper is to tease out some meaning from insights and reflections gained from transformative events that occurred while in art school. The structure of the essay weaves a tapestry of vignettes, insights, questions and reflections. This writing style has been adopted to explore the use of the subjective voice within the framework of academic writing and pedagogic discourse. The focus of the paper describes how the relationship between happiness and the development of 'the artist self' evolved within the tutor-student dynamics in the art studio. This is told from the student's viewpoint. It allows the reader a brief access into the private emotions of the student (writer). The inclusion of subjectivity is a deliberate strategy to contest the neat and tidy boundaries of the objectivity of academic writing. In my opinion, I think it also provides a certain level of realism to the discussion of emotions. The idea here is to put some 'flesh on the bones' regarding the issues under discussion. My question is this: Could this experimental writing style provide an alternative framework to illuminate the nuanced nature of tutor-student interactions in the art studio? This paper explores the potential. In order to streamline the narrative writing style, a narrow frame of reference is constructed around the writings of Austerlitz and Ben-Ze'ev.

Although the predominant voice within the paper is the student voice, the artist/teacher perspective is told with a second voice. This filters through intermittently. The common thread that connects the voices is the construction of meaning between the three factors under discussion. These are 'the artist self', happiness and the dynamics of the tutor-student interaction.

The artist self

In order to gain a good understanding of tutor-student interactions, it is important to get a good understanding of the art student. What is the essence of the art student? How is the art student's learning experience different from that of the non-art student? I am working from the assumption that there is a good understanding of the notion of the tutor. However, I think the definition of the art student requires some expansion. I have used the term 'the artist self' to explain the additional facet to the art student's learning experience .I think the art student has two aspects to their learner identity: the student identity plus the artist self.

Art student learner identity = student identity + the artist self

This definition is a working model to explain the learning experience of the art student. 'The artist self' could be defined as the intangible aspect of the artist. It is in a state of dynamic flux. In order to grow, the artist self has to develop an openness and flexibility of mind and spirit to constantly construct and reconstruct meanings about concepts, processes and ideas regarding a developing visual language within art practice. The artist self is mutable and fluid. In my case, it was experienced as elusive and mercurial, exciting and equally frustrating. It could be argued that it is this constant reconstruction and reframing of the learning experience that defines the artist self as opposed to other student learning experiences.

Another key difference of the artist self as opposed to other non-art learning experiences is its site of performance. The theatre of performance is in the public arena. The site of performance is the art studio. The event is either the student crit or the seminar. Other key players in this production are peers and tutors. At the centre of the production (the learning process) lies an unstable element of emotional arousal. An appreciation of this difference might assist in understanding tutor-student interactions in art school.

What have tutors got to do with it?

Although there is a general understanding of the role of tutors within the context of learning, the notion of the tutor is further scrutinised within this paper. In my experience of art education, it was apparent the system placed a high premium on intellectual and artistic progress. Intellectual and artistic developments existed as art artefacts, photographs and end-of-year reports. I gradually found the formal assessments of artistic and intellectual development were becoming less important to me. As a result of a series of encounters with tutors, I became increasingly aware of the intangible aspects of the impact tutors had on my learning process.

Why are these interactions important? I think they are important because they can be very memorable and powerful learning opportunities. In my experience, in addition to a vivid recollection of conversations and insights gained from seminars and desk crits, I can also remember the associative emotions of such encounters. This might be an indication of why they are powerful learning opportunities.

The acknowledgement of emotions is a key component of the unspoken interaction dynamics. I think the role emotions play in the student learning experience is somewhat overlooked. As a student, I did not place any value on my happiness within the context of my learning. If I was unhappy, I just got on with it. I took my cue from the system. The system was interested in academic and artistic progress. There did not appear to be any room for expression of messy emotions in the day-to-day learning in the studio. There is a myriad of emotions that might impact student learning in the studio. This paper will discuss the emotion of happiness. Happiness was the predominant emotion that had an impact on my artist self learning experience.

Happiness

This brings me to the most elusive part of this paper. How do I define happiness in relation to 'the artist self' learning experience in the art studio? More specifically, how do I relate happiness to the construction of the artist self? Since the notion of happiness is a personal interpretation, it is important to foreground a working definition of happiness.

Although there are a wide range of studies of happiness in philosophy and psychology, Ben-Ze'ev's (2000) explanations (based on cognitive psychology) are apt to contextualise how I relate happiness in the construction of the artist self. According to Ben-Ze'ev, there are two types of happiness, short-term emotion and long-term sentiment. Short-term feelings of happiness are joy and satisfaction. Short-term happiness is the most common perception of happiness. This aspect of happiness is normally perceived as transient. An example of a long-term sentiment associated with happiness is well-being. Ben-Ze'ev notes that this is a simplistic explanation of a complex emotion. Ben-Ze'ev further clarifies that it is the relationship between the two that creates the meaning of happiness.

> The acute emotion of happiness may be regarded as the occasional foreground reaction to specific positive events: happiness as a sentiment is the background framework.
> (Ben-Ze'ev, 2000, p. 450)

Why is happiness an important factor in the studio?

Ethnographic studies conducted by Austerlitz and Aravot (2007) indicate there is normally a short supply of happiness within the context of the studio. On balance, there was a higher report of negative incidences as opposed to positive incidences. 167/734 respondents indicated negative emotions of anger, insult and rejection, while 25/734 respondents indicated positive emotions of joy and relief.

I could never understand why I always had a constant low level of unhappiness while at art school. I would describe my personality as upbeat, optimistic and generally happy, however a personality transplant seemed to occur when I was in the studio. Austerlitz's studies on the logics of emotional relationships in the design studio offer insights as to why:

> It should not be a surprise that negative emotions have been found to be highly dominant. From the students' point of view, it is better to be attentive to changes, which might involve a threat to their well being, than overlook them. Positive emotions are generated due to improvement in well being, but failing to notice a positive change is not as pricey as in cases of negative ones.
> (Austerlitz & Aravot, 2007)

Austerlitz & Aravot described this high state of alert as the studio survival mechanism. In order to survive the constant scrutiny of the seminar, crit and development of projects, students need to have a rapid response rate to perceived threat to their well-being. Emotions serve as feedback indicators. As a result of the conventional art school tutor-student dynamics, tutor opinions and perceptions can potentially have a big impact on student well-being.

> When a change is recognised, the mental faculties go into an emotional mode. This operational mode's prime purpose is to appraise the received information about change, to evaluate its significance and to generate the best possible response.
> (Austerlitz & Aravot, 2007)

Therefore, contrary to popular misconceptions, my emotion of unhappiness was not an irrational response to the studio. It was an important studio survival strategy.

Three vignettes are used here to demonstrate scenarios that might occur in art school. The first example describes a critical emotional incident. This has been included in the paper as it gives a flavour of the student 'hurt voice'. This voice is not necessarily heard within the academic framework. It is more normal to hear something I have described as the 'veiled hurt voice'. I would describe the 'veiled hurt voice' as the angry anonymous comments found in student feedback forms. The second vignette is a snapshot of the dialogue of the critical incident. This has been included to examine the power relationship between tutor and student. The student's perception of this power relationship has an impact on student emotion. The third vignette illustrates a unique relationship possible between the art tutor and art student and it embodies all the concepts under discussion.

Scene one: Internal dialogue in Tracey Emin's Bed

> I lay there. Paralysed. I cannot eat. I cannot sleep. I just drink. Mind, body and spirit, frozen. The double duvet meekly attempts to thaw my being. Hovering between sleep and consciousness, I keep telling myself that I have to get up. I feel that if I don't get up now, I will become engulfed by 'The bed'. In the dark recess of my shattered mind, the same conversation keeps going round in my head. The visceral response intensifies. Moments before I finally drift off to sleep, I could not help thinking, it would have been far easier if I had just had a good cry and be done with it. I finally pass out.

This graphic description of an emotional episode adds another dimension to Austerlitz and Aravot's (2007) observations of the same phenomena. It adds a visceral subjective fleshiness to the language of academic bones.

> In cases where an intense emotional reaction was elicited, it often captured the whole of the student's attention and led him/her into an emotional turbulence lasting days or even weeks.
> (Austerlitz & Aravot, 2007)

This episode was the first inkling of how I had constructed an intimate relationship between 'the artist self' and happiness. My feelings of happiness had become bound to my notions of self-worth and self-esteem about my artwork. Short-term emotions of satisfaction were expressed when I felt a sense of accomplishment after solving a technical challenge. Sometimes snippets of joy were felt after a cursory nod of approval from a tutor. However, this never translated into the long-term sentiment of happiness, well-being. This tension existed because my creative process was intuitive, exploratory and nebulous. I found it difficult to contextualise and communicate the rigour within my work.

I could not always articulate my intentions clearly or perform the necessary public performance with a high level of confidence, therefore I had not been able to build up enough short-term currency of joy and satisfaction and convert it to the long-term sentiment of well-being. According to the theoretical approach applied to the study of the evaluation of happiness, happiness can be evaluated in the context of a baseline. The visual analogy of a volume slider on a stereo aids my understanding of the happiness evaluation scale. I imagine the baseline knob halfway on the volume slide. Anything above the baseline registers happy and below the baseline registers as unhappy. I can categorically state that, while at art school, the 'artist self' happiness was frequently perilously close to the lower end of the baseline.

Scene two: Seminar – a hot day in the studio

During the seminar, the tutor wanders around the studio, stopping intermittently to look through sketchbooks and artworks spewed around. The student talks excitedly about art. The tutor turns to the student.

Tutor: Are you serious?

Student: I don't understand. What do you mean am I serious?

Tutor: (looking at student with disdain, sneers) You can't be serious. You must be doing this course as a hobby.

Student: (unspoken) My heart sank. My dreams and aspirations of living the bohemian lifestyle evaporated in a flash. No sitting in cafes drinking coffee and talking about life, art and philosophy for me. I will have to work 9-5. Worse still, I might have to work the graveyard shift. Filled with terror, I tried to explain my intentions to the tutor. All I could muster was gibberish. Spirit crushed, I sat through the seminar. I pretended to listen. I pretended to care, but my soul had left the building; neatly tucked away under the duvet.

Under the duvet, this brief encounter grew into a looped conversation. I played it in slow motion, I played it in fast forward, I played it in rewind. In my mental exhaustion, I had to acknowledge that I was trying to resolve a feeling of unhappiness with critical thinking. The more questions I asked, the less understanding I gained, and the unhappier I got.

This experience had a negative effect on 'the artist self'. If the artist is not serious about his/her work, how does the artwork develop? 'The artist self' was still trying to find ways of dealing with issues of self-esteem about artwork. What does this new information mean? This statement was worse than concluding that the artwork is bad. If the artwork is bad, surely this implies that there might be some room for improvement? Apart from the upheaval and turmoil of 'the artist self', this had a profound effect on my relationship with the tutor. I was not interested in having a relationship with this tutor. I felt the tutor's comment was unfair, unconsidered and unprofessional. I was furious. I no longer had any respect for this tutor and I was not prepared to engage in dialogue. I terminated the relationship. There was no future dialogue. At best, there was an awkward aloof exchange of gazes. Still angry and requiring answers, I went in search of the sage.

Scene three: Conversations in Monet's garden – the sage as tutor; expanding the expectation of the notion of the tutor

We walked through the park. We passed the lake and hundreds of trees. For the first time in weeks, I remember feeling free. I was breathing again. For a couple of weeks, I felt like I had been holding my breath underwater.

Tutor: It's a nice day.

Student: (grunt) Um.

Tutor: How are you?

Student: Not very good.

Tutor: What are you looking for?

Student: Before I leave art school and embark on another journey,
I need to know what the truth is about my work.

Tutor: What do you mean?

Student: Is my work good enough? Will I become an artist?

Tutor: You are already an artist.

Student: How can I already be an artist when tutor x said my work looked like I was taking the course as a hobby.

Tutor: What do you think about your art?

Student: Well, I thought my art must be worthy of some attention, or you would not have accepted me onto the course. I work hard. I take my work pretty serious.

Tutor: So, you think your art is good then?

Student: Well, I don't think it is bad.

Tutor: How do you know your work is not bad?

Student: I feel that I started from a good position. So my work can only get better. I feel that my work might not be at its strongest or the most resolved at the moment. It is work in progress. Neither good nor bad ... Just work in progress.

Tutor: You say you feel that it is good. Do you think it is good

Student: I think that in comparison with my peers and within the context of the contemporary art scene, my artwork is engaging in meaningful enquiry. In addition, I feel that my work is constantly evolving.

Tutor: So it sounds like you think your art is OK at the moment and you feel that it will develop and get better. So, what is the problem? Why do you want to leave us?

The student thought about this for a couple of moments. Then something remarkable happened: the feeling of unhappiness dissolved. It seemed to evaporate. Puff ... It was gone.

Student: Now that you have put it like that, I feel much happier and I will finish the course. It all feels like so much fuss over nothing now.

Tutor: It is not fuss about nothing. It is important we had this chat about what is going on with you. What we are teaching you here is to develop an understanding about the difference between facts, opinions and the truth.

Student: (laughing) That sounds like philosophy. I must have signed up for the wrong course. I thought you were teaching us how to draw and paint.

Tutor: We are also teaching you how to see.

Student: What does that mean?

The tutor handed the student a piece of paper and told the student to read it out loud.

> Reality is what we take to be true
> What we take to be true is what we believe
> What we believe is based upon our perceptions
> What we perceive depends upon what we look for
> What we look for depends upon what we think
> What we think depends on what we perceive
> What we perceive determines what we believe
> What we believe determines what we take to be true
> What we take to be true is our reality.
> Zukav (1979, pp313)

Although the student had jokingly referred to the course not being a philosophy course, the above quote is from *The Dancing Wu Li Masters*. The book could be described as an East meets West collision of Buddhist wisdom, Einstein's theory of relativity and quantum physics.

The process of discussing concepts of opinions, beliefs and perceptions helped me gain a better understanding of how to deal with the emotion of happiness in relation to the context of the art studio. Within the context of the studio, there will be numerous opinions, perceptions and beliefs registered about my artwork. Firstly it is important to be able to remember the reference was to my artwork and not me. I found that, as an art student, there was a close association between who I was and what I produced. Therefore comments about my artwork had an impact on how I felt. Discussions with the guru helped the process of dissociation between me the person and the artist self. It was a moment of clarity. I witnessed the birth of my ' artist self'.

Conclusion

The process of writing this paper has been like an archaeological dig. The process of opening up academic writing conventions to include the subjective voice has provided additional insight to my understanding of the issue under discussion. Art school experiences have become internalised. Reflectivity and subjectivity have been important tools in enabling an understanding of the relationship between the issues. The most interesting discovery is the articulation of 'the artist self'. Although there might be an awareness or widespread knowledge of the existence of the artist self, it was never discussed or publicly acknowledged during my time at art school.

Although this paper focused on the relationship between tutor-student interactions, happiness and ' the artist self', I think it is safe to assume that even if one looked at another emotion, the relationship between the three elements will always be important to the art student learning experience. Unless there are imminent changes to art education in Britain, it is safe to assume that the context (art studio) will remain a constant; tutor-student interactions will also remain a constant.

I think it is important for students to have a cognitive understanding of these variables and their importance to their well-being and growth as artists. First of all, I think art students need to be made aware of, and be prepared for, a process of alchemy in the formation of the 'artist self' Some explicit intervention is required here. This area requires further research to indicate creative solutions whereby students can develop intelligent awareness and understanding of the internal processes applicable to their learning and development as artists.

The learner might be aware of cognitive and artistic development. This is explicit. Progress reports and end-of-year exhibitions provide empirical evidence. However, transformative development is implicit. I would argue that, in my experience, it is the awareness of the relationship between artistic, cognitive and transformative development in the formation of the artist self that sustains my practice as artist/teacher.

References

Austerlitz N., Aravot I. (2007). Emotions of Design Students: A New Perspective for the Design Studio, in Salama A. and Wilkinson, N. (Eds.), *Design Studio Pedagogy: Horizons for the Future.* (Chap. 3: Teaching Styles in the Studio) U.K.: Urban International Press pp. 233-246

Ben-Ze'ev, A. (2000), *The Subtlety of Emotions* (Cambridge, Mass.: MIT Press)

Zukav, G. (1979), *The Dancing Wu Li Masters* (New York: Bantan Books)

Janice Miller

Psychodynamic approaches to the study of pedagogy acknowledge the teacher-student relationship as emotional, empathetic, symbiotic and significant.[1] Here, Yewande Okuleye examines the specific correlation of this emotional relationship to the learning of art. This would seem a particularly prescient subject because, as a variety of art-specific studies on teaching and learning show[2] – as do cultural explorations of the artist in, for example, the work of Raymond Williams[3] – the emotional is a fundamental facet in the construct of the self-identity of the artistic individual. It is core to their understanding of themselves as creative people and a crucial factor within their definitions of creativity. Nonetheless, as the narratives contained here express so clearly, the emotional elements of the dual identity of learner and artist are something to be grappled with in the process of formal study.

Teachers are all too aware that learning is at times painful for their students; there are few who have not encountered students struggling with earlier negative classroom experiences or erroneous expectations of themselves or their subject that leave feelings of disappointment, despair, anger or fear. The challenge for both tutor and student is to recognise that such emotions are natural and perhaps even necessary to a truly transformative learning process, and to find strategies to navigate the obstacles that these feelings create. The kind of subjective voice adopted in this paper can give valuable insights. Ultimately, the conclusions here are optimistic, and the emotional experiences recounted present significant, painful but rewarding challenges.

Thus, this paper makes the important point that both learning and teaching is emotional labour. When transformative learning takes place, it is the artist who is worked on not the artefact, and what is discovered is an understanding of both the interrelatedness and separateness of the two.

Here, we are presented with learning as an emotional journey, echoing Freire's[4] notions of praxis, where it is a process of reflection and action and one closely allied to social discourses. In tracing this, Okuleye focuses in particular on the specific binary of happiness/unhappiness. While initially striving for short-term satisfaction and affirmation in the form of positive feedback and high grades, happiness is newly understood in situations that bring about more long-term rewards: the development of the critical abilities and objective viewpoints essential for creative work of all kinds. As philosophy plays such a significant part in this paper, it would seem appropriate to end here with some related sentiments from the work of A.C. Grayling, who considers happiness 'in itself ... a negative state, a passive condition which undermines things we value more: our striving and yearning, our improving and growing, our inventing and discovering' (Grayling, 2002, p. 72).[5]

Notes

1 See in particular the work of Roslyn Arnold: Arnold, R. (1994), 'The theory and principles of psychodynamic pedagogy', Forum for Education, 49 (2), pp. 21–33 and also Cotten, S.R. & Wilson, B. (2006), 'Student-faculty interactions: dynamics and determinants', *Higher Education*, 51, pp. 487–519

2 See, for example: Candlin, F. (2001), 'A dual inheritance: the politics of educational reform and PhDs in art and design', *International Journal of Art and Design Education*, **20** (3)

3 Williams, R. (1983), *Culture and Society: 1780–1950* (New York: Columbia University Press) (originally published 1958)

4 Freire, P. (2000), *Pedagogy of the Oppressed New York: Continuum* (originally published 1970)

5 Grayling, A.C. (2002), *The Meaning of Things: Applying Philosophy to Life* (London: Orion)

Section 3

Supporting the individual journeys in the emotional landscape

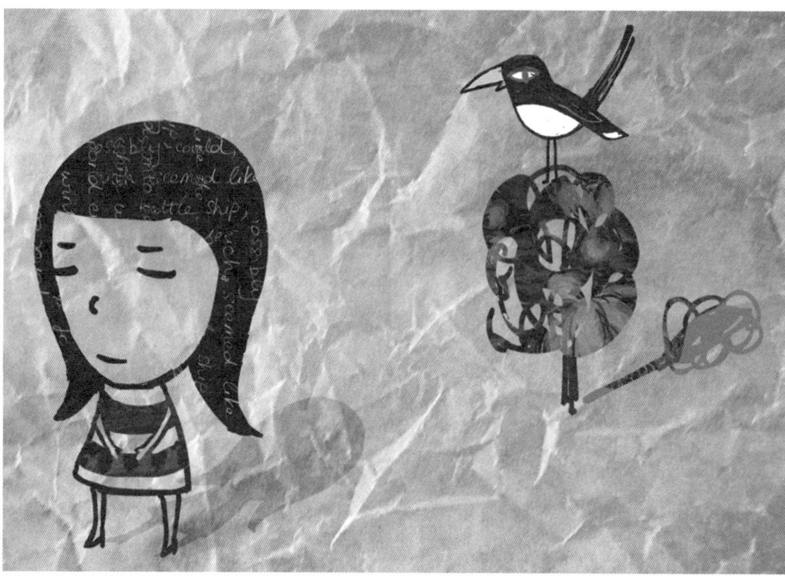

Sad girl — Su-Lynn Tan

Reproduced by permission of the artist

10

Arts students and the holding environment: reflections from a student counselling service

Author: Ken Ewings

Commentary: Jackie McManus

Keywords

student support,
self reported emotions,
art students,
holding environment

Ken Ewings

Introduction

The fact student counselling is outside of the teaching process but within the educational institution provides it with a particular perspective on the emotional aspects of pedagogy.

The thoughts presented here are based upon impressions gained from counselling conversations. It is not scientific evidence, but hopefully some of the observations will be of interest to those concerned with arts students' capacity to learn and be creative. In particular, the importance of the holding environment is discussed.

Students seek counselling because they find some aspect of life difficult. They talk about their fears, doubts, hopes, traumas, family backgrounds and relationship problems. They also talk about their experiences on their courses and the difficulties they are having with their work. The counsellor is curious about and interested in the student who, hopefully, feels safe to express pain and confusion. Counselling is a place to make connections, to play with ideas and to focus what can be done to make life and studying more manageable and rewarding.

Stresses of being an arts student

The arts are more subjective than other areas of study with less inherent solidity and certainty and fewer absolute yardsticks against which work can be judged. This is exciting, but the fluidity and lack of rules can also create almost constant uncertainty and anxiety, especially for the less confident student. It is particularly unsettling when conflicting reports on work are received from tutors. In such circumstances, students naturally look to each other for opinions or reassurance, but this isn't straightforward. Fear of ideas being stolen and anxieties about plagiarism, competition, envy and secrecy are commonly voiced in counselling.

For fine artists, it can feel as if their inner world is out there for all to see and comment on. They are encouraged to express something that is real for them, and what else can they draw on but their own experiences and feelings? This can connect some with distress, unhappiness or insecurity, and it may take a while to realise that art is not art therapy. If they can find ways of processing inner raw material, it is usually easier for others to engage with their work as art, rather than as a documentary or biographical piece.

Although such abstracting of experience enables students to keep aspects of themselves private, it is observed that there is often a desire by those who, for example, have been abused, to portray this in their work. As young adults, they don't want to hide away – as they may have had to do as children – and need their work to be stark and open and disturbing. For some developing artists who have experienced trauma, this is a stage that has to be gone through, and some find moving beyond it easier than others.

Occasionally, students who attend for counselling describe an obsession with their shadow side, which they express through their artwork. This can be extreme, with representations of pain and suffering and a morbid interest in death. In counselling, there is an opportunity for exploring and understanding these dark fascinations.

Many students find that being a good artist is not enough to get them through their course. They have to be able to write assignments and essays. This is a particular difficulty for foundation students who may have struggled at school. It can be because they are dyslexic (often undiagnosed), were written off by teachers and 'coped' by avoiding written work as much as possible. As Daphne Hampton points out: 'many art, design and communication students feel … anxious when they realise the extent of writing that is necessary on their degree courses' (Hampton, paper 11 in this book, p. 225). When they enter art college, the problems these students thought they had left behind reappear with all the attendant emotions and feelings of failure and inadequacy. This can also be an issue for first-year BA students who get through their foundation year (or sometimes skip the foundation year because of the excellence of their portfolios) and find they are expected to produce high-standard written material. Avoidance and denial are utilised as methods of coping, but sooner or later anxiety sets in and they often seek counselling. The following case study material will illustrate a typical trajectory.

Stacey

A 24-year-old student presented towards the end of the first term of her BA, saying she was unhappy but she didn't know why. She was passionate about art and had been accepted on the course on the basis of her portfolio. She had a good circle of friends and a loving boyfriend. She also had a good job in a photographer's studio. The counsellor encouraged her to talk and she mentioned, almost in passing, that she had an essay to hand in, the deadline for which was two days away. She said she hadn't even started to think about it and had been avoiding her tutor.

The counsellor asked more questions about her education and school experiences, and what emerged was a fear of anything academic or requiring the production of written material. When she talked about school and how stupid she felt when she was there, it was clear that the problem went back a long way. She also tearfully described being bullied for being 'stupid' and said that she tried not to think about it.

The counsellor saw this as the turning point, as the student had now begun to face her painful experiences at school, and could see and describe why she had poor levels of confidence on the course and in dealing with tutors. The student said she liked her tutor, but felt embarrassed and ashamed about not feeling confident about writing anything.

The counsellor suggested that she contact her tutor straight away to explain that she was stuck and that she was seeking help. The counsellor asked if she had ever been tested for dyslexia. The student said she hadn't; although this had been mentioned as a possible explanation several times at school, nothing had happened. The counsellor suggested that she make an appointment with study skills in her college and the dyslexia coordinator for an initial screening. This she did and, once she had developed some strategies for getting her ideas down on paper, she was able to engage more fully with her course assignments.

The counsellor contracted with Stacey for five more counselling sessions to help monitor her progress. It was also agreed that the student would use the sessions to talk about being bullied at school and other painful experiences connected with learning, something that she had never been able to talk to her parents or anyone else about before. This provided a release of feelings, freeing up emotions for more constructive use and expression.

Tough love and perfectionism

Stacey's tutor had high expectations and was interested, engaged and compassionate. Most tutors are, but in some areas of arts training some tutors, knowing that industry is fiercely competitive, may feel that being too 'soft' with students is not going to prepare them for the real world. Anecdotal evidence from conversations in the consulting room indicates that an approach of robust criticism is helpful, if leavened with support. Undiluted negativity or criticism, it appears, can further erode the confidence of those students who need a safe environment within which to develop.

Many arts students, or at least many who present for counselling, can be described as perfectionists. They want to be the best and cannot countenance anything less. They see mediocrity as failure and the resulting anxiety can inhibit their capacity to work and be creative, and a vicious circle sets in. Such negative loops can be broken by structured conversations with their tutor or with a counsellor.

Arts students, anxiety and the holding environment

An arts student has to operate at two very different levels. He or she has to be organised, adult, on top of the brief, earning money, dealing with the stresses of life AND be in touch with his/her creative, playful and childlike side. For this to be a realistic expectation, particularly for students who are highly stressed and with low levels of confidence, the institution needs to provide a good holding environment.

Anxiety is normal, but in excess it is uncomfortable and even dangerous, with the effects of heightened alertness, being on edge, irritability, and the inability to relax or concentrate. The sufferer may be weepy or dependent and there is often an overwhelming desire to seek the reassurance of others. Such experiences are seldom conducive to creativity as they impede the capacity to play with ideas. Above a certain level of anxiety it is difficult to react flexibly or imaginatively, although it is also the case that there are some students who experience such a low level of anxiety that they find it difficult to be motivated to work or to change (Yerkes Dodson, 1908). But, overall, it would appear that the biggest impediment to student functioning (particularly in the hectic complicated modern world) is high anxiety.

If this is the case, and it is accepted that excessive anxiety inhibits creativity, arts colleges should endeavour to reduce student anxiety by having good course structures and tutoring systems. If students feel secure enough, there is more psychological space for them to develop their own creative symbolisation.

The counselling service has noticed an apparent but clear correlation between the levels of anxiety a student reports and the extent to which he or she feels 'held' by the institution, specifically by the course and tutoring relationships, but also by other sections of the institution such as study skills, mentoring, counselling and advice and guidance.

The holding environment, as described by Donald Winnicott (1982), is a psychical and physical space within which the individual is protected – without knowing he or she is protected – and where anxiety is reduced. The role of a holding environment is primarily one of anxiety management and mirrors earlier transitional, separational and maturational processes (Winnicott, 1990). In this environment the student is more able to fully inhabit his/her 'negative capability' – a term originally coined by John Keats – described as ' the capability of being in uncertainty, mystery, and doubt without any irritable reaching after fact & reason' (Bate, 1963).

Some students are more vulnerable to the negative effects of not feeling held; particularly those from fractured backgrounds where there are self-esteem problems, self-damaging behaviours or a history of depression and loneliness. International students, from a different pedagogic culture, for whom English is not a first language and who are a long way from home, are another group that particularly benefit from a good holding environment (Elder, 2007; Sovic, 2007).

Vulnerable students who don't feel held, typically exhibit certain behaviours. They avoid their course and their tutors and find it difficult to engage with their work. They report creative blocks and low levels of confidence. Procrastination is commonly reported and this is often associated with a general disengagement or a fear of failure. Those who do their work at the last minute can continue believe that, if only they had started the work earlier, it would have been so much better.

Tutor-student relationship

The most important relationship for holding student learning anxieties is the tutor-student relationship. When students describe their tutor as accessible and reliable, less anxiety is generally reported. If the tutor gives honest, clear and timely feedback, students generally thrive; and if they report receiving a mixture of high support and high challenge with clear expectations they feel contained and able to learn. This is illustrated by a student voice from another paper in this book where Sovic quotes a student reporting: 'I am not sure what [tutors'] expectations are. So it stresses me; I don't know how I can work harder …' (Sovic, paper 3 in this book, p. 77).

The tutor's role is more than that of a teacher, as the boundaries tutors provide create stability in the student's learning and psychological environment. This is particularly the case in group learning, where the dynamics are extremely powerful. Group learning in art schools operates in the particular context of studio culture, small learning groups and a very public and competitive environment. The group that is mentioned more than any other in counselling is the 'crit' – a seminar where students present their work for discussion. It is important that such public criticism of work feels safe, with allowances made for different cultural experiences and with the tutor able to manage the group dynamic (Blair, Blythman & Orr, 2007).

Many students say that being in their learning groups is stressful, partly because they find it difficult to play with ideas and think around their work when they don't feel secure. Not knowing and puzzlement are an essential part of the process of learning, and a student's panic about not being in control can impede exploration and discovery (Austerlitz & Aravot, 2007). Stress occurs when control is low, but when the perceived need to be in control is high (Wheeler & Birtle, 1993). This conflict can only really be negotiated when there is sufficient trust in the process and in the relationship with the group leader for the students to be open and feel safe enough to take risks.

A case study will illustrate why talking in groups can be so difficult for some.

Dan

A final-year student came to counselling with a crippling fear of presentations. He would panic before every crit, feel paralysed and usually stay at home. He had managed to avoid most of them so far, but now had been told that it was essential to attend or there would be a detrimental impact on his final marks. His tutors had told him that he appeared aloof, but he felt this was unfair and just felt terrified when expected to present, going blank as a consequence. He therefore felt misunderstood by the tutors and was angry with them but had been unable to talk to them about this, or indeed about any of his feelings or difficulties.

In the first counselling session, he told the counsellor that he had a lot of unresolved and painful issues relating to his parents' separation when he was a teenager, but added, in a an aloof way, that there was no point in discussing this as there was nothing that could be done to change it. He was seeking counselling for the presentation problem only, he said. What he was communicating was that he was only willing to present certain aspects of himself to the counsellor, a bit like the tutors' perception of his presentations.

The counsellor said that the past issues must be very painful if he had decided they were a no go area, and made it clear that what he revealed was completely his choice

Over the next couple of weeks, Dan gradually began to tell the counsellor about the separation and how his father had left him with his mother, who then got together with someone else quite quickly, making it clear that he was no longer welcome in the house. As well as this rejection by both parents, neither parent was able or willing to acknowledge any of his feelings about the situation so he lapsed into a silent, depressive (and aloof) rage.

He felt that he could only present certain acceptable aspects of himself to his parents if he was going to retain any kind of relationship with them.

As the counselling progressed he recognised parallels with his current difficulties on the course, and once he began to express pain from his past he felt more able to open up a dialogue with his tutors, rather than remain silent, angry and misunderstood, as he had with his parents. He also began to face up to his fear of ending the course and having to present himself to the world beyond college.

Students who report feeling overwhelmed with hopelessness and frustration are often disengaged from their course and often do not appear to have an interested tutor steering them through the anxieties involved in learning. Helping students develop the capacity to bear uncertainties lies at the heart of both tutoring and counselling. This aspect of learning has been described as overcoming 'the three fears': the fear of impotence, the fear of chaos and the fear of ignorance (Salzberger-Wittenberg, 1983). Both tutoring and counselling can develop the capacity to think and to experience regardless of, and alongside, these fears.

Good boundaries help wobbly students know where they stand and tutors who are interested but don't get over-involved offer helpful psychological holding, paralleling a model of good parenting. Over-involvement by the tutor is occasionally reported by the student and is sometimes followed by a sudden retraction of interest when the tutor realises that he or she has got in too deep and overstepped professional boundaries.

Consistent teachers and tutors, who do not blow hot and cold, make the student feel valued and safe, and those who can offer the right level of timely support and guidance are prized. Arts students are often very passionate about their work and this appears particularly to be the case for students who feel that an academic staff member has engaged with their work and artistic endeavour.

Tutoring and counselling

Good student counselling and good tutoring normalise the uncertainty and stress of learning but in different ways. Neither one should avoid or prohibit the expression of emotions, as both are interpersonal processes that contain anxiety and encourage curiosity.

Tutors and counsellors alike are on the receiving end of projected feelings. These may be referred to as transferences (Freud, 1990) and are: 'redirected of feelings and desires especially of those unconsciously retained from childhood toward a new object' (Laplance & Pontalis, 1988). Transferences are powerful because they come from unconscious re-enactment of the students' earlier relationship patterns. The institution recapitulates many powerful connections, longings and meanings for students (usually rooted in their family of origin) and staff can be conduits of the transference process. For example, a student who has a critical and unsupportive parent will be 'tuned' to expect the tutor to be similarly negative, and mild criticism can be experienced as an attack. There are also positive transferences when the tutor can be experienced as the interested and talented parent they never had, sometimes manifesting as idolisation.

Such psychological expressions are common and normal, but to be on the receiving end of powerful positive or negative transference projections can be uncomfortable and even alarming. They are more easily managed if they can be understood for what they are.

It can also be useful to be curious about the nature of the feelings aroused (in staff) by the student. Such feelings can be opportunities to learn something about the student and his/her blocks to progress and creativity. In this process, feeling some of the mental pain connected with the student's learning and life stage is inevitable and an opportunity for role modelling. The tutor's capacity to be reflective and thoughtful can model what it is to be a thinking and creative person. This is part of what Okuleye refers to as: 'the relationship between artistic, cognitive and transformative development in the formation of the artist self' (Okuleye, paper 9 in this book, p. 191).

Like tutoring, counselling operates firmly within the holding environment of the institution, but, crucially and differently, it is outside academic assessment process. There is usually a collaborative focus to counselling and the process works because the active and benign attention of the counsellor enables students to make connections, and see themselves and their situation in new and helpful ways. It can be a critical intervention for very distressed or psychologically disturbed students, helping them manage their problems and their lives and to seek other help if necessary. But students who are not in serious difficulties can also benefit from a safe place to discuss their anxieties, the course, their relationships and decisions they need to make.

Conclusion

There are particular stresses for arts students related to the subjectivity of art and to its public and competitive nature. The fact that many have to draw deep from within themselves to produce work can connect them with personal disturbance. Such personal material is less likely to throw a student off balance and out of productivity if they are within a good institutional holding environment. This is the psychical and physical space within which the student is protected and anxiety is reduced. Such an environment is framed by good structures, systems and communications, but also by the quality of relationships, especially within personal tutoring. Regular, interested tutoring, with good boundaries, holds and guides the shaky student. Group tutoring, especially, needs to be safe and well organised as group dynamics can be very powerful, particularly when students feel exposed because their work is being discussed.

Counselling is also part of the holding environment, providing a neutral space outside the student's course where difficulties can be thought through. It is a place where emotional expression is welcomed, and connections and options can be explored. Mess and confusion can be brought, but it is also a place for goal setting and developing strategies.

Both tutors and counsellors alike can be on the receiving end of emotionally charged projections from students, or transferences. These are common and normal but some can be very powerful and are more easily managed if recognised as expectations of relationships powered from earlier in the student's life.

Tutors, counsellors and other support staff have different roles in relation to students, but what they have in common is the opportunity and responsibility to make real but professional connections with students, and not to be scared of the emotional dimension of their life and work.

References

Austerlitz, N. & Aravot, I. (2007), 'Emotions of design students: a new perspective for the design studio', in Salama, A. & Wilkinson, N. (eds.) *Design Studio Pedagogy: Horizons for the Future* (UK: Urban International Press)

Bate, W.J. (1963), *John Keats* (Harvard University Press)

Blair, B., Blythman, M. & Orr, S. (2007), *Critiquing the Crit* (The Higher Education Academy – Art, Design Media Subject Centre)

Elder, H. (2007), *The Silent Crit: Putting Thoughts into Word* (UAL)

Freud, S. (1990), *The Dynamics of Transference, reprinted in Essential Papers on Transference* (New York University Press)

Laplance, J. & Pontalis, J.B. (1988), *The Language of Psychoanalysis* (London: Karnac)

Salzberger-Wittenberg, I., Williams, G. & Osborne, E. (1983), *The Emotional Experience of Learning and Teaching* (Karnac)

Sovic, S. (2007), *The Experiences of First Year International Students* (UAL CLIP/CETL research project)

Wheeler, S. & Birtle, J. (1993), *A Handbook for Personal Tutors* (The Society for Research into Higher Education, Open University)

Winnicott, D. (1982), *Playing and Reality* (Routledge)

Winnicott, D. (1990), *The Maturational Processes and the Facilitating Environment: Studies in the Theory of Emotional Development* (Karnac)

Yerkes, R.M. & Dodson, J.D. (1908), first published in Journal of Comparative Neurology and Psychology, **18** pp. 459–482; online at: http://psychclassics.yorku.ca/Yerkes/Law/

Further reading

AUCC (2004), *Guidelines for University and College Counselling Services* (British Association for Counselling and Psychotherapy BACP)

Caldwell, L. (2000), *Art, Creativity, Living* (Winnicott Studies Monograph Series) (Karnac)

Coren, A. (1997), *A Psychodynamic Approach to Education* (Sheldon Press)

Earwaker, J. (1992) *Helping and Supporting Students – Re-thinking the Issues* (The Society for Research into Higher Education. Open University)

Klein, M. et al. (eds.) (1985), *New Directions in Psychoanalysis: The Significance of Infant Conflict in the Pattern of Adult Behaviour* (Karnac)

Kohut, H. (1977), *The Restoration of the Self* (New York: International Universities Press)

Noonan, E. (1983), *Counselling Young People* (Methuen)

Phillips, A. (2005), *Going Sane*

Rana, R. (2000), *Counselling Students: A Psychodynamic Perspective* (Basic Texts in Counselling & Psychotherapy) (Macmillan Press Ltd)

Stanley, N. & Manthorpe, J. (2002), *Students' Mental Health Needs Problems and Responses* (Jessica Kingsley)

Acknowledgements

Ideas and contributions from UAL counsellors were essential to the writing of this paper.

Anne-Marie Bradley, Cathy Bradley, Pat Griffiths, Sally Holder, Kevin Halon, Benedicta Kilburn, Alice Bulman

Jackie McManus

This paper focuses on the importance of good pedagogical and tutorial practices in supporting students. It offers rare and valuable insights into the world of student counselling and, in particular, draws comparisons between the counsellor-student relationship and the tutor-student relationship.

In spite of being modestly described by the author as 'not scientific evidence' this paper reminds us that the value of in-depth qualitative research is that it 'deals with meaningful talk and action ... in order to capture the complexities of the social worlds we seek to understand' (Coffey & Atkinson, 1996, pp. 3&5).

The author's perspective on the stresses of being an art student, and his focus on the holding environment, resonates with other work that challenges the remedial approach to student anxiety about assessment. Both Lillis (2001) and Burke (2002) shift the focus from the anxious student who needs to be 'fixed' by being sent to study support or student services, on to the importance of creating positive pedagogical practices and relationships (which ultimately benefit all students). The remedial approach views students' anxiety about their work as best dealt with by trying to teach the mechanics of academic life (Lillis, 2001) e.g. essay writing and presentation skills, or in the case of art and design, how to perform well in the 'crit'. However, this approach fails to take account of the emotional and socio-political context of learning and teaching, and assessment (ibid.). Burke (2007) highlights the importance of encouraging students to tolerate the uncertainties of producing academic work by challenging notions of the 'ideal student'. Moving away from models of the idealised perfect student helps to normalise anxiety about the struggle to write or make work and, using Ewing's counselling model, helps to create a 'holding' learning environment.

Moreover, as Ewing says, and Bowl (2003) points out in her research on 'non traditional' entrants to higher education, poor pedagogy and tutorial systems disproportionately affect students for whom the 'culture and norms of higher education' (Bowl, 2003, p. 124) are a mystery, because of their race, class or age, resulting in feelings of powerlessness and vulnerability in their dealings with the academy, but especially with the curriculum:

> … students blamed themselves for the failure of the education system to offer them support, make their studies manageable and to provide guidance about the rules of academic performance. (ibid. p. 124)

Ewing successfully argues that the emotional and the academic are not easily separated, and that the student counselling model of 'holding' students and creating good quality relationships to support them is one that could successfully be adopted pedagogically to provide better learning environments for all.

References

Bowl, M. (2003), *Non-Traditional Entrants to Higher Education: 'They Talk About People Like Me'* (Stoke-on-Trent: Trentham Books)

Burke, P.J. (2002), *Accessing Education: Effectively Widening Participation* (Stoke-On-Trent: Trentham Books)

Burke, P.J, & Jackson, S. (2007), *Reconceptualising Lifelong Learning* (London and New York: Routledge)

Coffey, A. & Atkinson, P. (1996), *Making Sense of Qualitative Data: Complementary Research Strategies* (London: Sage)

Lillis, T. (2001), *Student Writing: Access, Regulation, Desire* (London: Routledge)

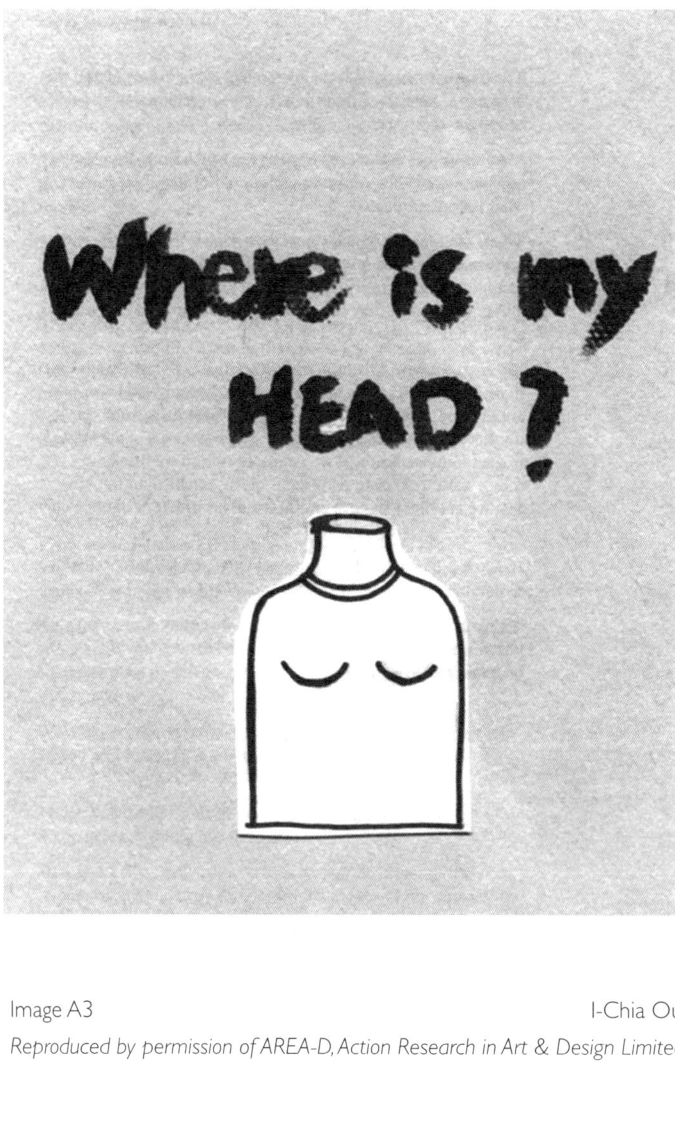

Image A3 I-Chia Ou

Reproduced by permission of AREA-D, Action Research in Art & Design Limited

11

The role of emotions in student support systems

Author: Daphne Hampton

Commentary: Margo Blythman

Keywords

feelings,
student support systems,
personal academic tutorial,
study support,
student mentoring,
student services

Daphne Hampton

Introduction

> Understanding what students are thinking and how they are feeling is the first step to getting retention results.
> (Noel & Levitz, 1999)

Students often have compelling stories to tell. Listening to them and then acting on their views is one way of improving their learning experiences in an age of diversity. Understanding student emotions and feelings is key to effective learning and good retention. The way students feel about student support systems is a determining factor in how successful these systems are in helping the students on their learning journey. One of the dimensions that make the student-tutor relationship important is the emotional dimension. Yorke and Thomas (2003) emphasise the importance of a supportive, friendly first-year climate, and point out that students' patterns of engagement with universities are changing. We need to know what makes our students perceive that the culture is friendly and supportive. Two pieces of research are discussed below, both recovering the student voice for art, design and communication students at LCC (London College of Communication), University of the Arts London. One piece of research discusses the student perspective on their first-term experience and pre-entry while the second looks at student use of, and attitudes and feelings towards, student support systems in year one. This essay will focus on aspects of the students' feelings about term one, especially their feelings towards student support systems.

Research methodology

My current research investigates student use of, attitudes towards, perceptions of and feelings about student support systems on the first year of art, design and communication foundation degrees at LCC. In particular, the current research looks at academic personal tutorials, study support, student mentoring and student services. The research uses semi-structured questions to elicit this information and follows on from my earlier research (Hampton & Blythman, 2006) into recovering the student voice on these degrees to discover student perspectives on the first term and pre-entry. The social world is understood through a variety of perspectives coming from multiple realities and this is best captured through social actors being able to 'name the world' (Freire, 1996, p. 69). For this reason, the research is reported with an emphasis on the students' own words.

Fifteen students on foundation degrees in interior design, visual design and display, and travel and tourism were interviewed for the original research. Fourteen students were female and one was male, reflecting the make-up of these courses that year. Six students were from the UK, five from Europe, two from China, one from Egypt and one from South America.

For the current research, 15 students were interviewed in the spring term of 2007. The courses involved were foundation degrees in journalism, media practice, interior design, creative advertising and travel and tourism. Six students were female and nine male; nine were from the UK and six from Europe; six were first generation students and nine had one or both parents who had been to university. This analysis will focus on the feelings expressed in both pieces of research, especially feelings about term one and those towards student support systems. Such feelings affect:

- engagement with learning;
- whether students come to the support systems in the first place;
- whether they recommend these support systems to their friends.

Students will have internal and external expectations of the systems, as will their tutors.

Student support systems at LCC

LCC has a long and proud tradition of student support systems. This includes the personal academic tutorial, study support, student-to-student mentoring schemes and student services. The personal academic tutorial monitors and supports the academic progress of the student across his/her whole course, Study support provides help with academic literacy, study skills, numeracy and academic support for students with dyslexia and other forms of disability. Student mentoring schemes enable second-year students to help first-year students settle into the course and college culture. Student services provides a comprehensive range of services such as financial advice, accommodation, counselling, health, disability support and careers. All of these are strands in the armoury of successful support to help aid retention and achievement.

Student support systems for art, design and communication students

Art, design and communication students have concerns that may differentiate them from students studying other disciplines. Many struggle with issues of identity and meaning. (Taylor & Littleton, 2007). They are worried by the dichotomy of the need to make creative work versus the need to 'work for a living'. Many feel guilty about enjoying their creative courses. Many perceive themselves as artists first and students second. The personal academic tutorial is a safe place where creative students can explore these dimensions, while student mentoring schemes can provide role models to help with these issues.

One in four art, design and communication students is dyslexic, or has another form of disability that leads them to want to work alone in concentrated bursts of activity rather than with the group in the studio or the lecture room. Study support provides support and mechanisms to help with these areas. Study support, personal academic tutorials and student mentoring can also help the many art, design and communication students who often struggle with written assignments as their main focus has always been visual. Whether dyslexic or not, many art, design and communication students feel very uncomfortable with the written word and can become very anxious when they realise the extent of writing that is necessary on their degree courses.

Art and design education often privileges ambiguity, leading these students to feel lost. It is common for such students to worry when different teachers give different or contradictory advice. The academic personal tutorial can provide a haven to discuss such issues, study support can supply strategies for coping, and student mentors can provide role models who discuss what happened to them so the mentees do not feel isolated and unique.

Art and design courses often ask their students to explore questions of identity. This can be troubling for some students, especially when they are undergoing a period of transition such as going to university, leaving home, coping in a new culture, and becoming an adult.

Austerlitz (2007) states:

> Therefore, we assume that studio participants, and students in particular, may experience a high level of cognitive stress and a tendency to emotionality.

Student support systems exist to help art, design and communication students explore and cope with all these issues, and we need to know the student voice regarding them.

The student voice: the research findings

The research into recovering the student voice (Hampton & Blythman, 2006) asked students to describe their experiences of their first term. Eight main themes emerged.

Feeling overwhelmed: the importance of support

One of the themes reported was a strong feeling of being overwhelmed by so many new experiences.

> Well, initially I found it all overwhelming. It was all new, and you're not quite sure what you are doing. Sometimes you're given a talk on something or you're given a brief and you don't always know what the tutor wants. You're doing your best but you're not always sure whether what you're doing is correct, but it seems to come right in the end.
> (Julie)

However, another of the eight main themes was that these feelings of being overwhelmed were ameliorated by the students' perception of good student support being available.

The personal academic tutorial

> I like the course because I have a fantastic tutor ... he's very nice and he makes you feel good when you are coming to the course, which stops you worrying about all the new things. The tutor is very special and he really likes what he does here.
> (Michelle)

These feelings link to the many feelings of positive support from a personal tutor reported in the 2007 research.

I feel the tutorials are very positive and useful at a time when you're pretty lost in the first term. I was also pretty lost coming from another country ... the tutor helped me integrate into the course.
(Juan)

I feel very positive about my tutor. I feel that even though there are so many students here, my personal tutor knows everything about me. We talk about how I can improve myself, we talk about where I'm strong, the areas in which I'm not strong yet, where I should improve myself, so it's very good.
(Phillippe)

The best support I get is from my tutor I feel it's wonderful as I get so much help and if I'm not strong on something I can find out how to get better. He helps me get organised and it's very good.
(Jack)

I feel it's fine, it's helpful and, yeah, it's really really good.
(Aldo)

Positive feelings about personal academic tutors were reported by 12 out of the 15 students but seemed especially strong for students coming to study from another country. However, support can have issues for some students. Much depends upon the personal tutor and the tutor-student relationship, illustrated by the fact that two students felt ambivalent towards tutorials.

I feel they are very useful if I go to them but I don't always bother to go.
(Susan)

I guess I feel the tutorials are helpful but I'm not sure how much my tutor knows me.
(Alex)

One student held hostile feelings to the tutorial:

I feel annoyed and stressed that I am not getting the individual help that my friends are getting from their tutors.
(Angela)

Following this up, it was discovered that this student had misunderstood how to contact her tutor and that help had been waiting for her all along, illustrating the need for all tutors to be proactive and follow tutorial policy to chase up any non-attendees. These student voices on their feelings about personal academic tutoring bear out the idea that 'Good advising may be the single most underestimated characteristic of a successful college experience' (Light, 2001, p. 81).

Study support

The importance of the student-tutor relationship in advising was also seen in feelings about study support.

> I feel just fine going to her. I feel very comfortable speaking to her. I can speak to her about anything else apart from course work as well.
> (Sally)

> I feel really good about tutorials and study support as they give advice and advice is good as it takes away a lot of the doubts you know. They don't tell you what to do but show you where to go or how to do it yourself and so it's good, it's good.
> (Pedro)

Pleasure from contact with staff

Another feeling spoken about in the 2006 research was pleasure. The students stressed how enjoyable the courses were, with good information and good staff.

> I enjoy the course. The staff are great. I enjoy coming to college every day and learning new stuff.
> (Miguel)

The importance of the staff was also emphasised in 2007.

> My tutor knows me personally and to get some kind of relationship is very good.
> (Phillippe)

In the 2006 research, students were asked what was the best experience in term one. Respondents reported a number of aspects, one of which was 'all the support to help integrate into the course and college', illustrating the importance of student support systems and the positive feelings towards them.

> Well, we were offered quite a lot of support which I found fantastic. I was worried to start with, as I am a mature student, but I found an incredible response from everyone.
> (Soraya)

In the 2007 research, all the students who had used study support held very positive feelings about it and would recommend it to a friend. Students who had not used this support stated they had no feelings about it.

> It's really good because sometimes you can read the brief and kind of understand it in a different way and then when you hand it in you have done something completely different to what the teachers expect. Study support helps you understand the brief so it's really fantastic.
> (Liz)

> I feel very positive about study support. It is lively, interesting, very helpful.
> (Diane)

> I feel it's really good, it's really helpful because it's good to have in the university a support centre for such help.
> (Aldo)

> I feel it's very useful. It's exciting as it's a great opportunity to improve my work.
> (Angela)

The contribution of mentoring to emotional integration

Topping (1996, quoted in Falchicov, 2001) defines mentoring as 'a supportive relationship between the student and another person of greater ability or experience'.

LCC has had some small-scale mentoring schemes on honours courses for several years and found them to be beneficial. Mentoring helps students settle into the course and college culture, while enabling them to fulfil their academic potential, with consequent good results for retention. With widening participation on institutional agendas, mentoring schemes provide an additional tool in the armoury of support for 'at risk' students.

In the 2006 research, the students were asked if they had ever heard of student mentoring schemes. Most students had, but none had participated in one. Before taking part in this aspect of the interviews, the students were given a brief description of the role of a mentor and were then asked what qualities were needed to be a good mentor. The following factors emerged:

- Good knowledge of the course and college.
- Being approachable.
- Good listening skills.
- Being motivating.
- Patience.
- Honesty and trustworthiness.
- Being hardworking.
- Helpfulness.
- Friendliness.
- Having time for the student being mentored as a person.
- Being encouraging.
- Intelligence.

The above list includes several qualities involving feelings and personal contact.

> I think that if I had some problems and maybe had some doubts in my own ability, maybe the mentor would say, 'look don't worry about that because I had the same problem but I've overcome it' ... and I think that it can be quite positive to think that other people have had the same problems and they've managed to overcome them.
> (Soraya)

The 2007 research also showed students who have experience of student mentoring find it very positive.

> It is great. The guy is so helpful, so useful, chatting, helping with my film course, structuring, giving me a hand, guiding me when I had a few doubts. He is really, really good.
> (Pedro)

> I feel he is very good. He's got more experience on films and doing cinematography and he makes me feel good. He removes my doubts about myself.
> (Colin)

> I feel quite fine about it. I know if there is anything that I want to enquire about, I can go to him.
> (Sally)

The contribution of student services to emotional integration

Most students expressed no feelings towards student services and several said they had no idea what they did. However, any students who had used them expressed very positive feelings towards them and would recommend them to others. Once the service had been explained to them, all the others felt it was very positive and stated that they would probably use it.

> I feel they are very helpful and that. They're nice and friendly and they have good ideas.
> (Colin)

> I feel they are really helpful and it's great support ... they help you with your doubts or questions so it's great, it's great. And they are really nice people.
> (Pedro)

One student, a mature student from Europe, felt students could do more to help themselves. He felt they should read all the material given in induction and go to the services.

> ... because I'm a guy that likes to use the resources that are around me so as soon as you got the information pack and everything, you know they explain you where to go, what to do, so you just go there you know.
> (Pedro)

> I have a friend of mine here who has loan problems. I said a hundred times to go to student services, they are so helpful. But he didn't go yet so, I mean, people must want to use the resources you know.
> (Pedro)

Pleasure and anxiety

Outley and Duncan's research (1992) on students of psychology found their most frequent emotions were happiness, fear, anger and sadness. From this list, only feelings of happiness were mentioned by the respondents in both pieces of research, for example when they were reporting feelings of enjoyment and pleasure on the course. However, some students did talk of 'anxiety' and 'worry', feelings less strong than fear.

> I was anxious before I went to study support, but now I'm really glad that I went along.
> (Sally)

> When I came for the interview, the building was full of end-of-year shows and it was quite an inspiration. There was some beautiful work on display and it's always had a really high reputation. So when I was accepted on to the course, I was really pleased that I would be doing work like that.
> (Julie)

Conclusion

Students need to feel that they are being taught by enthusiastic, knowledgeable and caring staff. The student voice tells us that they see this as a key factor in their success. Management should choose with care the staff teaching and managing first-year students. This is not without its own problems. Within today's higher education environment in the UK, research continues to have more status than teaching. Within teaching, any student nurturing activity can be perceived to hold even lower status. Morley (1998) points out that the 'emotional labour' of being caring and offering support is gendered as it often falls to female staff. This needs to be addressed in management and training policies.

The student voice shows us the importance of personal contact for emotional integration. However, increasing numbers of students and declining resources mean this is one thing students are getting less and less. Integration is one of the keys to retention and achievement so practitioners must find ways to keep personal contact within the current climate.

> It is becoming clear that relationships are at the heart of the issue of the students' experience of university.
> (Hixenbaugh et al., 2006, p. 55)

Mentoring, academic tutorials and study support are some ways of keeping the personal contact and building the relationships so we must ensure these support systems stay in place and grow rather than decline. We also need to explore other forms of providing this important personal contact. Taylor and Bedford (2004) suggest that, within retention discussions, academic staff tend to focus on student-based factors rather than issues of teaching and learning methodology and the curriculum. This should be pursued.

Peter Hill (2005, p. 93) refers to Joad's (1945) concept of the 'commuter university'. In London, 'Students have to travel relatively long distances to attend: because of this, they are not immersed in an educational or intellectual culture.' Personal contact via student support systems to enable emotional integration would help offset this.

University staff working within these student support systems recognise: 'that even the imparting of knowledge and social skills is highly dependent on the nature of the relationship between student and teacher, the individual and his fellow students, and the student and the institution as a whole' (Salzberger-Wittenberg et al., 1983, p. xi).

These two pieces of research listen to the student voice to elaborate on our knowledge of the nature of the relationship between student and tutor, especially the unspoken elements. The research shows the importance of student feelings in effective engagement with learning and, especially, with student support systems in term one. We can act on this voice to 'encourage the institution to organise their support activities around the needs of the students' (HEFCE, 2003/15, p. 17).

References

Austerlitz, N. & Aravot, I. (2007), 'Emotions of design students: a new perspective for the design studio', in Salama, A. & Wilkinson, N. (eds.) *Design Studio Pedagogy: Horizons for the Future*, pp. 233–246 (UK: Urban International Press)

Falchicov, N. (2001), *Learning Together: Peer Tutoring in Higher Education* (London: RoutledgeFalmer)

Freire, P. (1996), *Pedagogy of the Oppressed* (London: Penguin)

Hampton, D. & Blythman, M. (2006), 'Recovering the student voice: retention and achievement on foundation degrees', in Beaney, P. (ed.) *Researching Foundation Degrees: Linking Research and Practice* (Lichfield: Foundation Degree Forward Publications)

HEFCE (2003), *Supporting HE in FE Colleges: A Guide for Tutors and Lecturers*, April 2003/15, p. 17

Hill, P. (2006), 'Platoons to encourage social cohesion amongst a large and diverse undergraduate population', in Thomas, L. & Hixenbaugh, P. *Personal Tutoring in Higher Education* (Stoke-on-Trent: Trentham Books)

Hixenbaugh, P., Pearson, C. & Williams, D. (2006), 'Student perspectives on personal tutoring: what do students want?', in Thomas, L. & Hixenbaugh, P. *Personal Tutoring in Higher Education* (Stoke-on-Trent: Trentham Books)

Joad, C.E.M. (1945), *About Education* (London: Faber and Faber)

Light, R.J. (2001), *Making the Most of College: Students Speak Their Minds* (Cambridge, MA: Harvard University Press)

Morley, L. (1998), 'All you need is love: feminist pedagogy for empowerment and emotional labour in the academy', *International Journal of Inclusive Education*, **2** (1), pp 15–27

Noel, L. & Levitz, R. (1999), presentation given at the University of Missouri, Kansas City

Outley, K.T. & Duncan, E. (1992), 'Incidents of emotions in daily life', in Strongman, K.T. (ed.) *International Review of Studies on Emotion* (Chichester: Wiley)

Salzberger-Wittenberg, I. Williams, G. & Osbourne, E. (1983) *The Emotional Experience of Learning and Teaching*, p. xi (London: Routledge and Kegan Paul)

Taylor, J.A. & Bedford, T.(2004), 'Staff perceptions of factors related to non-completion in higher education', *Studies in Higher Education*, **29** (3), pp. 375–394

Taylor, S. & Littleton, K. (2007), 'Postgraduate study as validation or threshold? A discussion of a qualitative research project with current and recent art and design postgraduates', UAL Pedagogic Research Group seminar, 15 November

Yorke, M. & Thomas, L. (2003), 'Improving the retention of students from lower socio-economic groups', *Journal of Higher Education Policy and Management*, **25** (1)

Margo Blythman

This article raises several issues worthy of further exploration. First, it reminds us of the relationship between the affective domain and student retention and achievement. UK higher education came rather late to retention issues in comparison to other UK education sectors and to the US. UK further education was exploring retention in the 1990s (Martinez, 1997; Martinez & Munday, 1998) and American higher education, a mass system at a much earlier stage, identified early on the close relationship between retention and students' social and emotional integration into the university (Nora, 1987; Tinto, 1987). When UK higher education began to explore student retention (Yorke & Longden, 2004; Yorke & Thomas, 2003), there was less focus on the role of personal emotion in enabling the student to connect with the institution. More recently, Crosling et al. (2008) recognised the twin roles of engaging teaching and curriculum and the development of social relationships, but there is still considerable room for exploration of the emotional complexity underpinning such relationships. A clearer grasp of the affective domain might make a significant contribution to our understanding of student retention.

Second, this article also draws to our attention the potential of student peer mentoring. Mentoring as a model operates in the affective zone through human emotions such as happiness, confidence, sense of security and belonging, and building human relationships. This links closely with our understanding of reasons for student retention. Yet mentoring of this sort is relatively rare. Much study support activity in the UK has become rather instrumental. The focus is normally on academic writing, and support concentrates on helping students complete their assessed work, although some research (Devett et al 2006) into study support recognises that study support teachers see building confidence as central to their role. The underpinning academic literacies literature that is influential in study support does have a sophisticated understanding of the affective. It recognises difference and rejects ideas of the universal student. Multiple subjectivities and the tension there may be between different subjectivities are also recognised. The literature also foregrounds and explicates the underpinning power relations in any pedagogic relationship. However, this work tends to be limited to how this plays out through students' academic writing development (Clark & Ivanic, 1997; Lea & Street, 1998; Lillis, 2001). Increasingly, study support is also underpinned by ideas of cultural capital and social justice (Bourdieu, 1997; Margolis et al., 2001), but the focus is on the social and political rather than the emotional. Perhaps it is time for study support and, equally, personal tutoring to recognise more fully the role of underpinning emotions in student success in any arena.

References

Bourdieu, P. (1997), 'The forms of capital', in Halsey, A.H., Lauder, H., Brown, P. & Stuart Wells, A. (eds.) *Education: Culture, Economy and Society* (Oxford: Oxford University Press)

Clark, R. & Ivanic, R. (1997), *The Politics of Writing* (London: Routledge)

Crosling, G., Thomas, L. & Heagney, M. (eds.) (2008), *Improving Student Retention in Higher Education: The Role of Teaching and Learning* (Oxford: Routledge)

Devet, Bonnie, Orr, Susan, Blythman, Margo, & Bishop, Celia. (2006). Peering across the pond: The role of students in developing other students' writing in the US and UK. In Lisa Ganobcsik-Williams (Ed.), *Teaching academic writing in UK higher education* (pp. 196-211). Houndmills: Palgrave Macmillan.

Lea, M. & Street, B. (1998), 'Student writing in higher education: an academic literacies approach', *Studies in Higher Education*, 23 (2), pp. 157–172

Lillis, T. M. (2001), *Student Writing: Access, Regulation and Desire* (London: Routledge)

Margolis, E., Soldatenko, M., Acker, S. & Gair, M. (2001), 'Peekaboo', in Margolis, E. (ed.) *The Hidden Curriculum in Higher Education* (London: Routledge)

Martinez, P. (1997), *Improving Student Retention: A Guide to Successful Strategies* (Blagdon: FEDA)

Martinez, P. & Munday, F. (1998), *9000 Voices: Student Persistence and Drop-Out in Further Education* (Blagdon: FEDA)

Nora, A. (1987), 'Determinants of retention among Chicano students: a structural model', *Research in Higher Education,* 26 (1)

Tinto, V. (1987), *Leaving College* (Chicago: University of Chicago Press)

Yorke, M. & Longden, B. (2004), Retention and Student Success in Higher Education (Maidenhead: SRHE/Open University Press)

Yorke, M. & Thomas, L. (2003), 'Improving the retention of students from lower socio-economic groups', Journal of Higher Education Policy and Management, 25 (1), pp. 63–74

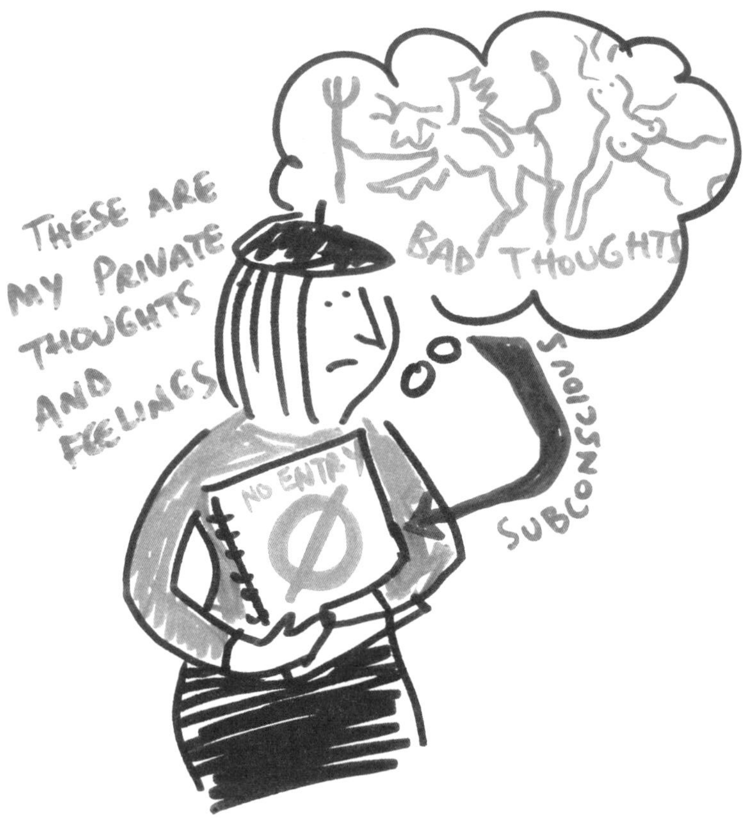

Private thoughts   Francesca Cassavetti

Reproduced by permission of the artist

12

Reflections on emotional journeys: a new perspective for reading fashion students' PPD statements

Authors: Alison James and Noam Austerlitz

Commentary: Linda Ball

Keywords

reflection,
emotional journeys,
personal constructs theory,
personal and professional development

Alison James and Noam Austerlitz

Introduction

This paper introduces work in progress on the presence of the emotions in reflective PPD (personal and professional development) statements at the London College of Fashion. The premise underlying our view of PPD activity is that by involving students in exploring how they represent themselves and their world – and the reliability of their perceptions – their reflective practices can be deepened.

This research is in its preliminary stages; at present defining a perspective on the emotions expressed in PPD and a way of analysing and reading statements that may be useful to researchers, tutors, educators and students. While our data to date has not been sufficiently analysed to draw categoric inferences, we are already able to suggest that PPD reflective statements offer narratives of personal improvement and individual emotional journeys. Using our case study from the London College of Fashion we will show how our emerging method of reading reveals a very different aspect of learning to the skills and employability orientation of other modes of analysis. Furthermore, it invites consideration as to the way PPD and critical reflection in a fashion context may differ from other subjects, in the intensity of personal creative investment and subjectivity.

The creative context for personal and professional development (PPD)

In recent years, PPD[1] has become a mandatory and explicit part of degree education in the UK, to help students develop critical self-awareness, understand how they learn and plan for their futures. Opinion is divided in the tertiary sector as to what PPD covers, which has implications for how students will express themselves in their reflective statements. Conceptions vary from a narrower model, which emphasises PPD as primarily about getting jobs, to a broader idea that is about personal identity and life view as well as skills.

Essential to PPD activities is the ability to reflect, often expressed in written logs, evaluations or statements. It is argued that critically reflecting, from concept through process to final production, is an inescapable part of designing, innovating and making. Through PPD, students can further elaborate these reflective practices – by looking inwardly at their personal goals, values and drivers, and outwardly at their thoughts about their industry and life trajectory.

PPD attracts a spectrum of believers and critics; the latter are often unconvinced that PPD is anything more than form filling to tick educational boxes. Our position is that, to be meaningful, PPD must consider the 'whole person' in a process of reflection and not simply be a tool for auditing skills. An integral part of this is understanding that the emotions add a significant dimension to students' learning experiences. Consequently we recommend ensuring opportunities to discuss how emotions affect the decisions learners make, the interpretations they place on their own capabilities and their self-worth as students and future practitioners. These activities go beyond an estimation of what went well or badly and why. In addition, it is clear from previous studies (e.g. James, 2007, Moon, 2005) that fundamental to the success of PPD is a shared understanding among students and tutors as to what critical reflection is, and how to do it effectively. Equally clear is that many universities do not invest time in enabling this kind of effectiveness through the teaching of explicit strategies. This lack is something that our work can address.

Conceptual frameworks for interpreting emotional data in students' PPD statements

In order to understand what the deeper meanings within PPD statements might be, we propose two theoretical standpoints, one emotional and one relating to personal construct theory (PCT). Both standpoints provide the basis for our method of critically reading PPD statements, as subsequently explained.

The emotions are currently well recognised as an inherent part of human everyday life and as a major factor in the socialising of individuals. This paper has neither the intention nor the scope to enter into the huge current debate on the philosophy of what is an emotion; however it will frame certain basic parameters for inquiry that seem to be particularly relevant for this discussion. Previous research into the role of the emotions in design students' learning (architectural design studio courses in particular) (Austerlitz, Aravot & Ben-Ze'ev, 2002;

Austerlitz & Aravot, 2007) adopted Ben-Ze'ev's (2000) approach, which stresses that emotions respond spontaneously to actual or potential changes in personal well-being and that emotions have a central role in giving meaning to one's experiences. These studies found that applying a content analysis methodology identifies dominant emotions (or a sequence of emotions) in student narratives of their studio learning experience.

Such an approach sees the emotions as a cognitive operational mode that involves the whole of the human being and can be applied to subjectively appraise information and generate action readiness towards dealing with information (Frijda, 1986). Furthermore, since emotions are related to the most precious human concerns and are required to operate within split seconds, they must therefore obey some kind of prestructured schemes (Oatley, 1982). These schemes obey a 'logical' pattern yet their rationality is different from intellectual rationality (De Sosa, 1990). One of these scheme's operations is to appraise a current personal situation according to previous standards, expectations and goals (Ortony et al., 1988). When a situation is appraised as fulfilling or exceeding expectations a positive emotional reaction will be elicited and in other cases one will probably experience a negative emotion. This pattern can be repeatedly detected in reflective PPD statements in relation to grading and assessment.

With this logic in mind, it is asserted that student emotions are not untrustworthy, inexplicable behaviours, but a set of reactions that can be subsequently analysed and interpreted. It is clear from a preliminary examination of PPD statements that many students articulate a narrative of development that is emotionally laden. PPD statements contain emotional expressions that often mix emotional memories together with later intellectual interpretations. Such emotional expressions may be explicit or implicit, with emotions suggested by implication or even conveying multiple contradictory emotions. Investigating the emotional composition of these statements reveals that very few PPD statements are free from emotions, as even numbness, indifference or neutrality may be said to be affective states.

Following Ben Ze'ev (2000), Austerlitz et al. (2002) have provided a model to establish the flow of emotions within a record of learning that can be adapted to analyse PPD statements. It refers to the:

A dominant emotion(s) reported;
B cause of the emotion (previous expectations, goals, behaviour of others, issues of identity etc.);

C object/focus of concern of the emotional response;
D reported emotional intensity;
E way the emotional response evolved;
F effects on aspects of learning.

These stages are not necessarily chronological and are illustrated in the following extract from a Year 1 Beauty Therapy student, marked up by their letter:

> I wrote in my journal the hardest part is removing the makeup (B). I get stressed out (A, D) trying to do it which therefore ruins my flow (F). I realised that the only way to overcome my problem was to not panic (C) and keep practising (F) until the movement becomes natural. I made it easier for myself (E) by breaking each step down into smaller steps, which as a result stuck in my memory better (F). As I began to remember the steps and the movements my confidence grew immensely (F).

This example shows how the application of an emotional framework to the reading of a complex episode can reveal two major aspects of learning (in addition to multiple effects on learning indicated by the letter F). The action taken by the learner was in response to the dominant emotion (panic/fears) elicited by a practical issue; however emphasis is often given to the resolution of the latter, rather than the former. It can be argued that it was the intensity of the specific emotion/quality (obstinacy leading to persistence) that spurred the individual to overcome the problem, rather than indifference or defeatism. The cause of the emotion will also have its roots in the ways the student has lived through and subsequently represented an event to himself/herself, through the memory of how it felt. Such memories infiltrate the way a student reviews his/her personal and professional identity, thus we suggest that personal construct theory (PCT) can be useful in understanding the review process underpinning a student's PPD statement.

Student statements as evidence of students' personal construct process

PCT posits that humans do not process their knowledge of their world through their experiences, but rather through their representations of these. Originally elaborated by the American psychologist George Kelly in 1955, PCT adopts a scientific approach in enabling individuals to express their view of their world through their own eyes, and not through the interpretation of a third party. This mirrors a change in assessment ethos concerning PPD from a model where tutors set the parameters for PPD to one in which the student takes responsibility for identifying what has been meaningful PPD and why. In PCT and PPD, responsibility for interpreting events and their consequences lies with the student, rather than the expert outsider (e.g. counsellor or tutor).

By twinning PCT and PPD, we offer a shift in what is being prioritised in a reflective statement – not just the things that someone says they can do, but rather the climate in which they became able to do them and consequences for self-revelation.

Eleven corollary statements (listed subsequently) explain the different dimensions of personal constructs and are organised around a fundamental postulate which argues that 'a person's processes are psychologically channelised by the ways in which he anticipates events' (Kelly, 1992, p. 3). Plank and Greene (1996, p. 29) describe PCT as elaborating 'that process of anticipation, perception, comparing the anticipation to reality and feedback', which in fact offers a remarkable parallel to the process of PPD.

Anticipation is part of a student attempting to define or predict future outcomes, such as the creation of an accessory or garment, conclusion of a project or competition success. For example a student on the foundation degree in buying and merchandising expressed anticipation and comparison with reality as follows:

My concerns were with the primary research. I was worried that there would be a lack of support. For my findings, I was surprised at the encouraging response from consumers but I was disappointed with the negative response from retailers.

Expectation of how things will be, based on memories of prior occurrences and how they felt, is a dimension within each corollary and in each emotional experience. It informs the ways representations of events are constructed, differ from another's version and are organised into personal hierarchies (construction, individuality, organisation corollaries). For example, PPD statements repeatedly reveal one of the most important learning experiences – that of dealing with dilemmas (often emotionally implicated) or challenges. Their personal constructions will both pre-empt and reveal how a student might respond, e.g. in terms of fearfulness of what is to come. Individuals will construct these responses in ways that best allow them to develop their view of the world, while inevitably having limitations on how they can perceive these events (choice and range corollaries):

> At the beginning I felt shy and slightly overwhelmed ... I knew I would have to overcome this as making pitches and addressing large numbers of people would be an everyday occurrence ...

The ways that students represent their reality will also be in relation to something else, in terms of contrast or opposing concepts (dichotomy corollary). The experience corollary also teaches about the validity of each construct – whether or not a prediction made about a response or experience has in fact turned out as expected. While individuals naturally and unconsciously revise their constructions with each new experience, capturing these on paper can make root causes of, and patterns in, situations explicit. Poor attendance caused one student to write 'Regret summarises my feelings', while others regularly record surprise in finding that an activity they expected to be superfluous had in fact been beneficial. The modulation and fragmentation corollaries allow for the individual to accept or reject new possibilities in their constructions while also juggling with competing or potentially incompatible constructions:

> I have been set in my ways, with immoveable opinions for years, and have grown to see that at such a young age, such stubbornness and a narrow-minded outlook is completely opposed to the industry I have chosen to work in.

In addition, inconsistent or contradictory emotions in certain constructs are not necessarily mutually exclusive. For example, a learner may feel passion for a subject, frustration at his/her progress, dread at the prospect of not achieving a desired outcome and the thrill of success in completing the task. A desire for completion may compete with resentment and boredom in having to see the mechanics of the process through, and so on. Finally, the commonality and sociality corollaries allow the individual to demonstrate how his/her representative processes may resemble those of another or facilitate empathy: 'I have become a lot more tolerant of others'.

An understanding of the basic principles of PCT can be helpful in two ways; as part of an introduction to PPD, which enables the learner to understand that their critical reflections will be constituted by their own personal and cultural history, and, for the reader of the statements, in shedding light on how the world seems to an individual student, rather than how the world 'is' in the eyes of another.

The case study at LCF

Although the suggested perspective could be employed in any higher education course, the authors have a particular interest in personal and professional development for students in the areas of design and related creative practices. In addition to technical competency and ways of thinking that result in workable and innovative solutions, fashion students' conceptions of self and work are often inextricably linked.

This interest has led to an examination of PPD statements produced by students from the London College of Fashion, on courses covering anything from the design and production of shoes, accessories and garments, cosmetic formulation, specialist make up, costume and image production of all kinds to fashion business management. Many modes of study are not traditionally academic, with a concentration on essays and examinations, but centre on studio and practical work, with outcomes exhibited through diverse media and on the catwalk, not just in written assessments. With work and industry related expertise also a priority, PPD can involve a range of areas. This context is important for the observations that are starting to emerge from our initial readings of 225 statements collected in 2006–07 and autumn term 2007–08. These statements came from undergraduate courses covering fashion journalism, cosmetic science, product design and development, fashion business management and beauty therapy and health studies. A further five learning journals from an access course were also included. Differentiating statements in terms of patterns of response within subject fields, levels of study and other factors was not included at this stage in the research. It was clear, however, that production of statements was affected by the guidance received from tutors and their interpretations of what constituted critical reflection. This sample will be continually added to, and a system of coding elaborated for a future in-depth analysis of data.

Overwhelmingly, data has been taken from the PPD reflective statements, with some examples from a small number of learning journals. The former are summative statements handed in at the end of each unit (often at the end of a term), read by tutors as part of assessing attainment of the learning outcomes as demonstrated by the students. These reflections are marked holistically, in company with the other learning outcomes on a unit, and do not receive specific marks; however, tutors do offer feedback on the quality of the reflection engaged in. They are retrospective summaries of what students feel have been their growth and development at that point in time, in line with Schön's concept of reflection on action. Learning journals obviously differ in that they are composed along the way, and have more in common with both this view and Schön's accompanying idea of reflection in action.

Two factors can affect the kind of reflection that students engage in. The first is whether or not time has been taken to fully brief them on the fullest possibilities of PPD discovery as outlined in this paper. Interactive workshops can be provided to course teams and their students on this, and a new compulsory first year unit, Introduction to Undergraduate Study, also enables understanding of PPD. Such support is critical, as earlier research (James, 2007) makes clear that strategies employed to encourage critical reflection are extremely diverse; in many cases there is assumption of a common understanding of what it is, as well as tacit modeling of reflection rather than explicit debate or trialling of techniques. This is partly because, as many tutor practitioners argue, creating and designing are by definition reflective processes. Such an argument, however, does not resolve some of the variation and ambiguity that colour interpretations of reflection. The second factor is the timing of the production of these statements – their primarily summative character inevitably impacts on the kind of reflection produced, although tutors do advise that where learning journals are also in use, these provide excellent raw data for the final, shorter statement. The fact that statements are submitted with assignments for tutor scrutiny may also explain the relatively positive tone that the vast majority have; even where fears or difficulties are referred to, overwhelmingly statements end on an optimistic note that is future facing. There is, inevitably, more material in a learning journal (which describes an emotional journey in detail) than in a PPD statement, but the two documents can be mutually supportive.

A particular mode of reading has been applied to students' reflective PPD statements, recognising that the statement will have been composed through the filter of the student's own personal constructs. This reading prioritises identification of emotional content, using the A–F framework already described as a set of reference points, rather than 'factual data', telling the reader how an individual's IT skills have improved or his/her practical capabilities been enhanced. Phrases indicating emotion were highlighted and extracts illustrating the emotional climate extrapolated from texts. Statements were subsequently considered against the categories of the A–F emotional framework and PCT corollaries; read in this context they provided multiple instances of emotional narratives and evidence that these had an ultimate effect on learning outcomes and reflections on development.

Even at this early stage, emotional themes were detected in students' commentaries, relating to various foci of concerns such as:

- acquiring skills;
- interactions with others (tutors and peers);
- pace of teaching and learning;
- self-improvement as learners;

- self-mastery and gaining emotional control;
- growth in capability and independence;
- personal maturing and coping with challenges;
- understanding of the profession.

Recurrent in students' narratives is the emotional roller coaster, with dominant emotions including stress rising from difficulty in coping with a new way of life and learning, passion for creating, pride of achievements, pleasure in learning, frustration at plans thwarted, self-doubt and fear: 'Nervous, anxious, scared, I can see my future but it will be hard work getting there'. Numerous comments on the prospect of a major piece of writing illustrate this sense of trepidation. Standards, expectations and anticipations were also common and dominant factors could be detected which linked emotional theory and PCT in determining both the kind of elicited emotion and its intensity: 'The thought of having to complete the dissertation was incredibly overwhelming'. Of critical importance to many students is the way in which their confidence has increased (or not) in the wake of an experience:

> I was so excited that I really did finish an English essay and it was truly my idea ... I was proud of myself and felt confident.

In addition to fearfulness, the new, different or unexpected often provoked surprise, conflict or confusion. These unanticipated responses to expectations often resulted in a revised view of things, which is in line with the nature of the experience corollary:

> Working in a team was far harder than I had initially foreseen. The lack of control scared me and the constant worry that I may let others down certainly played on my mind ...

Good fortune brought by the unexpected was also noted by a student who wrote of a new addiction to photography, which she never could have imagined developing before going to the Lee Miller exhibition. Expectations are often also overturned:

> When I saw the title of this unit on the timetable I thought that it may be a lesson that would not be important to my learning this term. I thought that it would be the lesson that nobody went to. I was very mistaken.
>
> Brain freeze. What have I got myself into?

A sense of loss or disquiet can often be hidden within student behaviours and invisible to tutors, as described by Ariel Peng-Chun Koo:

> He is really sad that no tutors really understand his work well, which has an impact on his understanding of their feedback. He feels too challenged and pushed during crits and one-to-one tutorials. He keeps nodding without really learning … although he is listening, he knows he does not understand because his emotions are garbled. This makes him feel guilty which in turn puts even more emotional stress on him.
> (*The Written Stuff*, 2007, pp. 50–51)

Using an approach that focuses on emotional references in PPD statements helps to plot some of these disjunctures in communication and the weight of the internal struggle the learner – here an international student – is engaged in. Such statements also provide evidence that they are the place where students become aware of things about themselves (extract 1 below) as opposed to purely summarising things they can do (extract 2):

> Delivering the presentation was one of my proudest moments as public speaking is something that fills me with great apprehension ... I came off well as my nerves were visible to no one but me. I now know that no matter how difficult something may be, practice, practice and more practice will win the day! (extract 1)

> While working on this project I have learnt numerous things. I am now more confident with my IT skills ... I have gained a deeper understanding of instrumental and sensory evaluation techniques. (extract 2)

Both kinds of realisation have value, however, the first extract demonstrates an evolving self-awareness that has a specific significance. This final example contains in a single paragraph the student's developmental cycle, expectations, emotions and outcomes:

> I was incredibly nervous about doing my end of term presentation towards my image project. This was my first presentation I had ever done and being in front of other people was going to be quite daunting. Despite this I went up and did my presentation 3rd and I managed to get everything that I wanted to say out. I had my notes on cards and I felt calmer after id [sic] started. I was still anxious about getting my feedback the next week however, when I did receive it was so pleased that I accomplished some fantastic feedback and a proud grade. I overcame this fear and

> it has given me more confidence for any other public speaking which I may need to [do] in the future.

PPD statements are often compiled retrospectively, in a time of review; we suggest however, that asking students to record their expectations from the outset, to compare with their actual experience and emotions along the way, amplifies understanding of progress.

Conclusions and potential benefits

We are developing a method of reading PPD statements that prioritises the identification of emotion within the narrative, a framework for understanding the root and context for such emotions, and what they have led to. It can be used by tutors, students and their peers to bring a different perspective to PPD reviews. These reviews depend on students defining the terms of their growth and development. Of fundamental importance to this is encouraging students to understand what critical reflection is and how to do it, emphasising that PPD is more than form filling. It is an opportunity for individuals to reflect on their personal educational progress including their emotional development. Being able to further analyse that reflection afterwards is an important stage in identifying the critical 'eureka' moments of all sizes and intensities that demarcate learning. Introducing students to the basic principles of PCT as a tool within an armoury of critical and reflective practices can offer a useful mode of self-analysis. Often associated with repertory grid techniques, which can be unwieldy to implement, PCT can be presented in simpler activities that will mean more to students than the terminology of science or philosophy.

The many different things that impact on a period of learning and living are easily forgotten and their significance missed if not noted down. A genuine, honest and thoughtful statement that a student is happy to share is also a way of keeping communication going between the learner and his/her peers/mentors. Retrospective plotting of the emotional trajectories that students have followed during learning can enable staff and students alike to understand the triggers for crises or successes, as well as the motivating factors and variables that affect learning. Similarly, identifying with students their expectations and standards at the outset of a learning experience and revisiting these will offer insight into the emotional journey undertaken. Seeing the emotions that accompany different events or interactions may also be a part solution to identifying ways of dealing with such situations in the future, very much in line with the anticipatory premise of PCT. Positively identifying the specific value that this activity can bring may also serve to strengthen the appreciation of PPD within the institution and staff/student mindset, where it is not always universally accepted or understood. Collecting such statements or compiling them within the format of a log or diary can also create a unique store of personal knowledge that the individual can draw on for all kinds of future uses or considerations.

From a tutor point of view, an insight into the student's emotional journey may also provide invaluable data on the ways in which tutors and the learning experiences they orchestrate can impact on student learning. It is already accepted that what students learn and what a tutor intended to teach them do not always match up; this analysis may serve as a means of closing the gap (if so desired). The reflective statement is both a dialogue with the self and also a tool to engender a supportive conversation with staff. We suggest that applying emotional/PCT analyses of PPD statements could be a means by which staff can realise that students often understand where they are and why better than they are given credit for. Analysing student anticipation of events and the emotional journey they experience gives a whole new understanding to the stories that students are telling.

Note

Across UK universities PPD is diversely referred to, either as synonymous with personal development planning (PDP), or as a process within which PDP plays a part. We recognise that, in many cases, PDP is seen as the process relating specifically to critical self-reflection, however there is not always a clear-cut separation between this and some of the review processes relating to professional skills. Ideas of self-actualisation and personal identity are at the heart of PDP, and yet are inextricable, for many, from the act of making. Making, designing and creating in the creative arts are both central to the professional element of PPD and act as a referent to the self, which welds PDP and PPD together. With this in mind, as well as the inelegance of shifting between such similar acronyms, and the fact that at LCF PPD is taken to encompass PDP, the referent PPD is used in this paper for ease of reading. The authors further believe that it will be helpful in the future to achieve an understanding of both activities, which makes the use of one of these acronyms obsolete

References

Austerlitz, N., Aravot, I. & Ben-Ze'ev, A. (2002), 'Emotional phenomena and the student-instructor relationships', *Landscape and Urban Planning*, **60** pp. 105–115

Austerlitz, N. & Aravot, I. (2007), 'Emotions of architecture students: a new perspective for the design studio', in A. Salama and N. Wilkinson (eds) *Design Studio Pedagogy: Horizons for the Future, Gateshead*, (UK Urban International Press)

Austerlitz, N. & Aravot, I. (2007), 'Emotions of design students: a new perspective for the design studio', in Salama, A. & Wilkinson, N. (eds.), *Design Studio Pedagogy: Horizons for the Future* (UK: Urban International Press)

Bannister, D. & Fransella, F. (1989), 3rd edition, *Inquiring Man: The Psychology of Personal Constructs* (London: Routledge)

Bannister, D. & Mair, J.M.M. (1968), *The Evaluation of Personal Constructs* (London and New York: Academic Press)

Ben-Ze'ev, A. (2000), The Subtlety of Emotions (Cambridge, Mass.: MIT Press)

Butler, R. & Green, D. (1998), *The Child Within: The Exploration of Personal Construct Theory with Young People* (Oxford: Butterworth Heinemann)

De-Sosa, R. (1980), 'The rationality of emotions', in Rorty, A. *Explaining Emotions* (Berkeley: University of California Press)

Dewey, J. (1910), *How We Think* (New York: Dover Publications Inc.)

Frijda, N.H. (1986), *The Emotions* (New York: Cambridge University Press)

James, A. (2007), 'Reflection revisited: perceptions of reflective practice in fashion learning and teaching', *Art, Design and Communication in Higher Education*, **5** (3), pp. 179–196

Kelly, G. (1992), *The Psychology of Personal Constructs. Volume 2: Clinical Diagnosis and Psychotherapy* (Routledge, Taylor and Francis)

Moon, J. (2005), 'We seek it here ... a new perspective on the elusive activity of critical thinking: a theoretical and practical approach', *ESCalate Discussion Series*, available (accessed 11 February 2008) at: http://escalate.ac.uk/2041

Oatley, K. (1992), *Best Laid Schemes: The Psychology of Emotions* (Cambridge: Cambridge University Press)

Ortony, A., Clore, G.L. & Collins, A. (1988), *The Cognitive Structure of Emotions* (New York: Cambridge University Press(

Peng-Chung Kuo, A. (2007), in Lioy, A. (ed.) *The Written Stuff: An Anthology of Art and Design Students' Stories from a Writing Workshop, Area-D* (Cambridge University Press)

Plank, R.E. & Greene, J.N. (1996), 'Personal construct psychology and personal selling performance', *European Journal of Marketing*, **30** (7), pp. 25–48

This paper was first published in Art, Design and Communication for Higher Education, pp 209–219, Volume 6, number 3, June 2008. Reprinted by permission of Intellect Books, The Mill, Parnall Road, Bristol BS16 3JG, UK, © 2008

Linda Ball

The emotional dimension of any learning situation is rarely formally acknowledged, although we all experience it. My own emotional journey for writing this piece involved initial pleasure at being asked to contribute, the positive impact on my self-esteem at being invited and, as the deadline approached, considerable uncertainty: what exactly was I being asked to do? Anticipation involved some fear and anxiety – would I be able to understand the paper? Am I capable of writing an intelligent and worthy response? Will they like what I write? How will it fit into my workload? Now, as I write, I am enjoying the highs of juggling thought processes, ideas, concepts and my own learning experiences in response to what I have read, reflected on and reread. This triggers the cognitive processes - thinking about the many aspects of reflection – understanding it, how we do it ourselves, how we instruct or teach others to do it, how feelings enter into it, how we give it value, and its role in creative practice learning.

In creative subjects, creative practice itself is the pivotal component of experiential learning, through which learners develop and refine high-level intellectual skills and entrepreneurial attributes such as formulating ideas, testing concepts, learning from mistakes, applying analysis and decision-making. Reflection plays a critical part in this process and, at best, provides an opportunity for a more holistic expression of learning – valuing what has been 'learned' from the experience, rather than placing emphasis on 'product' outcomes or competencies.

For creative practitioners, the role of critical reflection is central to building confidence in expressing achievement and speaking positively about creative practice – 'what they can do.' Transfer of the creative process – applying creativity in other settings – what students are required to do when they graduate – does not automatically occur, unless reflection on the experience takes place, first in the academic context, preferably shared in critical reflection (staff – student – peer – employer – external professional), so that personal and creative learning can be articulated and related to future progression, new goals or ideas to be developed and explored.

Many factors come into play in relation to the role of reflection, and are raised here by the authors: i.e. how reflective learning is introduced to students by academics, the appropriateness of the reflective tool for the reflective task, the problems in assessing 'reflection' when creative practice and personal identity are so inextricably bound up with self, the authenticity of the narrative (if produced for assessment purposes), how the emotional journey is interpreted.

Boyatzis and Goleman (2005) offer a process for raising awareness and exploring the emotional dimension of learning, in which they provide an inventory of more than 60 statements to which students respond, on four dimensions: self awareness (personal development), self management (development of autonomy), social awareness and relationship management (working with others). James and Austerlitz go further with their innovative proposition in this paper, relating to raising student awareness of the simple principles of personal construct theory as a means of reflecting on and interpreting emotional learning and developing emotional resilience. As an advocate of 'letting students in on the theory', the rewards of trusting students as co-learners are many. Try debating with them a rationale for learning activities: Why are we doing this? What are we learning? (Modelling reflection in briefings by bringing in earlier cohorts is beneficial for all – reflecting, articulating, motivating and celebrating.)

And now, I experience profound relief that I am writing the final statement, although, looking back, it has not been a linear writing experience and, in the order of things, this is not the last paragraph I am writing. Nor is it a straightforward narrative. It has involved much cutting and pasting to order the sequence and flow to satisfy logical conventions, indicating for me the haphazardness and unpredictability of reflection. What happens? It is sparked off by feelings, thought processes, prompts and ideas that pop into the brain, often when one least expects. It's not something that can be done to order, and this is a thought to bear in mind when we seek to encourage ourselves and our students to reflect on how we feel about what we are learning, as well as on the progression of our learning.

References

Boyatzis, R.E. & Goleman, D. (2005), *The Emotional Competence Inventory: University Edition II* (London: Hay Group)

Author's Biographies

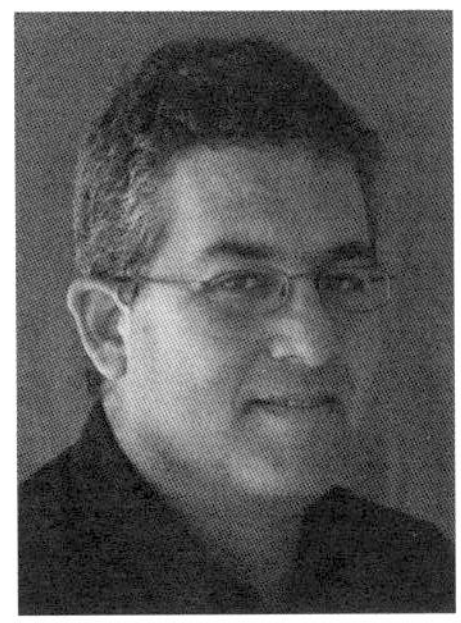

Dr Noam Austerlitz
n.austerlitz@gmail.com

Dr Noam Austerlitz holds a PhD degree from the faculty of architecture and town planning, Technion, IIT (Haifa, Israel). He graduated from the faculty of architecture, Bezalel Academy of Arts, Jerusalem, in 1996, and has been a practising architect since then. He taught design in the faculty of architecture and has 18 years of experience of teaching, in varied educational settings, including as a field guide in the Israeli nature society and on training courses for guides. For the last ten years he has also been teaching yoga. In his academic research, Noam is merging his interests in education, social interactions and design. Since 1999 he has been conducting studies into the emotional and social aspects of design education. Noam has been a research fellow at the CLIP CETL between 2006 -2008 and is currently a visiting professor at the University of the Arts London.

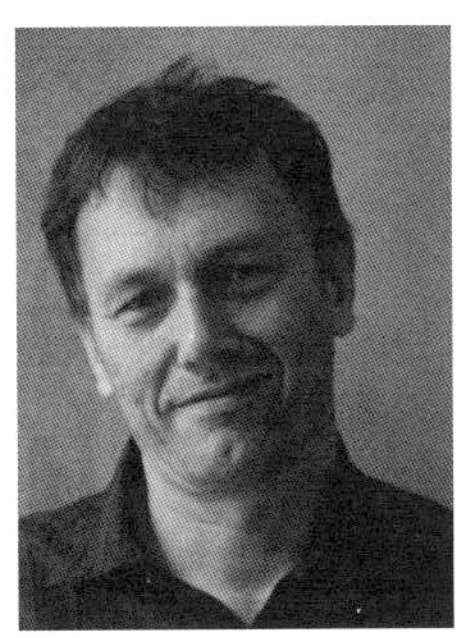

Ken Ewings
k.ewings@arts.ac.uk

Ken Ewings is Head of Counselling, Health Advice and Disability for University of the Arts London. He has worked in student support in higher education since 1993, managing services and counselling students in Queen Mary University, London, Sheffield University and, for the past three years, the University of the Arts London. Prior to that he worked for alcohol and drug services, training projects and in the supportive housing sector. He has been a professional counsellor since 1988, having trained at Westminster Pastoral Foundation in brief psychodynamic therapy and clinical supervision.

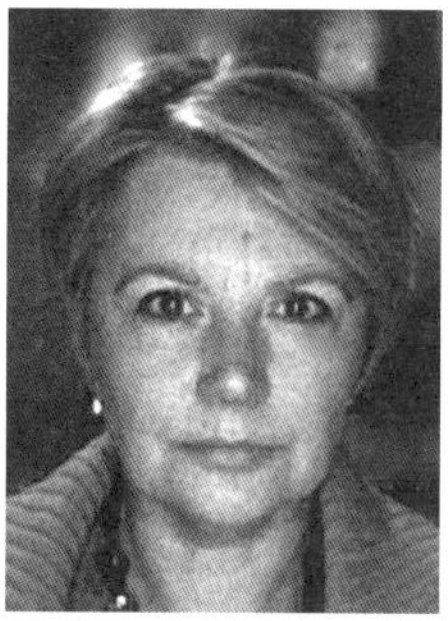

Dr Julia Gaimster
j.gaimster@fashion.arts.ac.uk

Dr Julia Gaimster EdD is the Head of eLearning at the London College of Fashion. Her background is in fashion design and she has 20 years' experience in the delivery of fashion education at all levels from FE to postgraduate. Her research interests are in the areas of pedagogy and eLearning. She has contributed to the development of a number of eLearning projects including Seeing Drawing, an interactive DVD, and the Textiles Online Resource Guide. She is currently developing an online visual research resource funded by the Art, Design and Media Subject Centre and the University of the Arts London. Her particular area of expertise is in the use of virtual learning environments to enhance the teaching and learning experience. Recently this has expanded to include the use of virtual worlds as educational spaces.

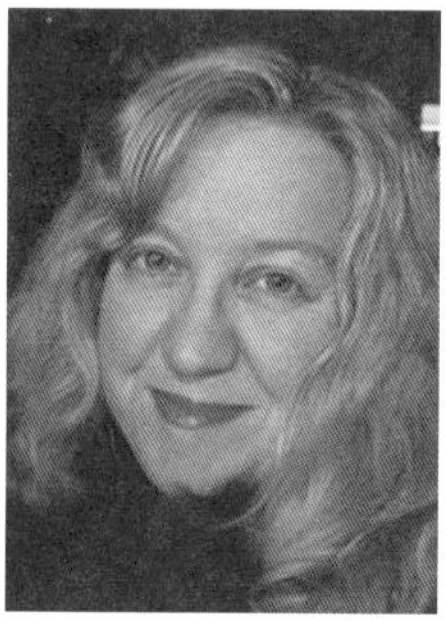

Cathy Greenhalgh
c.greenhalgh@lcc.arts.ac.uk

Cathy Greenhalgh originally trained at the National Film and Television School and worked as a cinematographer for years in the British film industry. She now directs films which incorporate choreography, documentary and animation elements, using a combination of media for film / gallery spaces. Her lastest film, Aftermath (2006) showed in many venues, gaining 1st prize at Strange Screen Festival in Greece. As an experienced writer, she is influenced by ethnographic work with feature film cinematographers undertaken over ten years, and has contributed to publications on cinematography and filmmaking practices, performance and narrative, creative collaboration and practice language, film aesthetics and cinematographic phenomena. She is author of Cinematography (Wallflower Press, 2010 forthcoming) and co-founder of UAL's Film and Phenomena Creative Laboratory, which promotes discussion and collaborative film works with scientists. Cathy is currently Head of Film and Television at the London College of Communication, University of the Arts London.

Daphne Hampton is an academic member of staff at LCC, University of the Arts London. Her role is split into two parts - Quality Assurance and Marketing Unit (QAM) and the School of Creative Enterprise, where she is the Tutorial Co-ordinator. Daphne is the Student Mentor Co-ordinator for the college and the LCC rep on the UAL Student Health Forum. She is also involved in staff development and training. She combines research into student mentoring with the practical experience of running student mentoring schemes over several years, and has acted as a consultant in this field. She has also acted as a consultant in the field of academic personal tutoring. Her research interests are both, the first year experience on foundation degrees as well as student mentoring and she has published in these areas. Her research project for 2007/8 aims to investigate the student voice and assessment on Foundation degrees.

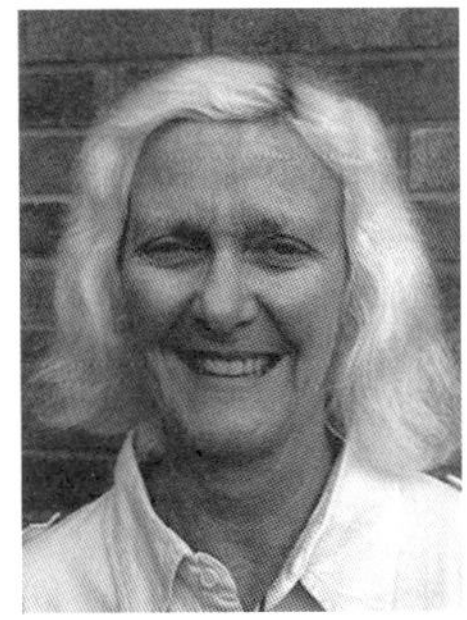

Daphne Hampton
d.hampton@lcc.arts.ac.uk

Katrine Hjelde is an artist, lecturer and research student. After graduating with an MA in Fine Art from The Slade in 1995, she has exhibited regularly in Great Britain and Europe. Her practice is largely site-specific, with architectural installations exploring the intersection between physical space and discursive sites. From 2000, her practice includes a collaboration with Norwegian architects b+r, and since 2007, she also works with the Future Reflections Research Group. Teaching part-time since 1997, Katrine is currently an Associate Lecturer at Chelsea College of Art and Design, where she also holds a CLIP CETL Studentship for doctoral research into the relationship between art practice and teaching practice. Her current research intersects practice and pedagogy, and includes collaborative research, conceptions of practice, and the mediated possibilities within site-specific practice. Katrine was born in Norway and currently lives and works in London.

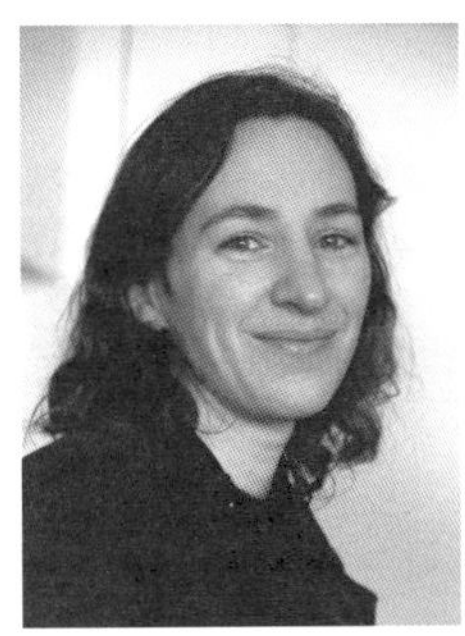

Katrine Hjelde
k.hjelde@chelsea.arts.ac.uk

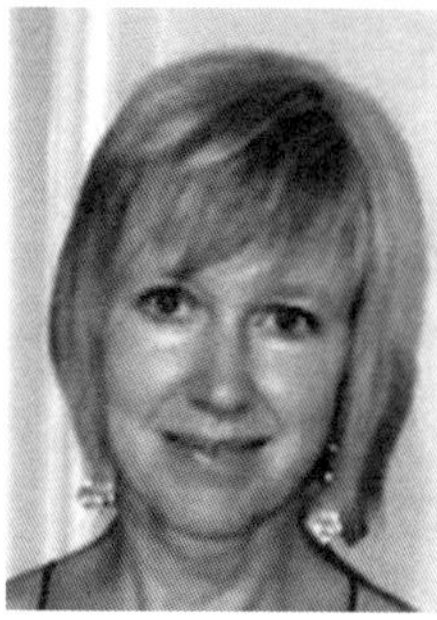

Dr Alison James
a.james@fashion.arts.ac.uk

Dr Alison James is Head of Learning and Teaching at the London College of Fashion and coordinator of the College Pedagogic Research Hub. Her primary research interests lie in theories of auto/biography, identity and narrative construction in creative arts education, critical reflection, personal development planning and the emotions in learning. Of particular interest in pedagogic terms is the way in which conceptions of identity and self-construction permeate learning experiences – formal and informal. This theoretical interest in the life of the individual also informed her PhD, which provided a biographical analysis of the life and work of the artist Dod Procter RA. A monograph on Procter was also published in September 2007.

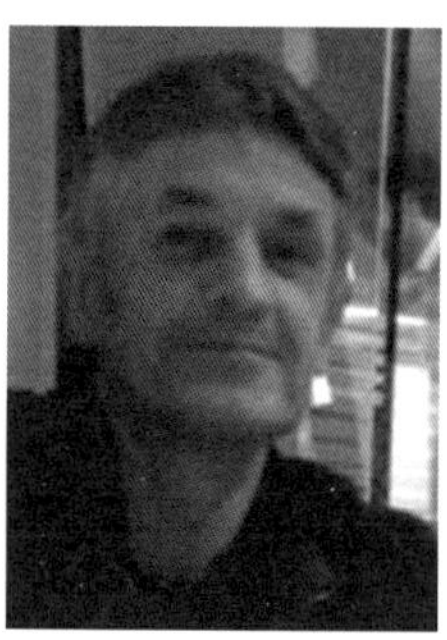

Ben Jonson
b.jonson@csm.arts.ac.uk

Ben Jonson is a London-based artist designer engaged in professional practice, education and creative/academic research. He studied at Central School of Speech & Drama, London College of Printing, Chelsea College of Art and Design, The Bartlett School of Post Graduate Studies, Central St Martins College of Art and Design, and Goldsmiths University College. His doctoral thesis (Goldsmiths, 2004) illuminates ideation across a broad spectrum of design, focusing on the impact of digital technology on conceptual tools and drawing in particular. A visiting lecturer (PGCEHE), and member of the pedagogic research network of the University of the Arts London, his research interests include studio culture, communication design, ideation and conceptual tools, architectonics, and sustainable and inclusive designs. For an extended profile, go to: http://ideation.mysite.orange.co.uk

Andrea Lioy (Italy, 1966) is currently Contextual Studies coordinator on the BA (Hons) in Graphic Design at Central Saint Martins College of Art and Design. He is a playwright and scriptwriter, and is also active as script consultant. His research interests include narrative structures, interactive narrative, community stories, folktales and myths, education in the arts, and writing. He is working on a book on the relationships between creative writing and graphic design.

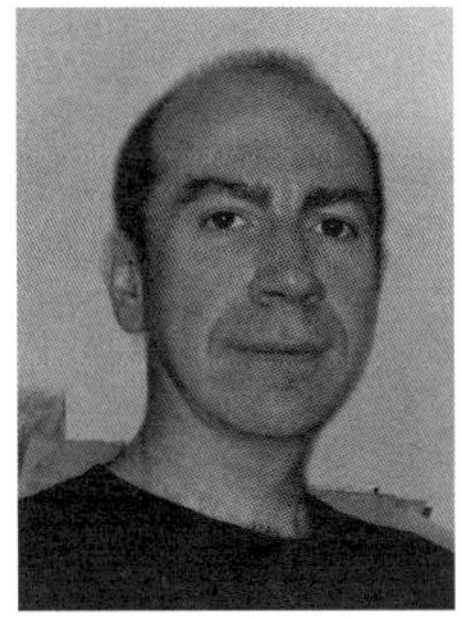

Andrea Lioy
a.lioy@csm.arts.ac.uk

Yewande Okuleye was born in Manchester in 1963, She was educated in Nigeria and the UK, trained as a scientist and worked in the cosmetics industry. Yewande returned to university as a mature student and studied fine art at University of East London and The Slade School of Fine Art. Yewande became interested in learning and teaching while lecturing in Cosmetic Chemistry at University of the Arts and maintains an interdisciplinary art practice. Yewande currently lives in London.

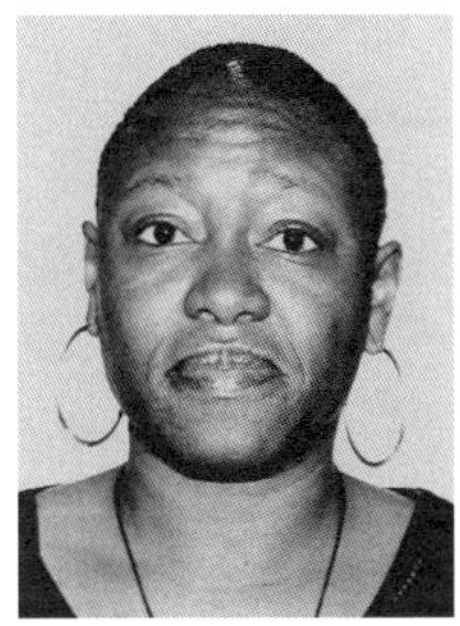

Yewande Okuleye
yewyokuleye@yahoo.co.uk

Dr Olivia Sagan is currently a Senior Research Fellow in Pedagogy at UAL, Olivia is involved in a range of research projects across the university that investigate learners' lives and experience. She is enjoying the challenge and irony of coming back to an art and design environment having left it many years ago to work in education and therapy in community, forensic, voluntary and FE settings, work in which she focused on the extreme ends of learner disadvantage. Her main interests remain in mental health and learning; creativity and social disadvantage – and her methodologies of choice and passion are biographic narrative, auto/ethnography and psychosocial approaches to interpreting social phenomena. (Which means, basically, she's just very nosey about what makes us tick… or not.)

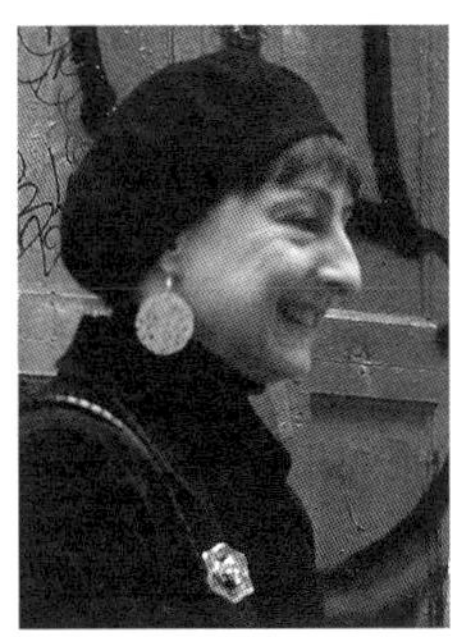

Dr Olivia Sagan
o.sagan@arts.ac.uk

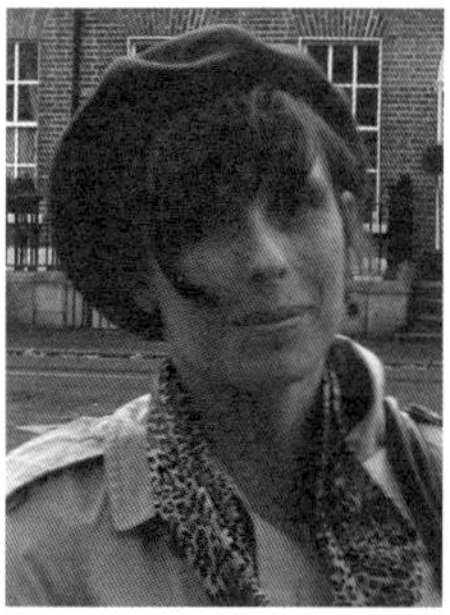

Dr Silvia Sovic
s.sovic@fashion.arts.ac.uk

Dr Silvia Sovic is Research Project Coordinator at the Creative Learning in Practice Centre for Excellence in Teaching and Learning at the University of the Arts London, where she is running a project on the experiences of first-year international students. Her background is in history; she took her BA in history and ethnology at the University of Ljubljana, Slovenia, her MA at the Institute of Historical Research, University of London, and her PhD in historical demography at the University of Essex. She has worked as Research Training Development Officer at the School of Advanced Study, University of London, and as researcher at the Cambridge Group for the History of Population and Social Structure. She is Senior Research Fellow at the Institute of Historical Research, where she also teaches statistics for historians.

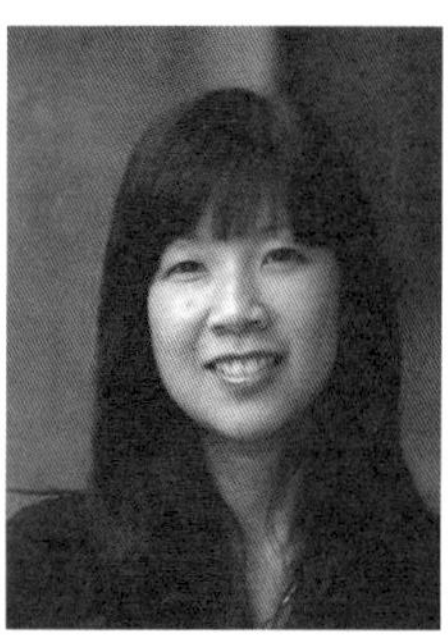

Su-Lynn Tan
s.tan@lcc.arts.ac.uk

Su-Lynn Tan combines her passion for learning with her experience of working in further and higher education in teaching, support and research roles. She is currently the course leader on the ABC Diploma in Image Production (Animation) at the London College of Communication. Her teaching on two other (undergraduate) animation courses at LCC accents and supports diversity in the student cohort. This offers her a challenging and rewarding experience. Her recent research project, 'Are sketchbooks still relevant to student learning?' was presented at the CLIP CETL & cltad Learning & Teaching Symposium in January 2008. Her career spans many commercial design disciplines from editorial illustrator to art director in advertising and has seen her produce successful published work for children's books, print campaigns and TV commercials. Her animation work synergises and reflects her interests in fashion, textiles and children's book illustration.

Commentator's Biographies

Sarah Atkinson is Director of Programmes for the Foundation Diploma in Art and Design at the London College of Fashion. In addition to her role as course director, she is also the Coordinator for Teaching and Learning for the School of Media and Communication and has been an active participant in a number of research initiatives within the university since joining the team in 2006.

Sarah Atkinson
s.j.atkinson@fashion.arts.ac.uk

Linda Ball has a background as researcher, writer, academic and educational developer and works in the Centre for Learning and Teaching in Art and Design at the University of the Arts London. Her research interests include professional development, enterprise and employability in higher education creative arts subjects. She is currently project director for a study of the career patterns of UK graduates involving 24 higher education institutions.

Linda Ball
l.ball@arts.ac.uk

Dr Margo Blythman is the Academic Director of Teaching and Learning at the London College of Communication, where she has responsibility for quality enhancement initiatives including study support, tutorial and student retention. Her current research interests include the micropolitics of organisations, lecturers' conceptions of their working practices and students' approaches to design and

Dr Margo Blythman
m.blythman@lcc.arts.ac.uk

Rebecca Fortnum read English at Oxford before gaining an MFA from Newcastle University and taking up a fellowship at the Skowhegan School of Painting and Sculpture, USA. She has been a Visiting Fellow in Painting at Plymouth University and at Winchester School of Art, a visiting artist at The School of the Art Institute of Chicago, and a Senior Lecturer at Norwich School of Art and Wimbledon School of Art.

Rebecca Fortnum
r.fortnum@camberwell.arts.ac.uk

Antony Johnston is a Principal Lecturer at the London College of Communication within the School of Printing and Publishing, where he supports developments in learning and teaching and teaches mainly within digital media based disciplines. Recent research interests have included an investigation into disciplinary differences in art and design, as well as exploring students' experience of assessment and feedback practices.

Antony Johnston
a.johnston@lcc.arts.ac.uk

Geoffrey Makstutis is a practising architect and course director at Central Saint Martins College of Art and Design. Originally from the US, he has both educational and professional experience in the US and UK. At Central Saint Martins he is engaged in the development of curriculum and promoting widening participation projects. He is currently engaged in a funded research project looking at student motivation in relation to social engagement.

Geoffrey Makstutis
g.makstutis@csm.arts.ac.uk

Jackie McManus is Acting Head of Widening Participation at University of the Arts London. She is especially interested in issues of equity and social justice in arts education, both in terms of access and the curriculum.

Jackie McManus
j.b.mcmanus@arts.ac.uk

Janice Miller is Lecturer in Cultural and Historical Studies at the London College of Fashion. She has previously taught at Central St Martins College of Art and Design, Kingston University and University of the Creative Arts at Epsom. She has recently published essays, book chapters and conference papers concerned with Cultural Studies learning in art and design education, make-up, hair and performance, and dress in literature. She is currently working towards the publication of a book on fashion and music with the publisher Berg.

Janice Miller
j.miller@fashion.arts.ac.uk

Dr Tony Sullivan is a lecturer in Cultural and Historical Studies at the London College of Fashion. He is currently working on a book proposal Consuming Brands and has spoken on his PhD research at a number of recent international conferences as well as contributing to The Journal Of Consumer Culture and to Critical Psychology.

Dr Tony Sullivan
t.sullivan@fashion.arts.ac.uk

Dr Alison Shreeve is the Director for Creative Learning in Practice Centre for Excellence in Teaching and Learning (CLIP CETL). Alison is responsible for the strategic direction of the CLIP CETL and for ensuring that the centre's planned activities contribute to understanding more about the nature of learning in practice for the creative industries.

Dr Alison Shreeve
a.shreeve@fashion.arts.ac.uk

Professor Teal Triggs BFA (Hons), MA, MA, PhD, FiSTD is Professor of Graphic Design and Head of Research, School of Graphic Design, London College of Communication, University of the Arts London. As a graphic design historian, critic and educator, she has lectured widely and her writings have appeared in numerous edited books and international design publications.

Professor Teal Triggs
t.triggs@lcc.arts.ac.uk

Jane Tynan is a senior lecturer in cultural studies at Central Saint Martins College of Art and Design. She has taught cultural and historical programmes for art and design courses in the National College of Art and Design in Dublin, Goldsmiths College and London College of Fashion.

Jane Tynan
j.tynan@csm.arts.ac.uk